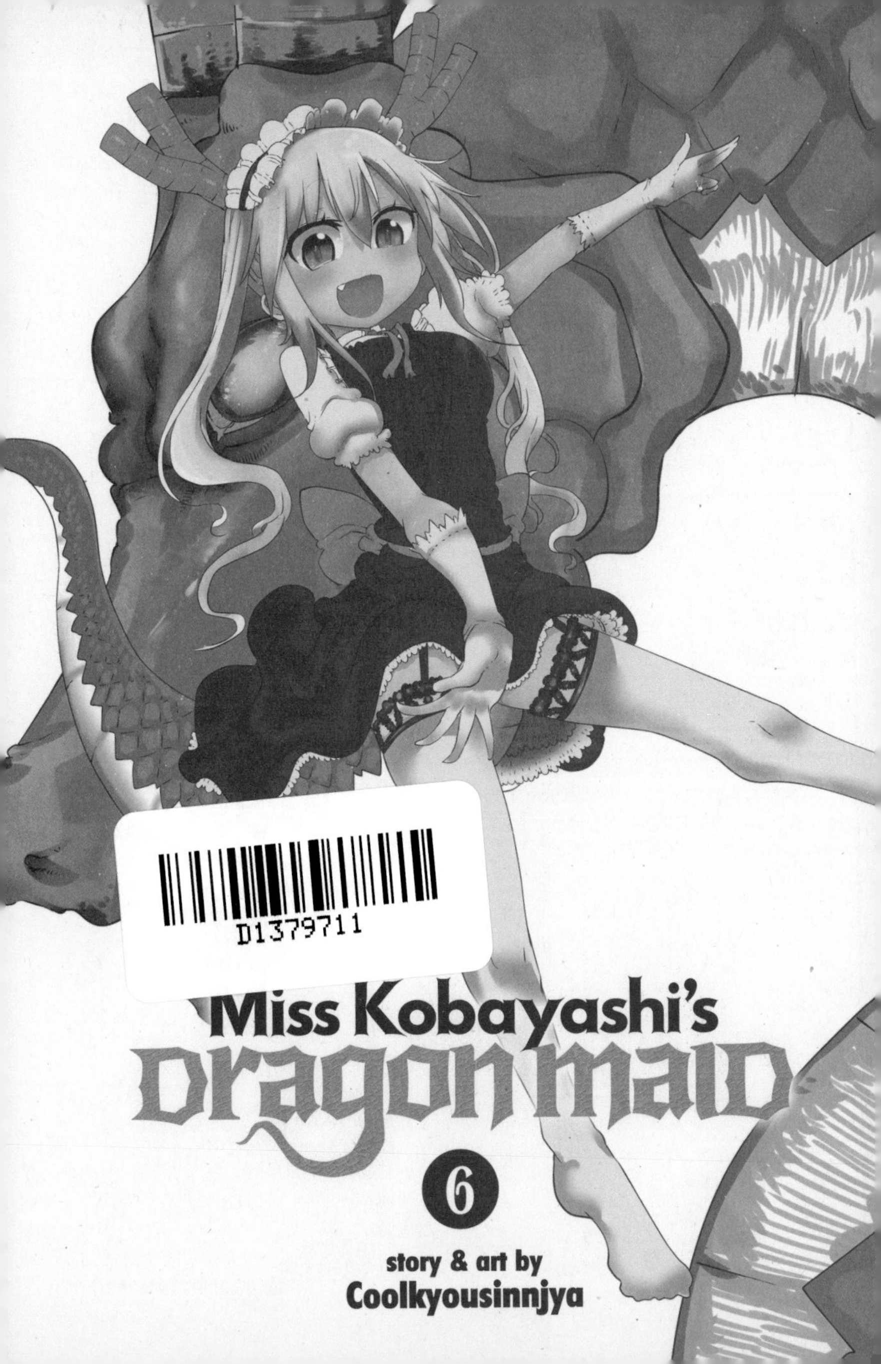

Miss Kobayashi's Dragon Maid

6

story & art by
Coolkyousinnjya

Miss Kobayashi's Dragon Maid

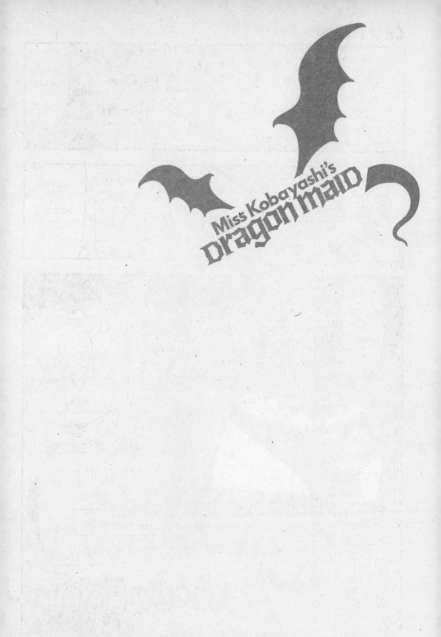

CHAPTER 49

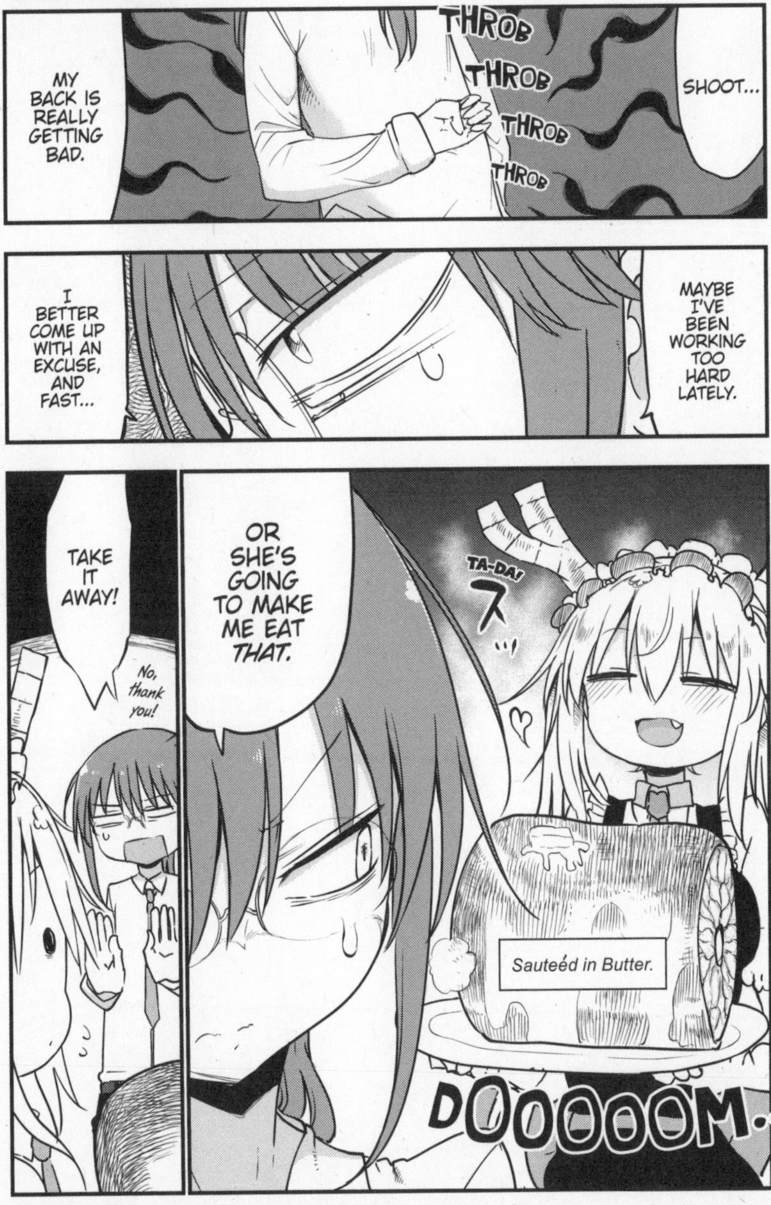
SHOOT...
THROB
THROB
THROB
THROB
MY BACK IS REALLY GETTING BAD.
MAYBE I'VE BEEN WORKING TOO HARD LATELY.
I BETTER COME UP WITH AN EXCUSE, AND FAST...
TA-DA!
ス
OR SHE'S GOING TO MAKE ME EAT *THAT.*
Sauteéd in Butter.
DOOOOOOM...
TAKE IT AWAY!
No, thank you!

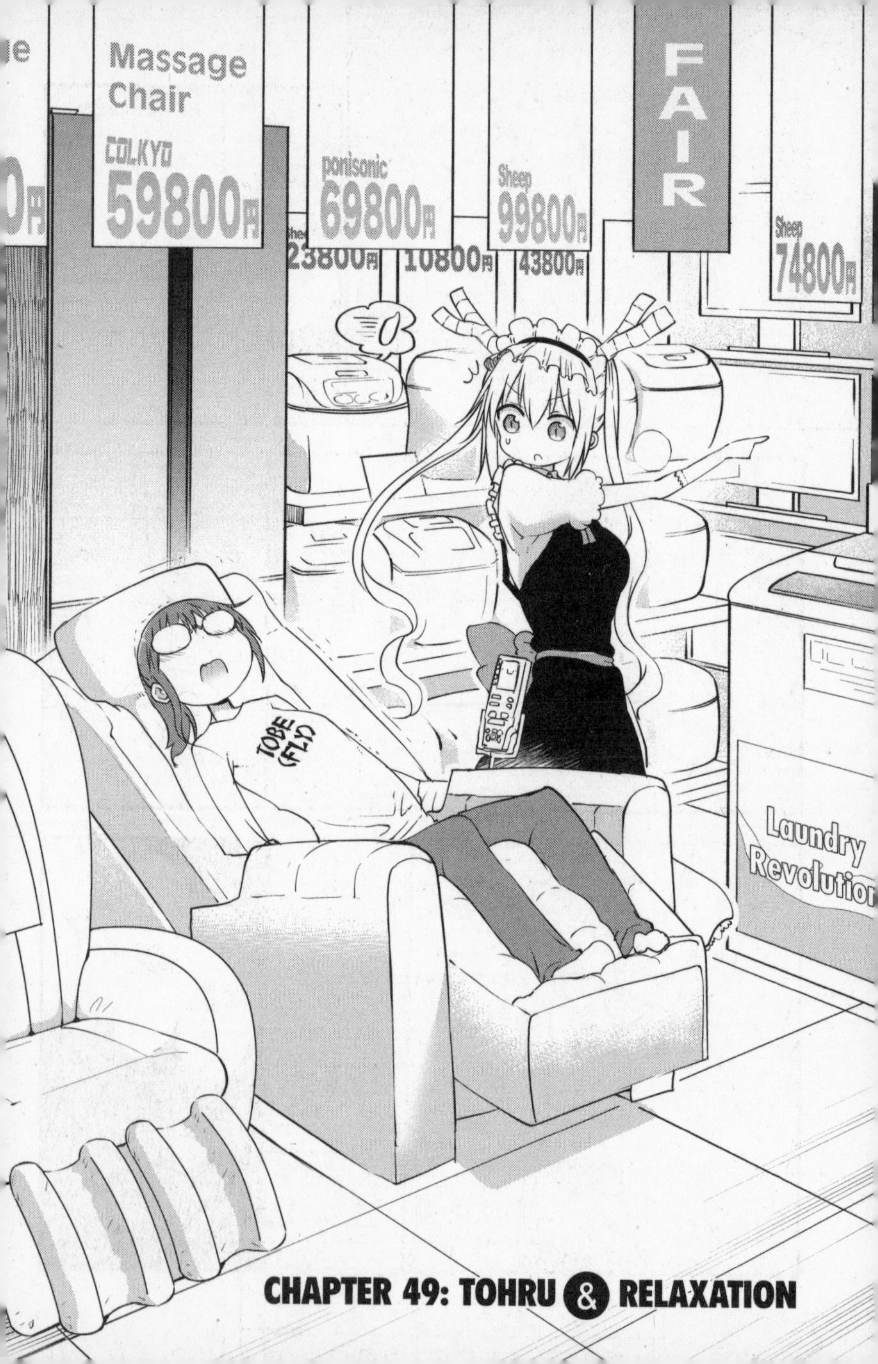
Massage Chair
COLKYO
59800円
ponisonic
69800円
Sheep
99800円
FAIR
23800円
10800円
43800円
Sheep
74800円
TOBE (FLY)
Laundry Revolution

CHAPTER 49: TOHRU & RELAXATION

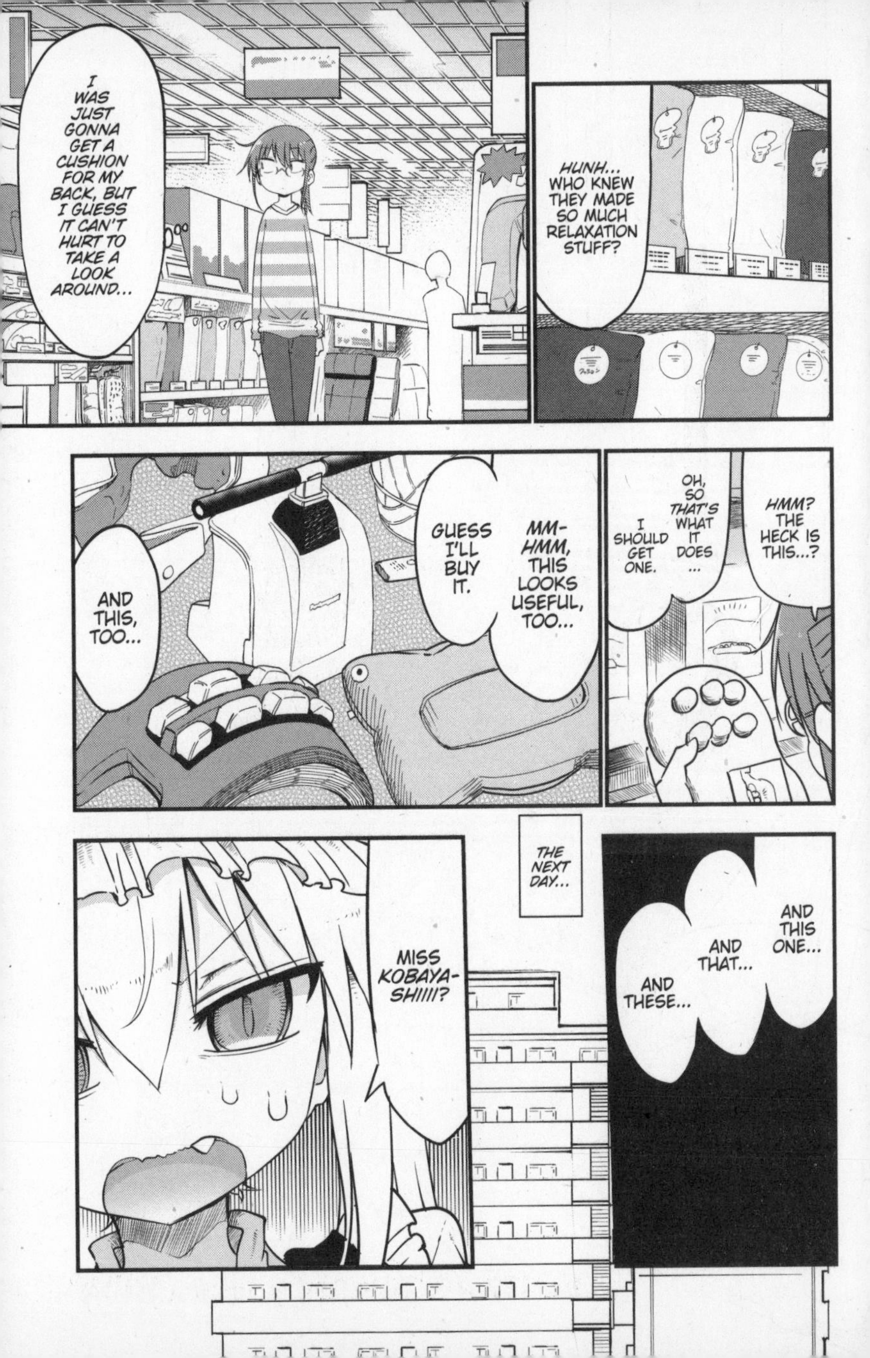
HUNH... WHO KNEW THEY MADE SO MUCH RELAXATION STUFF?
I WAS JUST GONNA GET A CUSHION FOR MY BACK, BUT I GUESS IT CAN'T HURT TO TAKE A LOOK AROUND...
HMM? THE HECK IS THIS...?
OH, SO THAT'S WHAT IT DOES...
I SHOULD GET ONE.
MM-HMM, THIS LOOKS USEFUL, TOO...
GUESS I'LL BUY IT.
AND THIS, TOO...
AND THIS ONE...
AND THAT...
AND THESE...
THE NEXT DAY...
MISS KOBAYA-SHIIII?

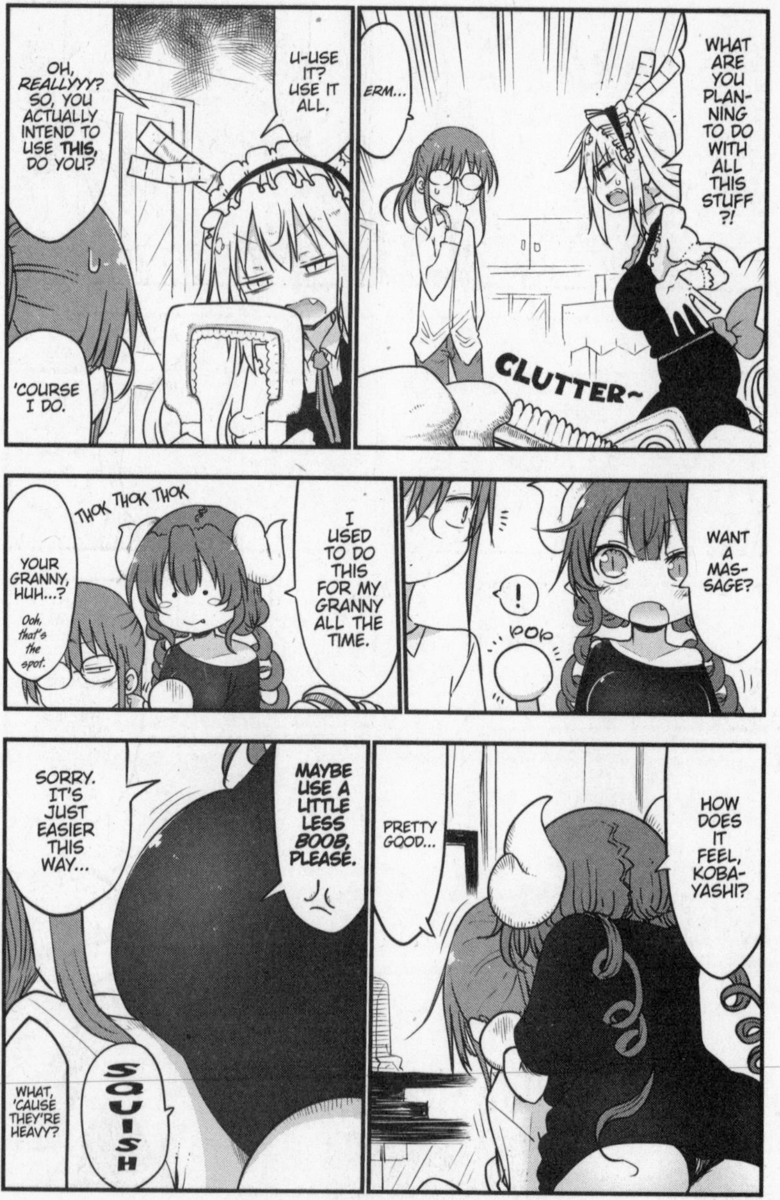
WHAT ARE YOU PLAN-NING TO DO WITH ALL THIS STUFF?!
CLUTTER~
ERM...
U-USE IT? USE IT ALL.
OH, *REALLYYY?* SO, YOU ACTUALLY INTEND TO USE **THIS,** DO YOU?
'COURSE I DO.
WANT A MAS-SAGE?
!
POP
I USED TO DO THIS FOR MY GRANNY ALL THE TIME.
THOK THOK THOK
YOUR GRANNY, HUH...?
Ooh, that's the spot.
HOW DOES IT FEEL, KOBA-YASHI?
PRETTY GOOD...
MAYBE USE A LITTLE LESS *BOOB,* PLEASE.
SORRY. IT'S JUST EASIER THIS WAY...
SQUISH
WHAT, 'CAUSE THEY'RE HEAVY?

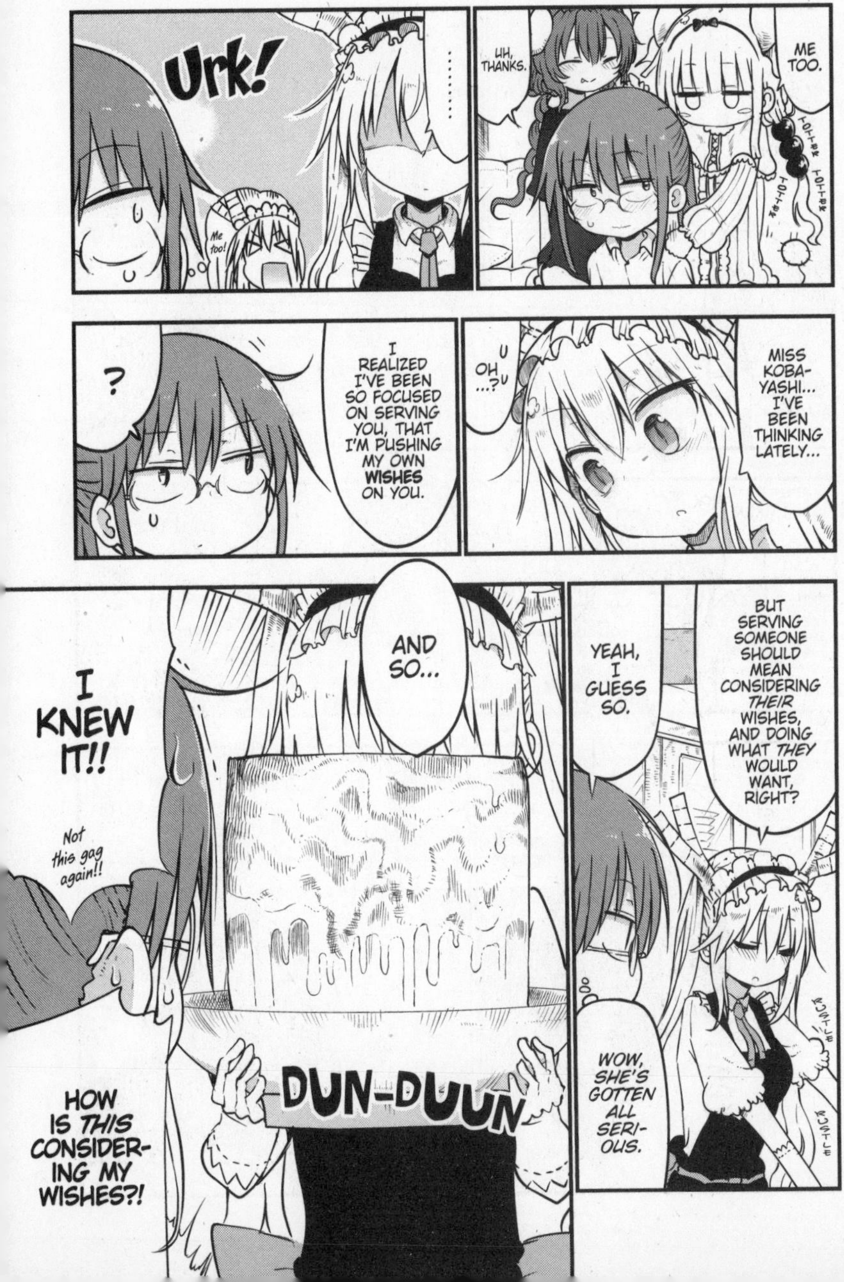
ME TOO.
TOTTER TOTTER
UH, THANKS.
......
Urk!
Me too!
MISS KOBA-YASHI... I'VE BEEN THINKING LATELY...
OH ...?
I REALIZED I'VE BEEN SO FOCUSED ON SERVING YOU, THAT I'M PUSHING MY OWN **WISHES** ON YOU.
?
BUT SERVING SOMEONE SHOULD MEAN CONSIDERING *THEIR* WISHES, AND DOING WHAT *THEY* WOULD WANT, RIGHT?
YEAH, I GUESS SO.
WOW, SHE'S GOTTEN ALL SERI-OUS.
RUSTLE
RUSTLE
AND SO...
I KNEW IT!!
Not this gag again!!
DUN-DUUN
HOW IS *THIS* CONSIDER-ING MY WISHES?!

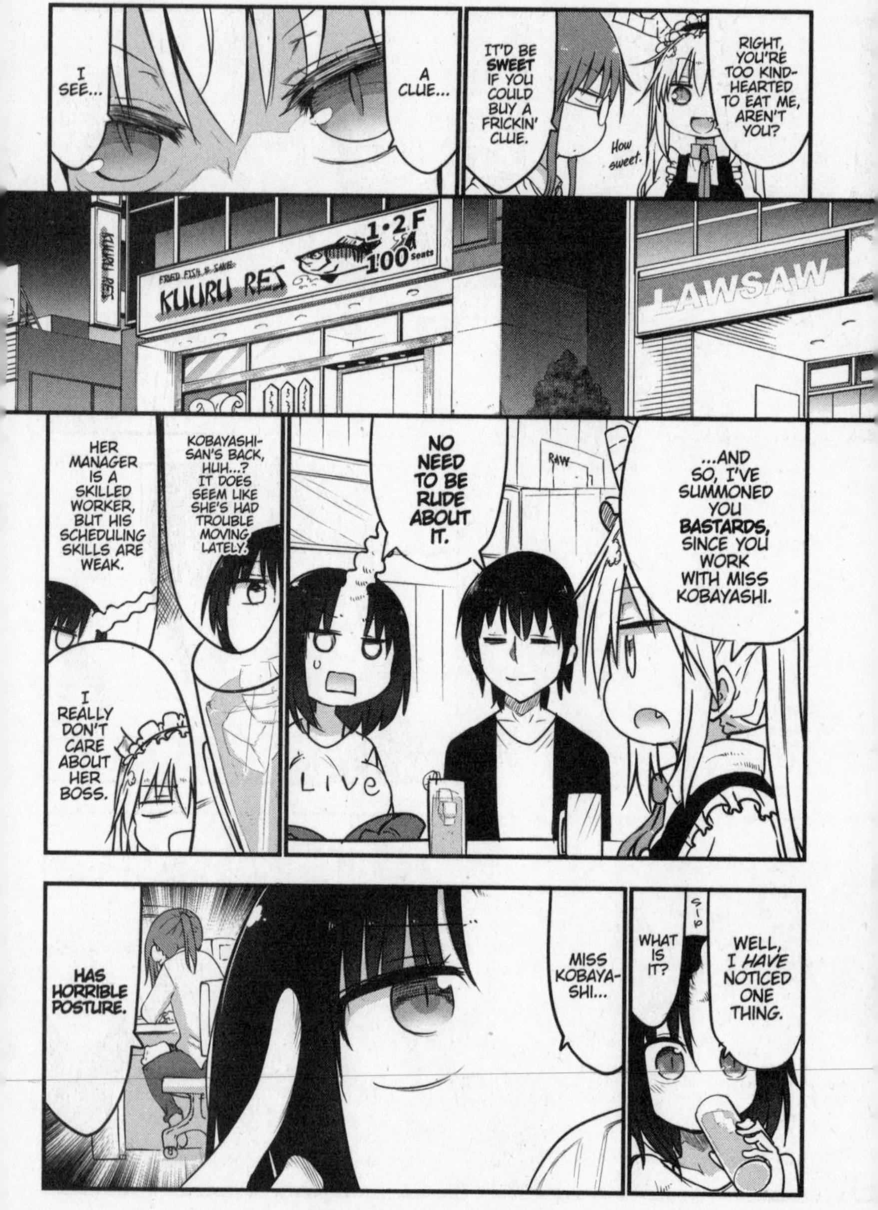
RIGHT, YOU'RE TOO KIND-HEARTED TO EAT ME, AREN'T YOU?
How sweet.
IT'D BE **SWEET** IF YOU COULD BUY A FRICKIN' CLUE.
A CLUE...
I SEE...
1·2F
100 Seats
FRIED FISH & SAKE
KUURU RES
LAWSAW
...AND SO, I'VE SUMMONED YOU **BASTARDS**, SINCE YOU WORK WITH MISS KOBAYASHI.
NO NEED TO BE RUDE ABOUT IT.
RAW
KOBAYASHI-SAN'S BACK, HUH...? IT DOES SEEM LIKE SHE'S HAD TROUBLE MOVING LATELY.
HER MANAGER IS A SKILLED WORKER, BUT HIS SCHEDULING SKILLS ARE WEAK.
I REALLY DON'T CARE ABOUT HER BOSS.
WELL, I *HAVE* NOTICED ONE THING.
WHAT IS IT?
sip
MISS KOBAYASHI...
HAS HORRIBLE POSTURE.

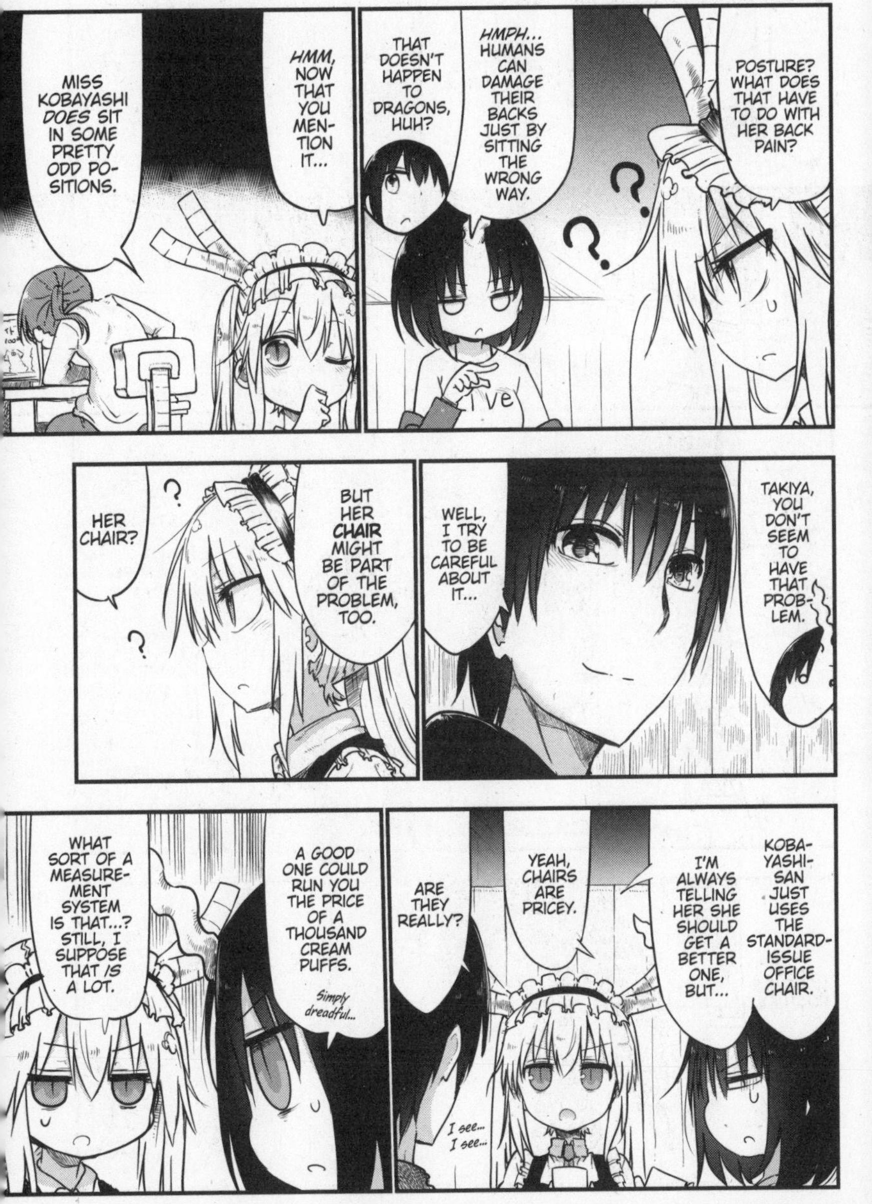
POSTURE? WHAT DOES THAT HAVE TO DO WITH HER BACK PAIN?
HMPH... HUMANS CAN DAMAGE THEIR BACKS JUST BY SITTING THE WRONG WAY.
THAT DOESN'T HAPPEN TO DRAGONS, HUH?
HMM, NOW THAT YOU MENTION IT...
MISS KOBAYASHI DOES SIT IN SOME PRETTY ODD POSITIONS.
TAKIYA, YOU DON'T SEEM TO HAVE THAT PROBLEM.
WELL, I TRY TO BE CAREFUL ABOUT IT...
BUT HER CHAIR MIGHT BE PART OF THE PROBLEM, TOO.
HER CHAIR?
KOBAYASHI-SAN JUST USES THE STANDARD-ISSUE OFFICE CHAIR.
I'M ALWAYS TELLING HER SHE SHOULD GET A BETTER ONE, BUT...
YEAH, CHAIRS ARE PRICEY.
ARE THEY REALLY?
I see... I see...
A GOOD ONE COULD RUN YOU THE PRICE OF A THOUSAND CREAM PUFFS.
Simply dreadful...
WHAT SORT OF A MEASUREMENT SYSTEM IS THAT...? STILL, I SUPPOSE THAT IS A LOT.

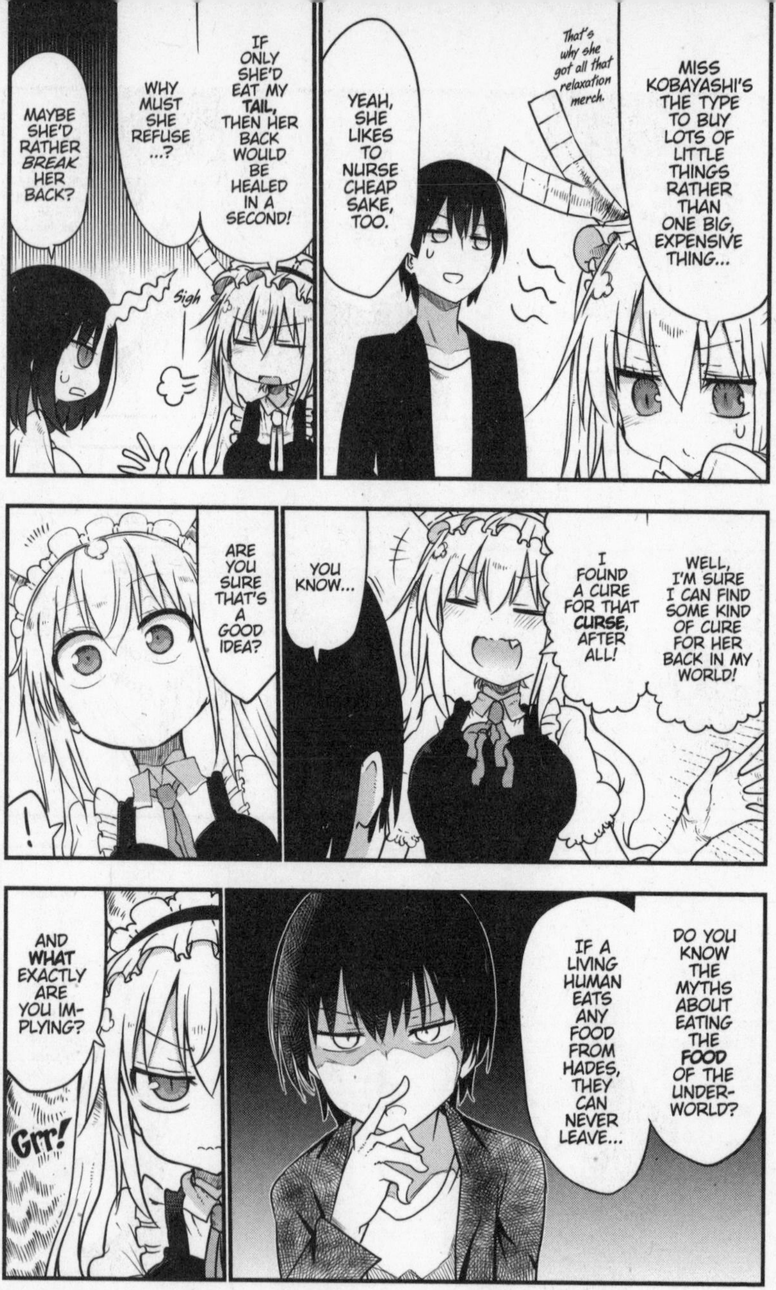
MISS KOBAYASHI'S THE TYPE TO BUY LOTS OF LITTLE THINGS RATHER THAN ONE BIG, EXPENSIVE THING...
That's why she got all that relaxation merch.
YEAH, SHE LIKES TO NURSE CHEAP SAKE, TOO.
IF ONLY SHE'D EAT MY **TAIL**, THEN HER BACK WOULD BE HEALED IN A SECOND!
WHY MUST SHE REFUSE ...?
Sigh
MAYBE SHE'D RATHER *BREAK* HER BACK?
WELL, I'M SURE I CAN FIND SOME KIND OF CURE FOR HER BACK IN MY WORLD!
I FOUND A CURE FOR THAT **CURSE**, AFTER ALL!
YOU KNOW...
ARE YOU SURE THAT'S A GOOD IDEA?
!
DO YOU KNOW THE MYTHS ABOUT EATING THE **FOOD** OF THE UNDER-WORLD?
IF A LIVING HUMAN EATS ANY FOOD FROM HADES, THEY CAN NEVER LEAVE...
AND **WHAT** EXACTLY ARE YOU IM-PLYING?
Grr!

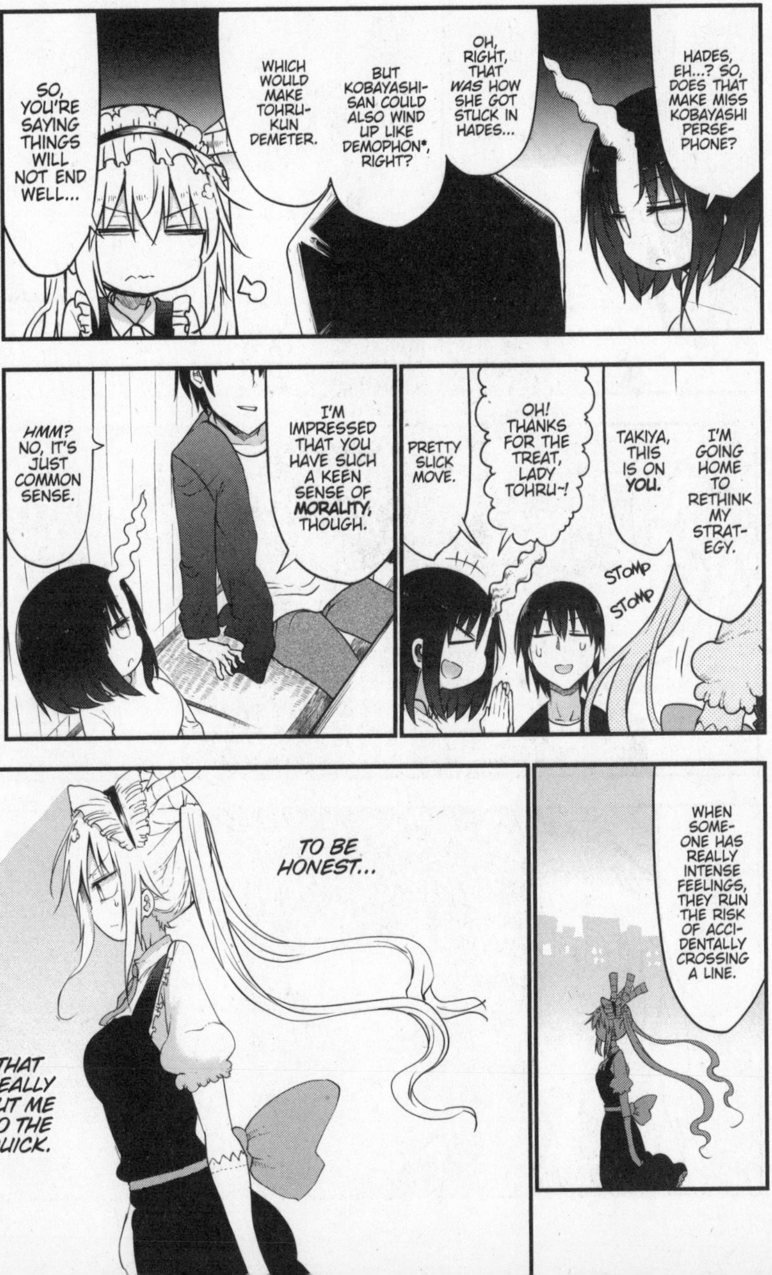
HADES, EH...? SO, DOES THAT MAKE MISS KOBAYASHI PERSE-PHONE?
OH, RIGHT, THAT WAS HOW SHE GOT STUCK IN HADES...
BUT KOBAYASHI-SAN COULD ALSO WIND UP LIKE DEMOPHON*, RIGHT?
WHICH WOULD MAKE TOHRU-KUN DEMETER.
SO, YOU'RE SAYING THINGS WILL NOT END WELL...
I'M GOING HOME TO RETHINK MY STRAT-EGY.
TAKIYA, THIS IS ON YOU.
OH! THANKS FOR THE TREAT, LADY TOHRU~!
PRETTY SLICK MOVE.
STOMP
STOMP
I'M IMPRESSED THAT YOU HAVE SUCH A KEEN SENSE OF MORALITY, THOUGH.
HMM? NO, IT'S JUST COMMON SENSE.
WHEN SOME-ONE HAS REALLY INTENSE FEELINGS, THEY RUN THE RISK OF ACCI-DENTALLY CROSSING A LINE.
TO BE HONEST...
THAT REALLY CUT ME TO THE QUICK.

*In Greek mythology, the goddess Demeter tried to make the human prince Demophon immortal by burning away his mortality in a hearth-fire. It did not end well.

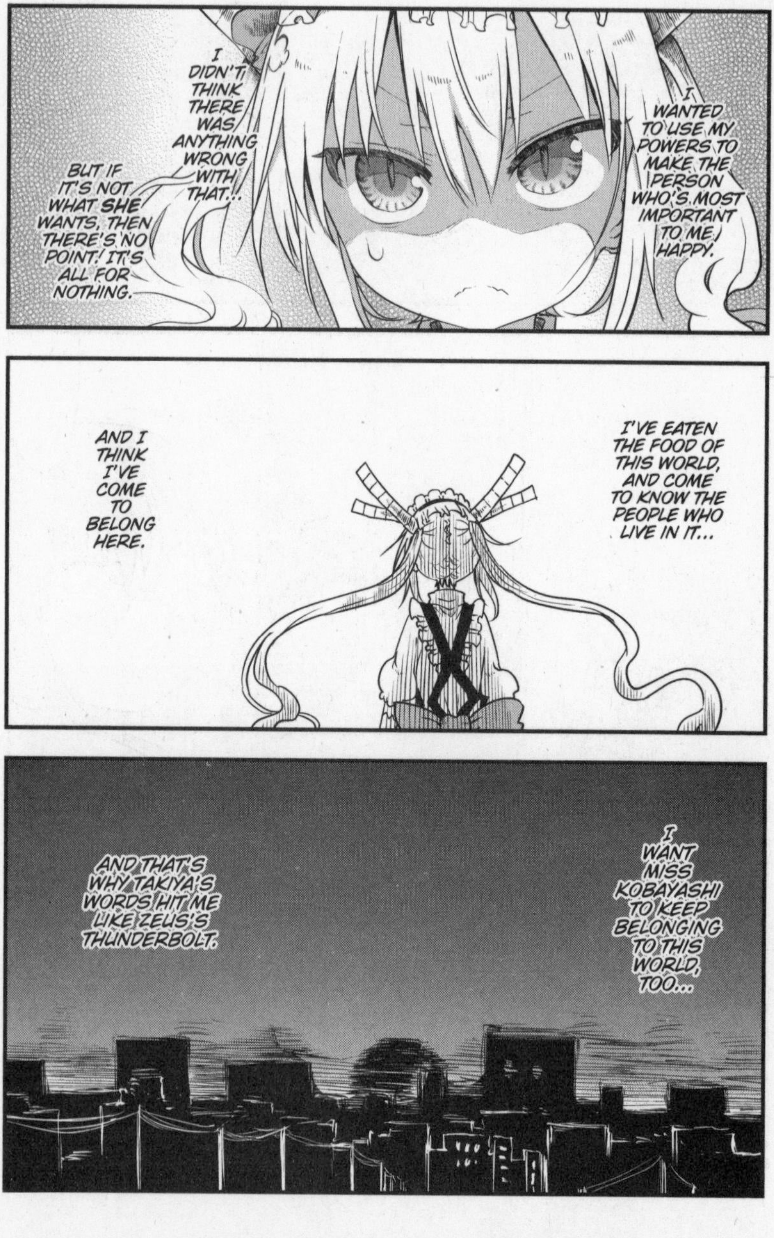
I WANTED TO USE MY POWERS TO MAKE THE PERSON WHO'S MOST IMPORTANT TO ME HAPPY.
I DIDN'T THINK THERE WAS ANYTHING WRONG WITH THAT...
BUT IF IT'S NOT WHAT SHE WANTS, THEN THERE'S NO POINT! IT'S ALL FOR NOTHING.
I'VE EATEN THE FOOD OF THIS WORLD, AND COME TO KNOW THE PEOPLE WHO LIVE IN IT...
AND I THINK I'VE COME TO BELONG HERE.
I WANT MISS KOBAYASHI TO KEEP BELONGING TO THIS WORLD, TOO...
AND THAT'S WHY TAKIYA'S WORDS HIT ME LIKE ZEUS'S THUNDERBOLT.

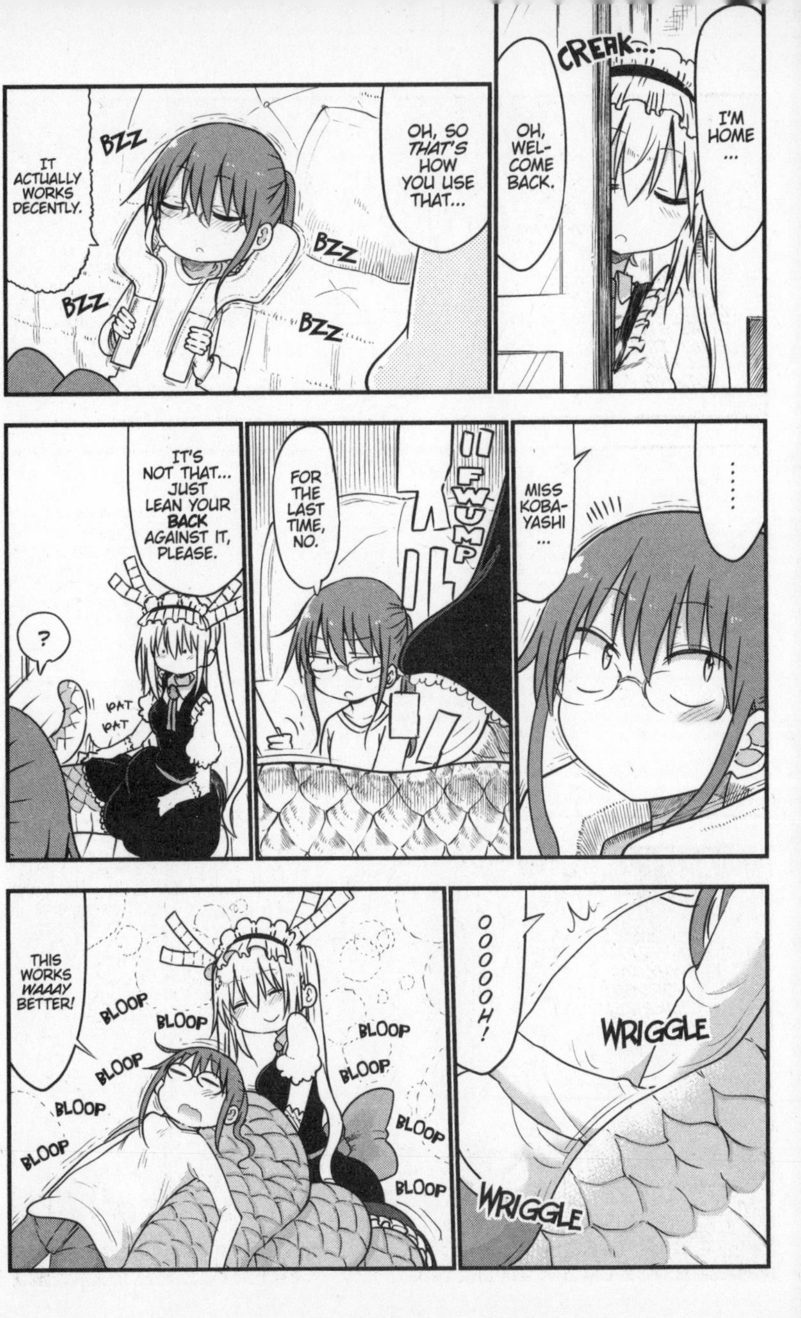
CREAK...
I'M HOME...
OH, WEL-COME BACK.
OH, SO THAT'S HOW YOU USE THAT...
BZZ
BZZ
BZZ
BZZ
IT ACTUALLY WORKS DECENTLY.
......
MISS KOBA-YASHI...
FWUMP
FOR THE LAST TIME, NO.
IT'S NOT THAT... JUST LEAN YOUR BACK AGAINST IT, PLEASE.
?
PAT PAT
OOOOOOH!
WRIGGLE
WRIGGLE
THIS WORKS WAAAY BETTER!
BLOOP
BLOOP
BLOOP
BLOOP
BLOOP
BLOOP
BLOOP
BLOOP
BLOOP

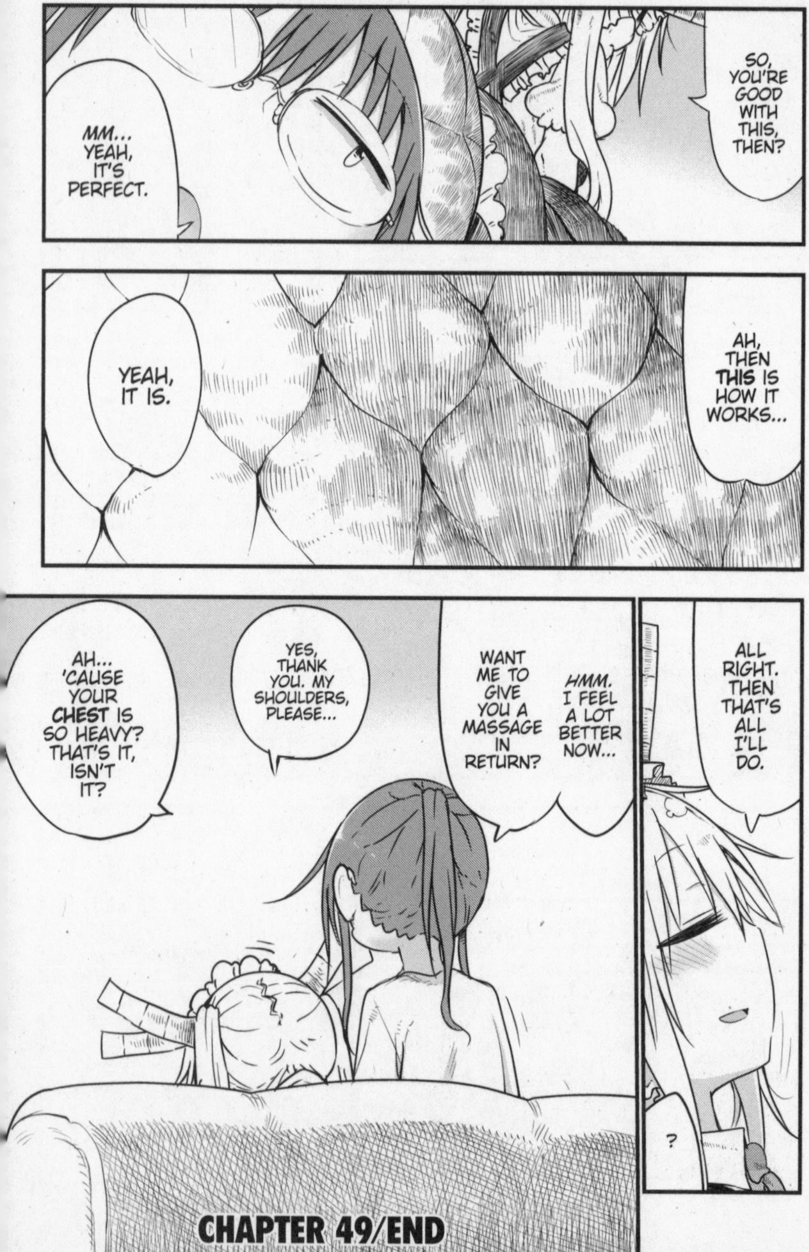
SO, YOU'RE GOOD WITH THIS, THEN?
MM... YEAH, IT'S PERFECT.
AH, THEN **THIS** IS HOW IT WORKS...
YEAH, IT IS.
ALL RIGHT. THEN THAT'S ALL I'LL DO.
?
HMM. I FEEL A LOT BETTER NOW...
WANT ME TO GIVE YOU A MASSAGE IN RETURN?
YES, THANK YOU. MY SHOULDERS, PLEASE...
AH... 'CAUSE YOUR **CHEST** IS SO HEAVY? THAT'S IT, ISN'T IT?
CHAPTER 49/END

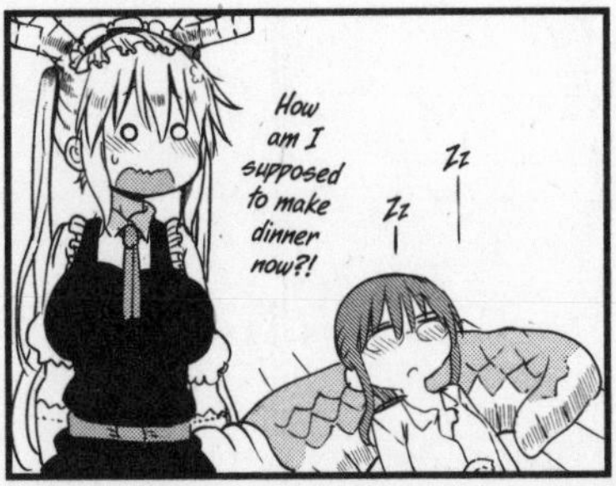
How am I supposed to make dinner now?!
Zz
Zz

Miss Kobayashi's
DRAGON MAID

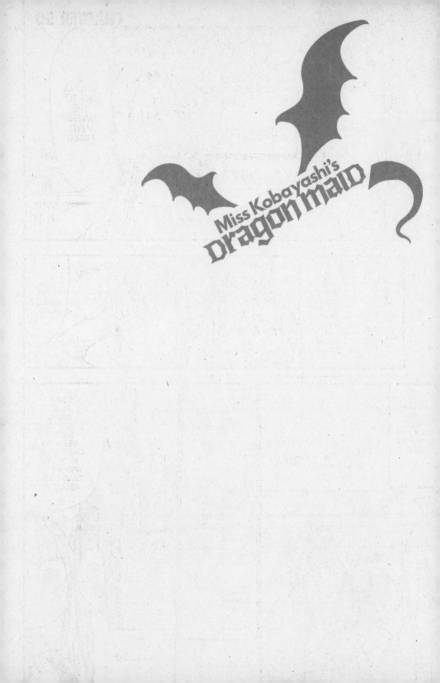

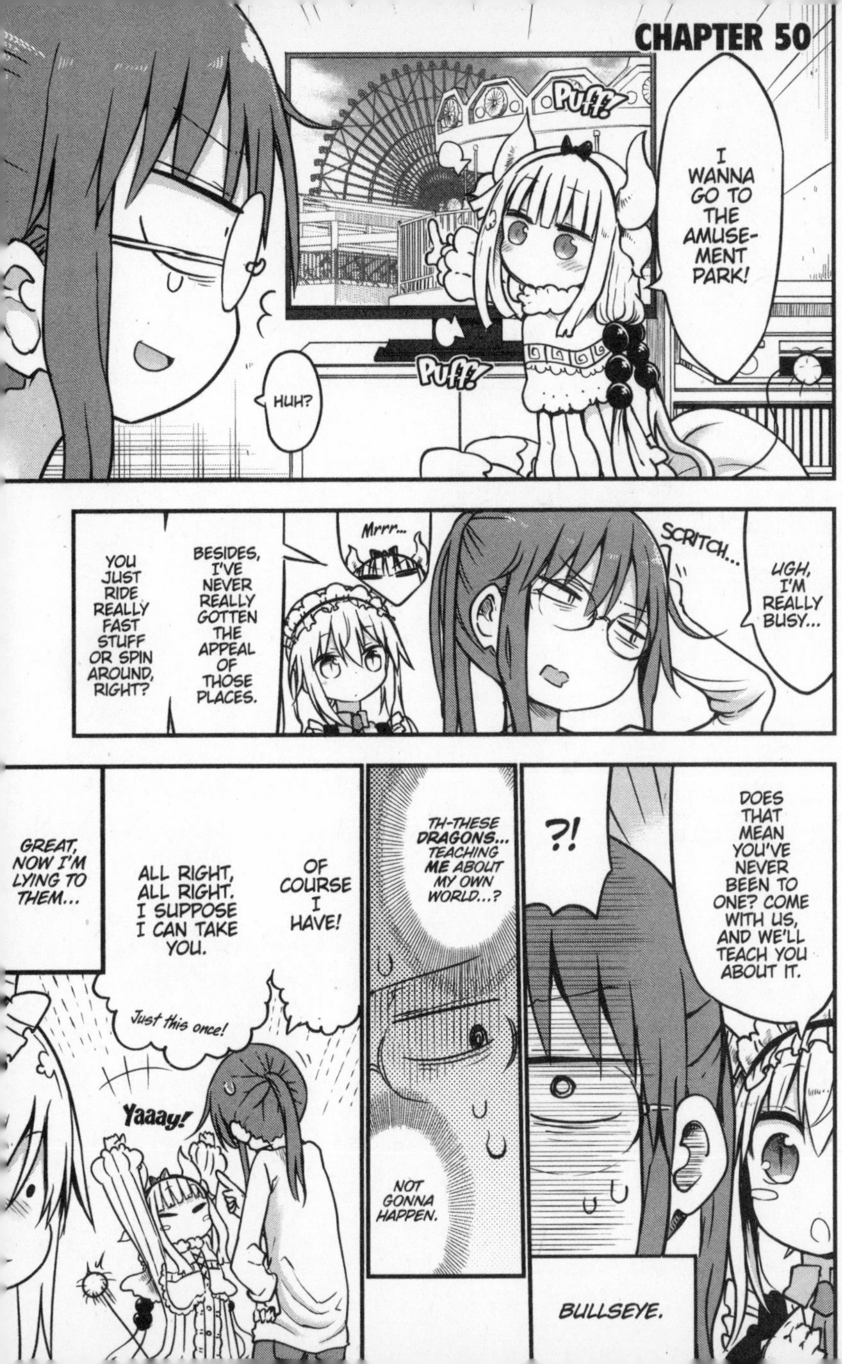
CHAPTER 50
PUFF!
I WANNA GO TO THE AMUSEMENT PARK!
PUFF!
HUH?
UGH, I'M REALLY BUSY...
SCRITCH...
Mrrr...
BESIDES, I'VE NEVER REALLY GOTTEN THE APPEAL OF THOSE PLACES.
YOU JUST RIDE REALLY FAST STUFF OR SPIN AROUND, RIGHT?
DOES THAT MEAN YOU'VE NEVER BEEN TO ONE? COME WITH US, AND WE'LL TEACH YOU ABOUT IT.
?!
BULLSEYE.
TH-THESE DRAGONS... TEACHING ME ABOUT MY OWN WORLD...?
NOT GONNA HAPPEN.
OF COURSE I HAVE!
ALL RIGHT, ALL RIGHT. I SUPPOSE I CAN TAKE YOU.
GREAT, NOW I'M LYING TO THEM...
Just this once!
Yaaay!

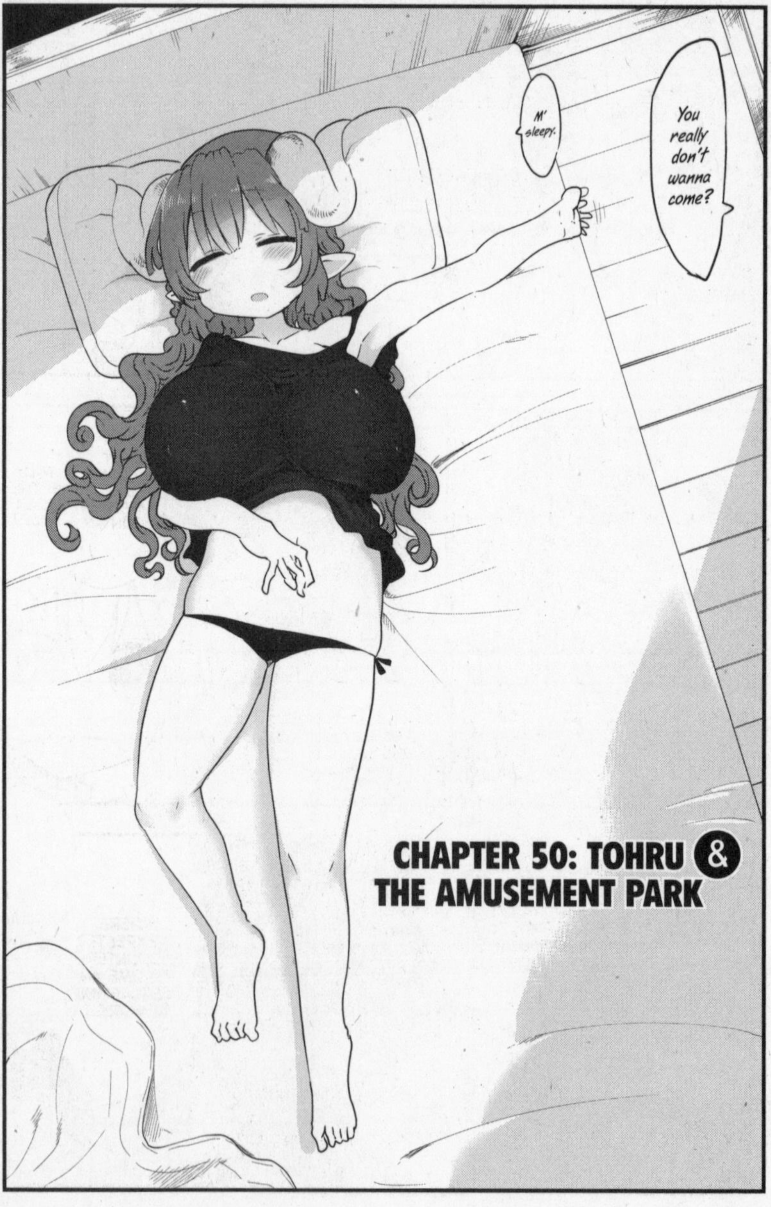
You really don't wanna come?
M' sleepy.

CHAPTER 50: TOHRU & THE AMUSEMENT PARK

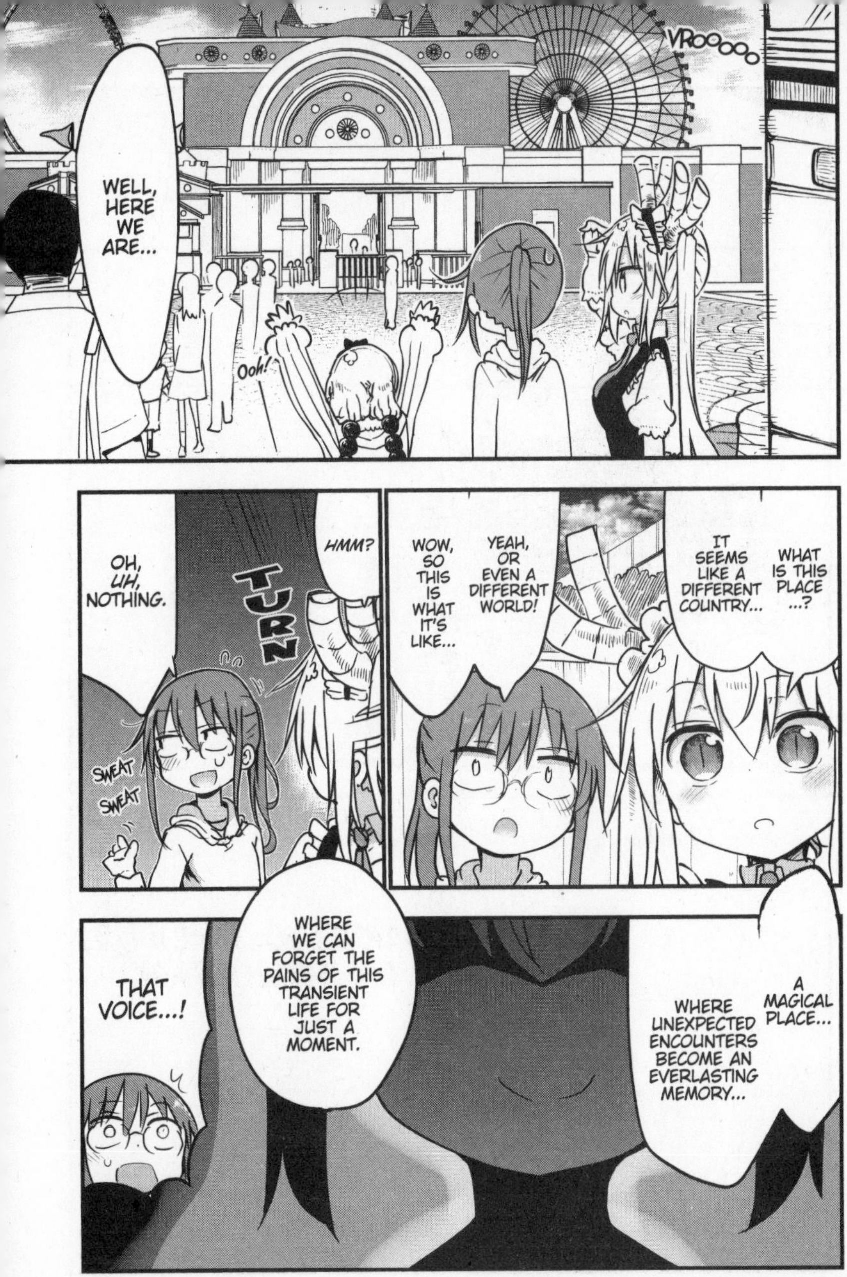
VROOOOOO
WELL, HERE WE ARE...
Ooh!
WHAT IS THIS PLACE ...?
IT SEEMS LIKE A DIFFERENT COUNTRY...
YEAH, OR EVEN A DIFFERENT WORLD!
WOW, SO THIS IS WHAT IT'S LIKE...
HMM?
TURN
OH, UH, NOTHING.
SWEAT SWEAT
A MAGICAL PLACE...
WHERE UNEXPECTED ENCOUNTERS BECOME AN EVERLASTING MEMORY...
WHERE WE CAN FORGET THE PAINS OF THIS TRANSIENT LIFE FOR JUST A MOMENT.
THAT VOICE...!

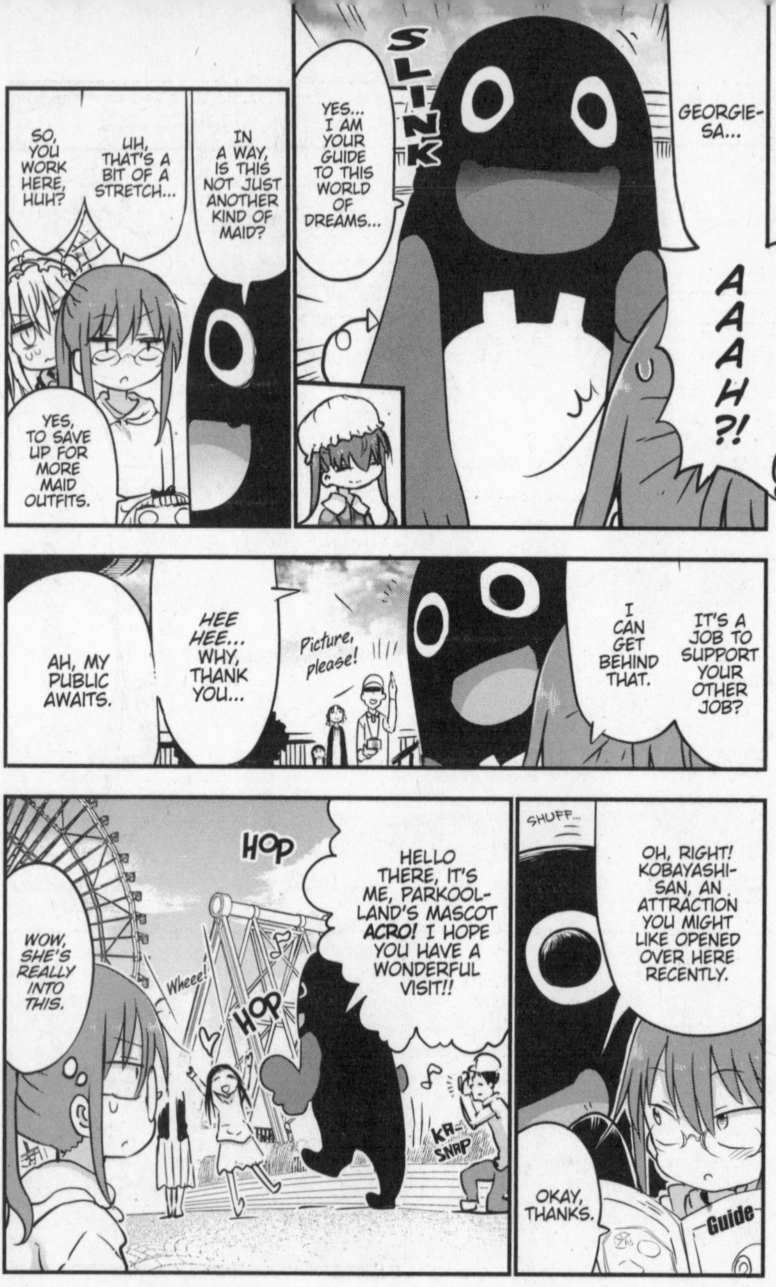
GEORGIE-SA...
AAAAH?!
SLINK
YES... I AM YOUR GUIDE TO THIS WORLD OF DREAMS...
IN A WAY, IS THIS NOT JUST ANOTHER KIND OF MAID?
UH, THAT'S A BIT OF A STRETCH...
SO, YOU WORK HERE, HUH?
YES, TO SAVE UP FOR MORE MAID OUTFITS.
IT'S A JOB TO SUPPORT YOUR OTHER JOB?
I CAN GET BEHIND THAT.
Picture, please!
HEE HEE... WHY, THANK YOU...
AH, MY PUBLIC AWAITS.
SHUFF...
OH, RIGHT! KOBAYASHI-SAN, AN ATTRACTION YOU MIGHT LIKE OPENED OVER HERE RECENTLY.
Guide
OKAY, THANKS.
HELLO THERE, IT'S ME, PARKOOL-LAND'S MASCOT ACRO! I HOPE YOU HAVE A WONDERFUL VISIT!!
HOP
HOP
Wheee!
KA-SNAP
WOW, SHE'S REALLY INTO THIS.

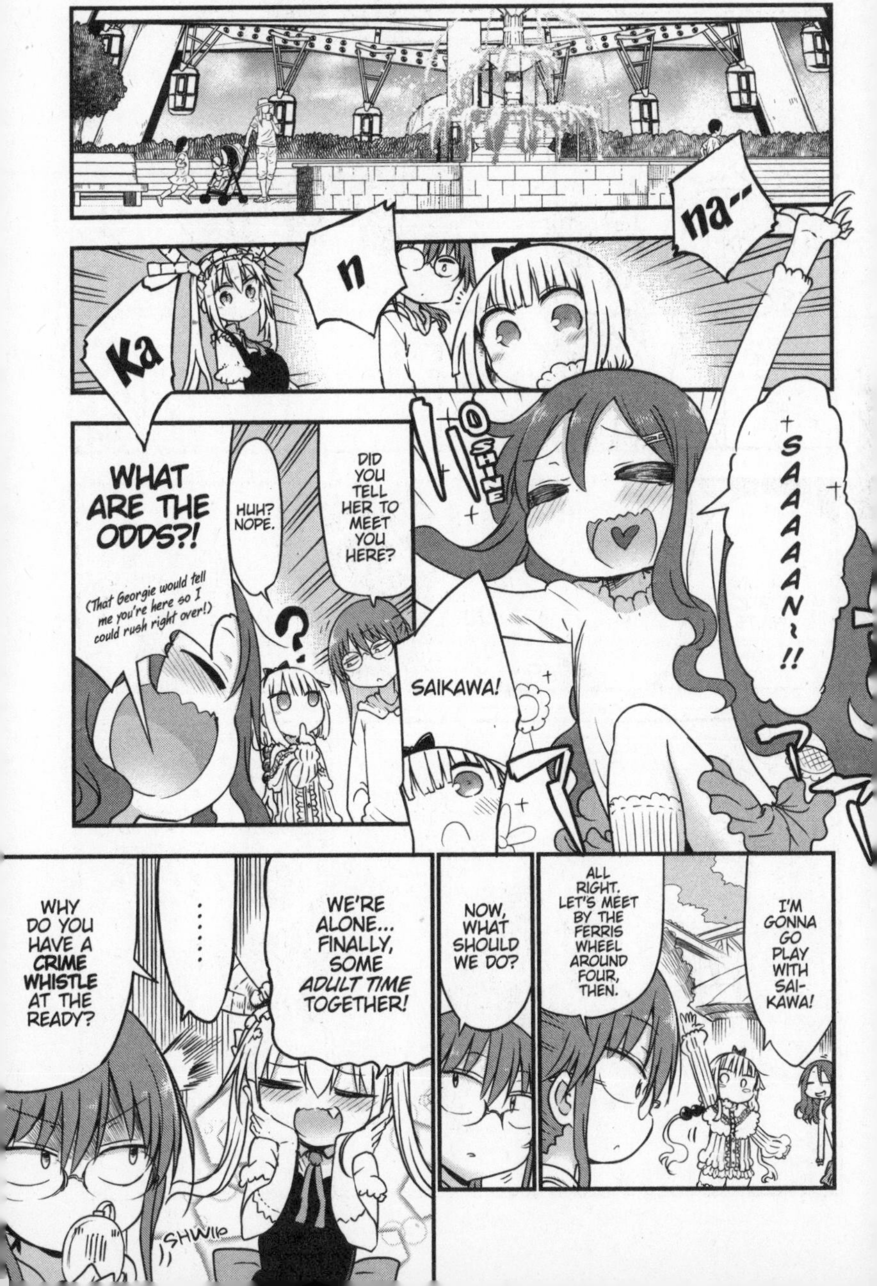
Ka
n
na--
SAAAAAN~!!
SHINE
SAIKAWA!
DID YOU TELL HER TO MEET YOU HERE?
HUH? NOPE.
WHAT ARE THE ODDS?!
(That Georgie would tell me you're here so I could rush right over!)
I'M GONNA GO PLAY WITH SAI-KAWA!
ALL RIGHT. LET'S MEET BY THE FERRIS WHEEL AROUND FOUR, THEN.
NOW, WHAT SHOULD WE DO?
WE'RE ALONE... FINALLY, SOME *ADULT TIME* TOGETHER!
......
WHY DO YOU HAVE A **CRIME WHISTLE** AT THE READY?
SHWIP

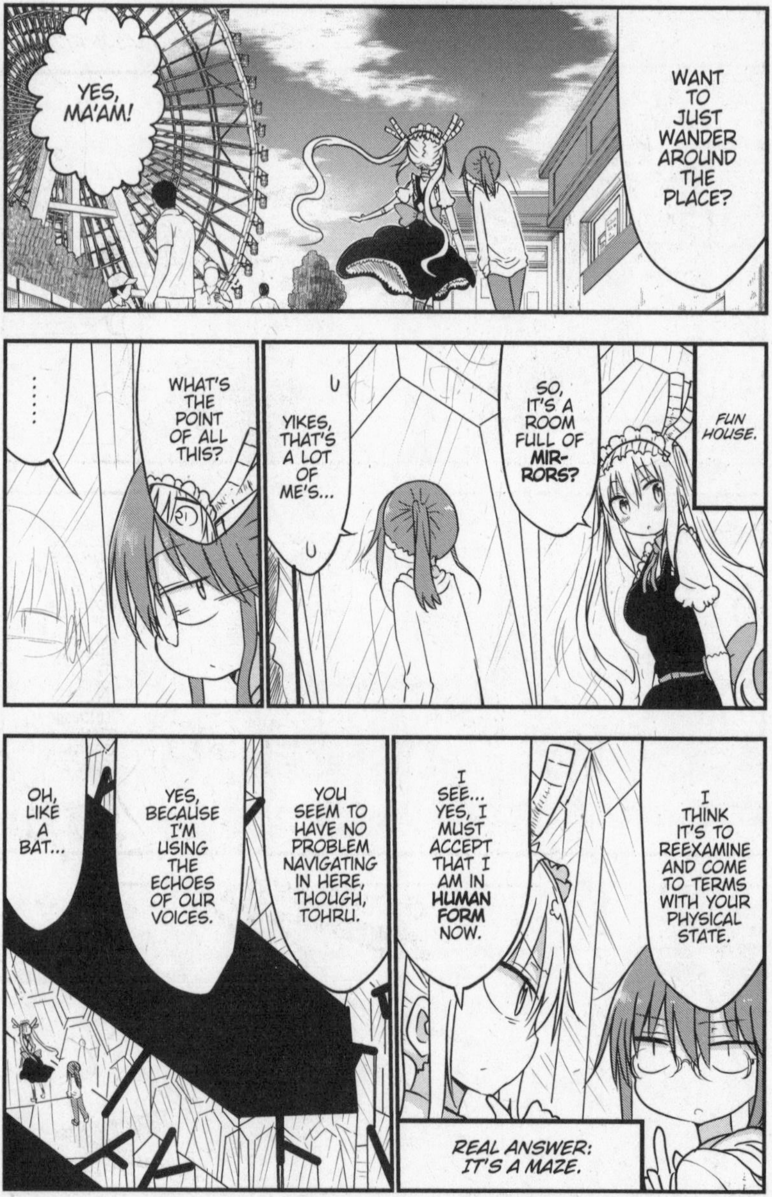
WANT TO JUST WANDER AROUND THE PLACE?
YES, MA'AM!
FUN HOUSE.
SO, IT'S A ROOM FULL OF MIR-RORS?
YIKES, THAT'S A LOT OF ME'S...
WHAT'S THE POINT OF ALL THIS?
......
I THINK IT'S TO REEXAMINE AND COME TO TERMS WITH YOUR PHYSICAL STATE.
I SEE... YES, I MUST ACCEPT THAT I AM IN HUMAN FORM NOW.
REAL ANSWER: IT'S A MAZE.
YOU SEEM TO HAVE NO PROBLEM NAVIGATING IN HERE, THOUGH, TOHRU.
YES, BECAUSE I'M USING THE ECHOES OF OUR VOICES.
OH, LIKE A BAT...

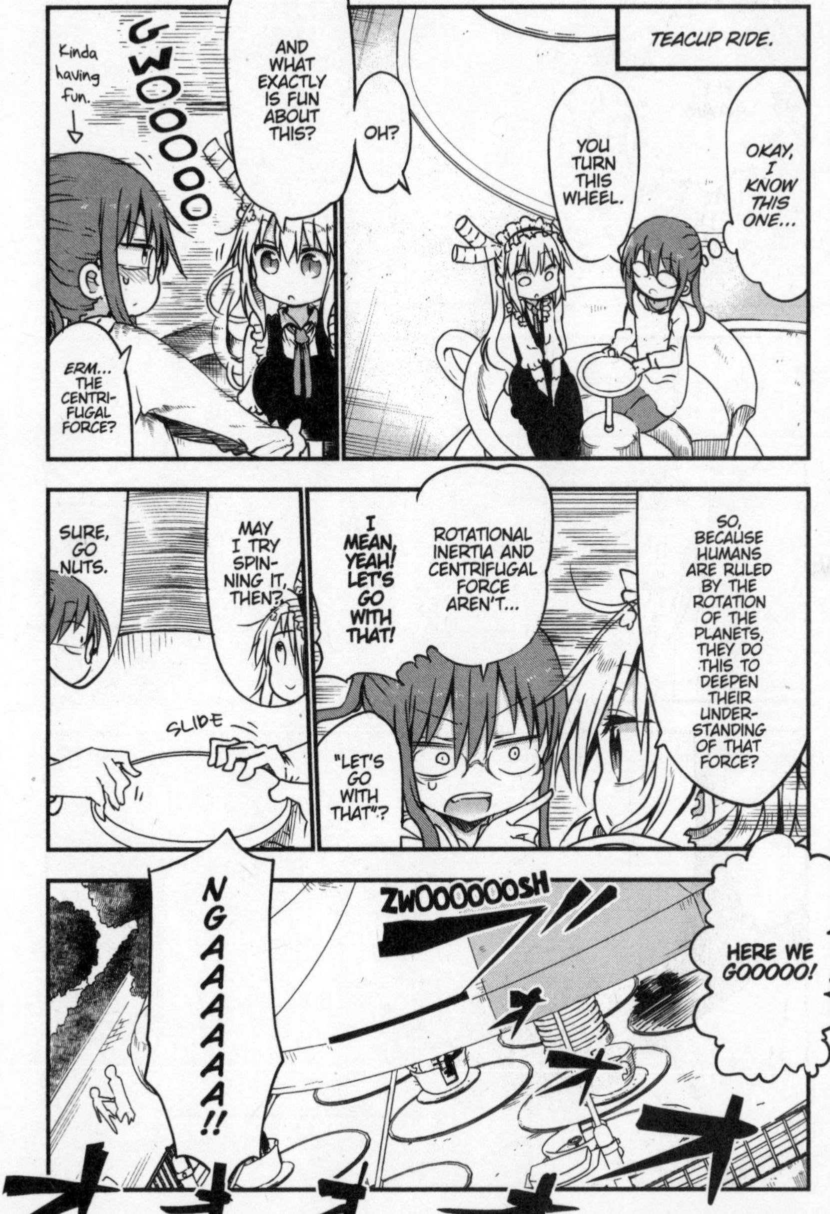
TEACUP RIDE.
OKAY, I KNOW THIS ONE...
YOU TURN THIS WHEEL.
OH?
AND WHAT EXACTLY IS FUN ABOUT THIS?
UWOOOOOO
Kinda having fun.
ERM... THE CENTRIFUGAL FORCE?
SO, BECAUSE HUMANS ARE RULED BY THE ROTATION OF THE PLANETS, THEY DO THIS TO DEEPEN THEIR UNDERSTANDING OF THAT FORCE?
ROTATIONAL INERTIA AND CENTRIFUGAL FORCE AREN'T...
I MEAN, YEAH! LET'S GO WITH THAT!
"LET'S GO WITH THAT"?
MAY I TRY SPIN-NING IT, THEN?
SURE, GO NUTS.
SLIDE
HERE WE GOOOOO!
ZWOOOOOOSH
NGAAAAAAAA!!

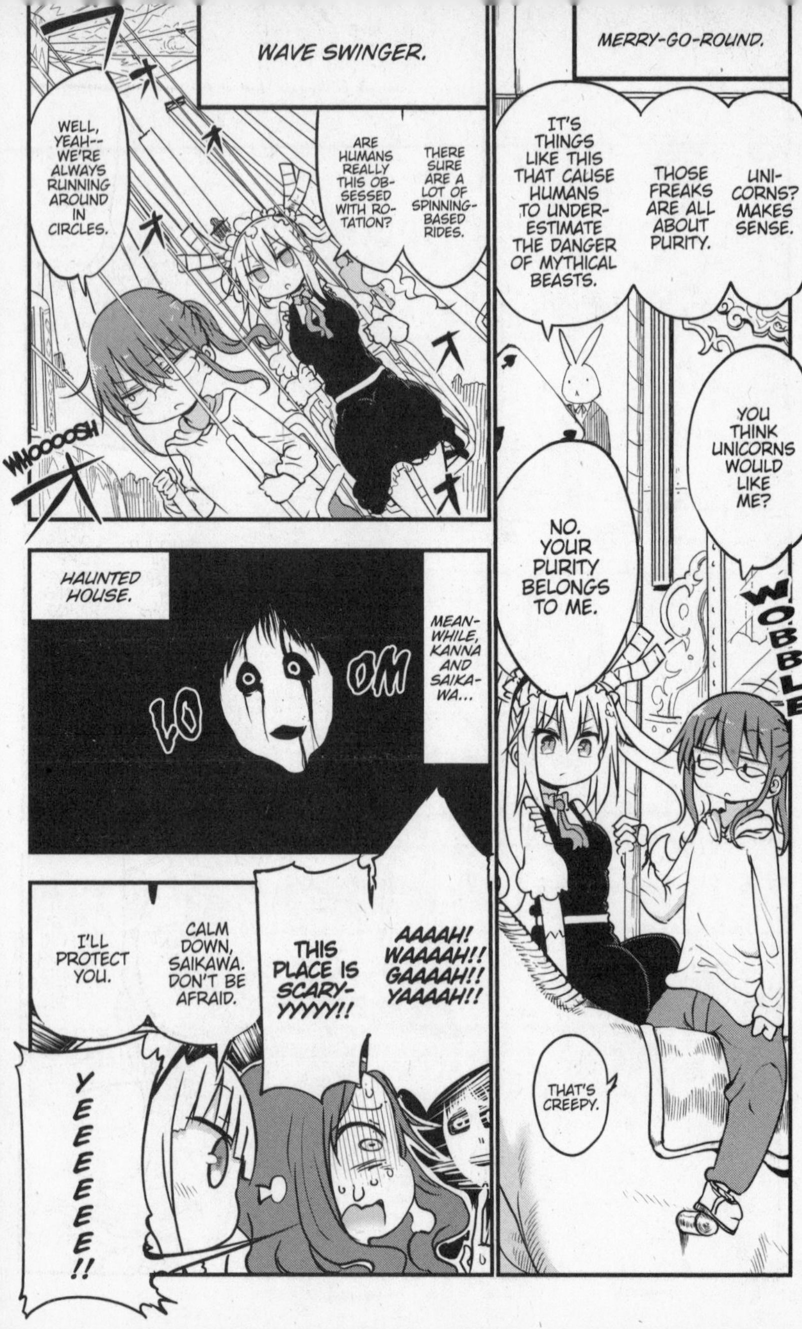
MERRY-GO-ROUND.
UNICORNS? MAKES SENSE.
THOSE FREAKS ARE ALL ABOUT PURITY.
IT'S THINGS LIKE THIS THAT CAUSE HUMANS TO UNDERESTIMATE THE DANGER OF MYTHICAL BEASTS.
YOU THINK UNICORNS WOULD LIKE ME?
NO. YOUR PURITY BELONGS TO ME.
WOBBLE
THAT'S CREEPY.
WAVE SWINGER.
THERE SURE ARE A LOT OF SPINNING-BASED RIDES.
ARE HUMANS REALLY THIS OBSESSED WITH ROTATION?
WELL, YEAH-- WE'RE ALWAYS RUNNING AROUND IN CIRCLES.
WHOOOOSH
HAUNTED HOUSE.
MEANWHILE, KANNA AND SAIKAWA...
LO OM
AAAAH! WAAAAH!! GAAAAH!! YAAAAH!!
THIS PLACE IS SCARY-YYYYY!!
CALM DOWN, SAIKAWA. DON'T BE AFRAID.
I'LL PROTECT YOU.
YEEEEEEE!!

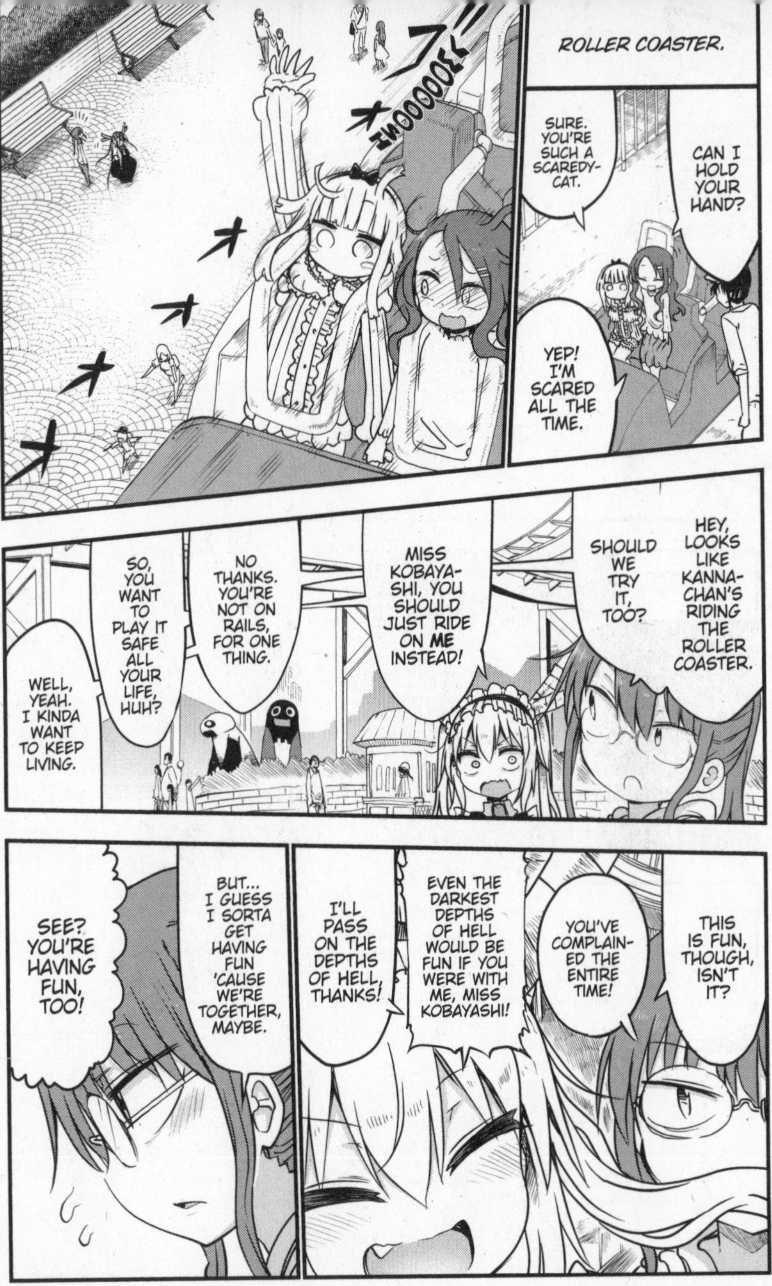
ROLLER COASTER.
CAN I HOLD YOUR HAND?
SURE. YOU'RE SUCH A SCAREDY-CAT.
YEP! I'M SCARED ALL THE TIME.
HEY, LOOKS LIKE KANNA-CHAN'S RIDING THE ROLLER COASTER.
SHOULD WE TRY IT, TOO?
MISS KOBAYASHI, YOU SHOULD JUST RIDE ON **ME** INSTEAD!
NO THANKS. YOU'RE NOT ON RAILS, FOR ONE THING.
SO, YOU WANT TO PLAY IT SAFE ALL YOUR LIFE, HUH?
WELL, YEAH. I KINDA WANT TO KEEP LIVING.
THIS IS FUN, THOUGH, ISN'T IT?
YOU'VE COMPLAIN-ED THE ENTIRE TIME!
EVEN THE DARKEST DEPTHS OF HELL WOULD BE FUN IF YOU WERE WITH ME, MISS KOBAYASHI!
I'LL PASS ON THE DEPTHS OF HELL, THANKS!
BUT... I GUESS I SORTA GET HAVING FUN 'CAUSE WE'RE TOGETHER, MAYBE.
SEE? YOU'RE HAVING FUN, TOO!

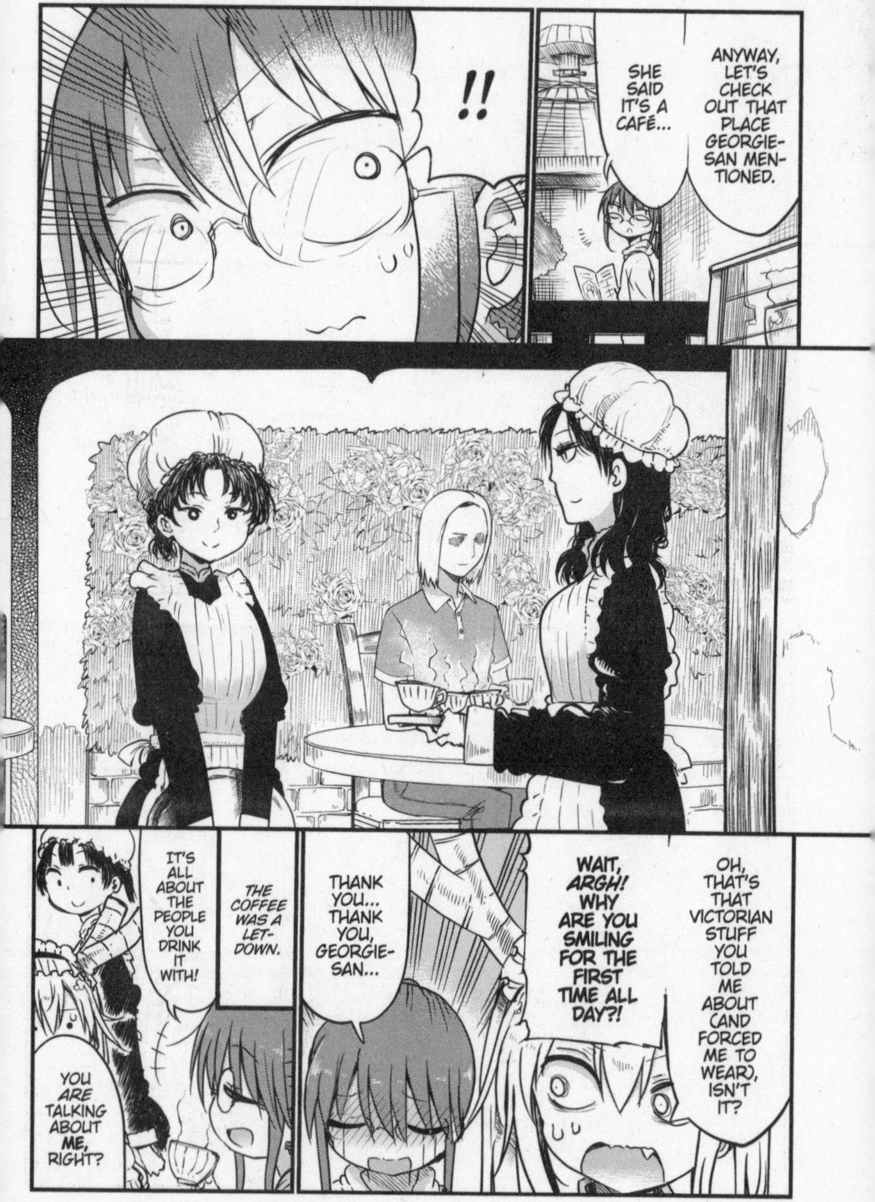
ANYWAY, LET'S CHECK OUT THAT PLACE GEORGIE-SAN MENTIONED.
SHE SAID IT'S A CAFÉ...
!!
OH, THAT'S THAT VICTORIAN STUFF YOU TOLD ME ABOUT (AND FORCED ME TO WEAR), ISN'T IT?
WAIT, *ARGH!* WHY ARE YOU SMILING FOR THE FIRST TIME ALL DAY?!
THANK YOU... THANK YOU, GEORGIE-SAN...
THE COFFEE WAS A LET-DOWN.
IT'S ALL ABOUT THE PEOPLE YOU DRINK IT WITH!
YOU *ARE* TALKING ABOUT *ME*, RIGHT?

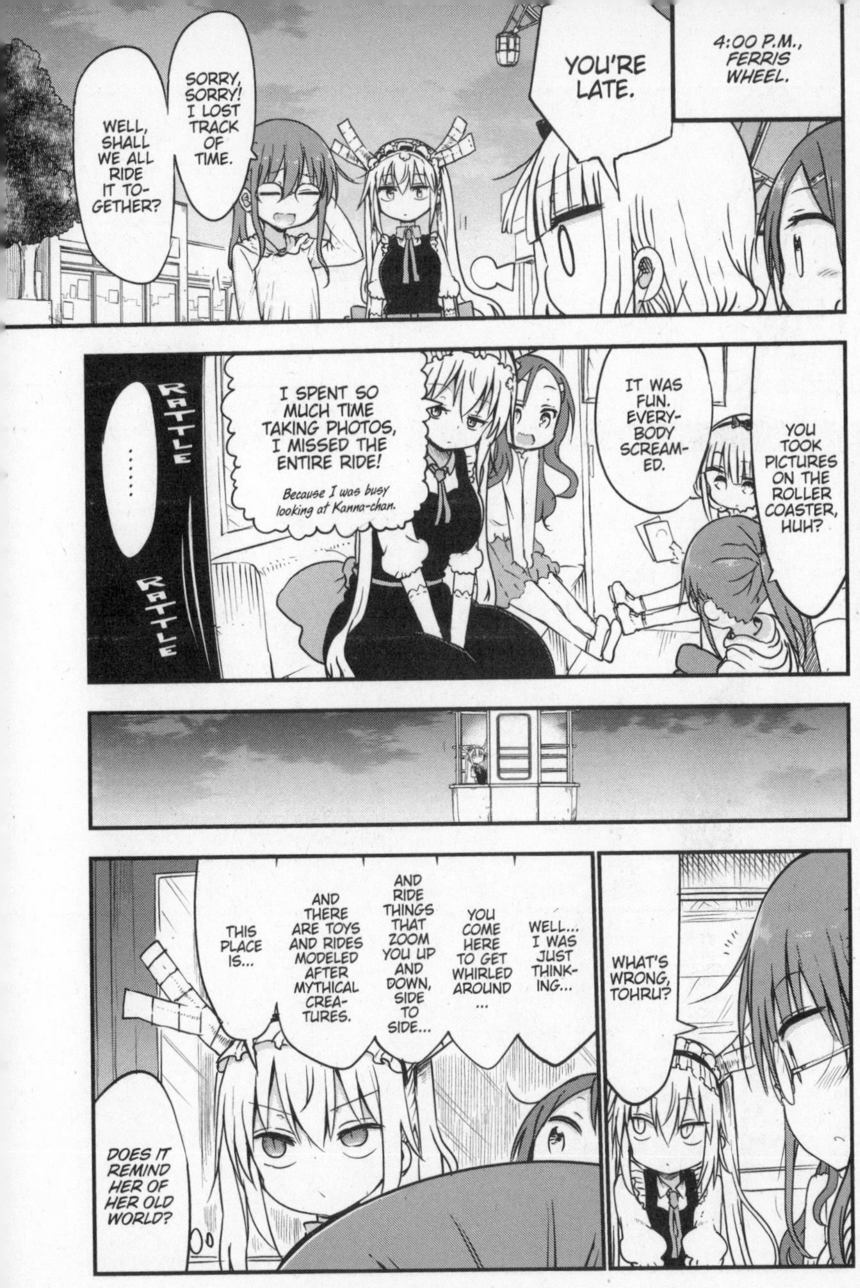
4:00 P.M., FERRIS WHEEL.
YOU'RE LATE.
SORRY, SORRY! I LOST TRACK OF TIME.
WELL, SHALL WE ALL RIDE IT TOGETHER?
YOU TOOK PICTURES ON THE ROLLER COASTER, HUH?
IT WAS FUN. EVERYBODY SCREAMED.
I SPENT SO MUCH TIME TAKING PHOTOS, I MISSED THE ENTIRE RIDE!
Because I was busy looking at Kanna-chan.
......
RATTLE
RATTLE
WHAT'S WRONG, TOHRU?
WELL... I WAS JUST THINKING...
YOU COME HERE TO GET WHIRLED AROUND...
AND RIDE THINGS THAT ZOOM YOU UP AND DOWN, SIDE TO SIDE...
AND THERE ARE TOYS AND RIDES MODELED AFTER MYTHICAL CREATURES.
THIS PLACE IS...
DOES IT REMIND HER OF HER OLD WORLD?

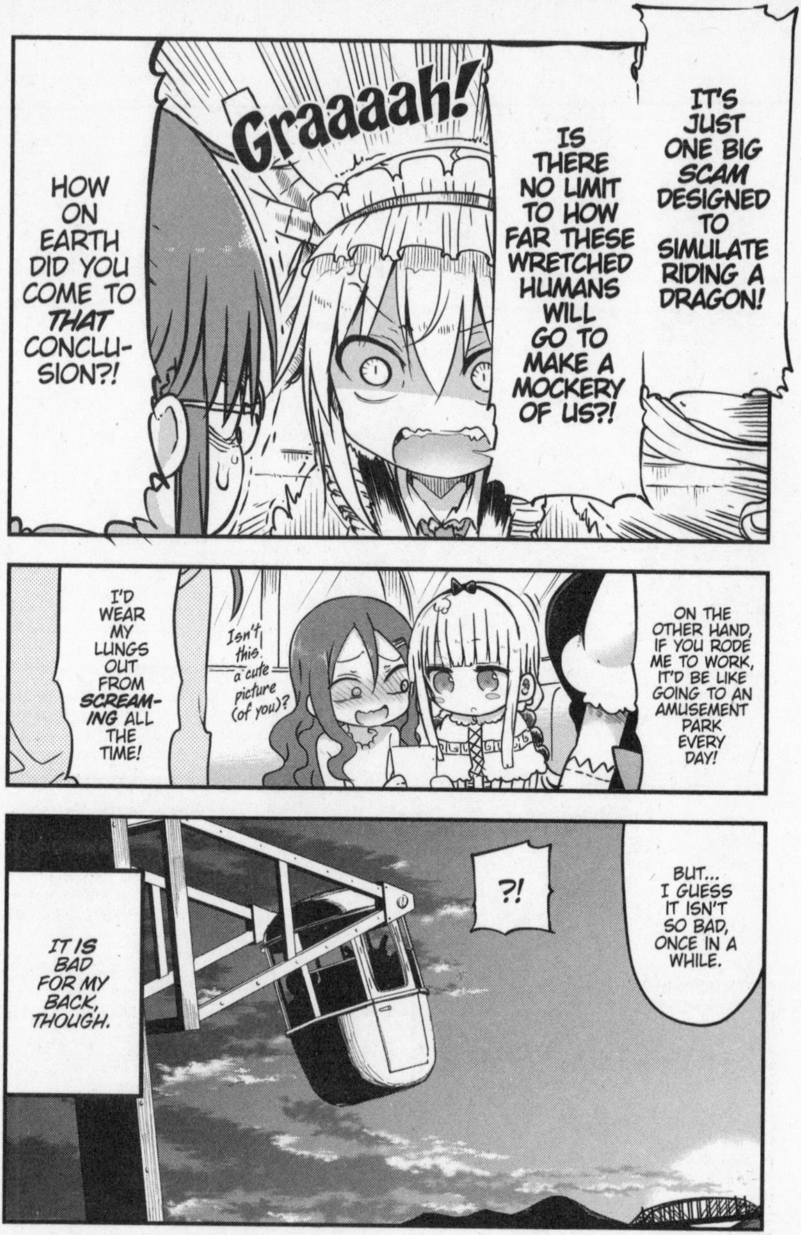
IT'S JUST ONE BIG SCAM DESIGNED TO SIMULATE RIDING A DRAGON!
Graaaah!
IS THERE NO LIMIT TO HOW FAR THESE WRETCHED HUMANS WILL GO TO MAKE A MOCKERY OF US?!
HOW ON EARTH DID YOU COME TO THAT CONCLUSION?!
ON THE OTHER HAND, IF YOU RODE ME TO WORK, IT'D BE LIKE GOING TO AN AMUSEMENT PARK EVERY DAY!
Isn't this a cute picture (of you)?
I'D WEAR MY LUNGS OUT FROM SCREAMING ALL THE TIME!
BUT... I GUESS IT ISN'T SO BAD, ONCE IN A WHILE.
?!
IT IS BAD FOR MY BACK, THOUGH.

Georgie in a school uniform.

Miss Kobayashi's
DRAGON MAID

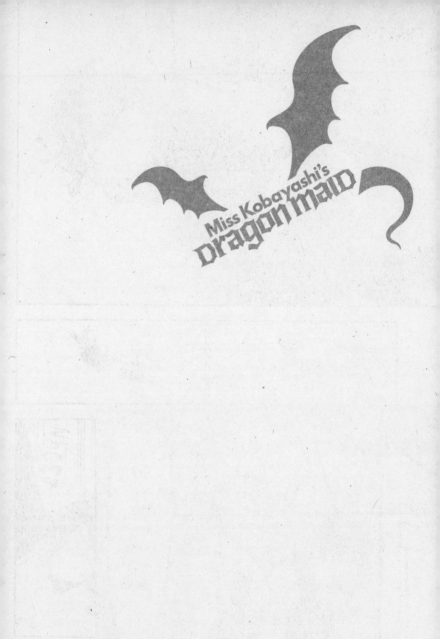

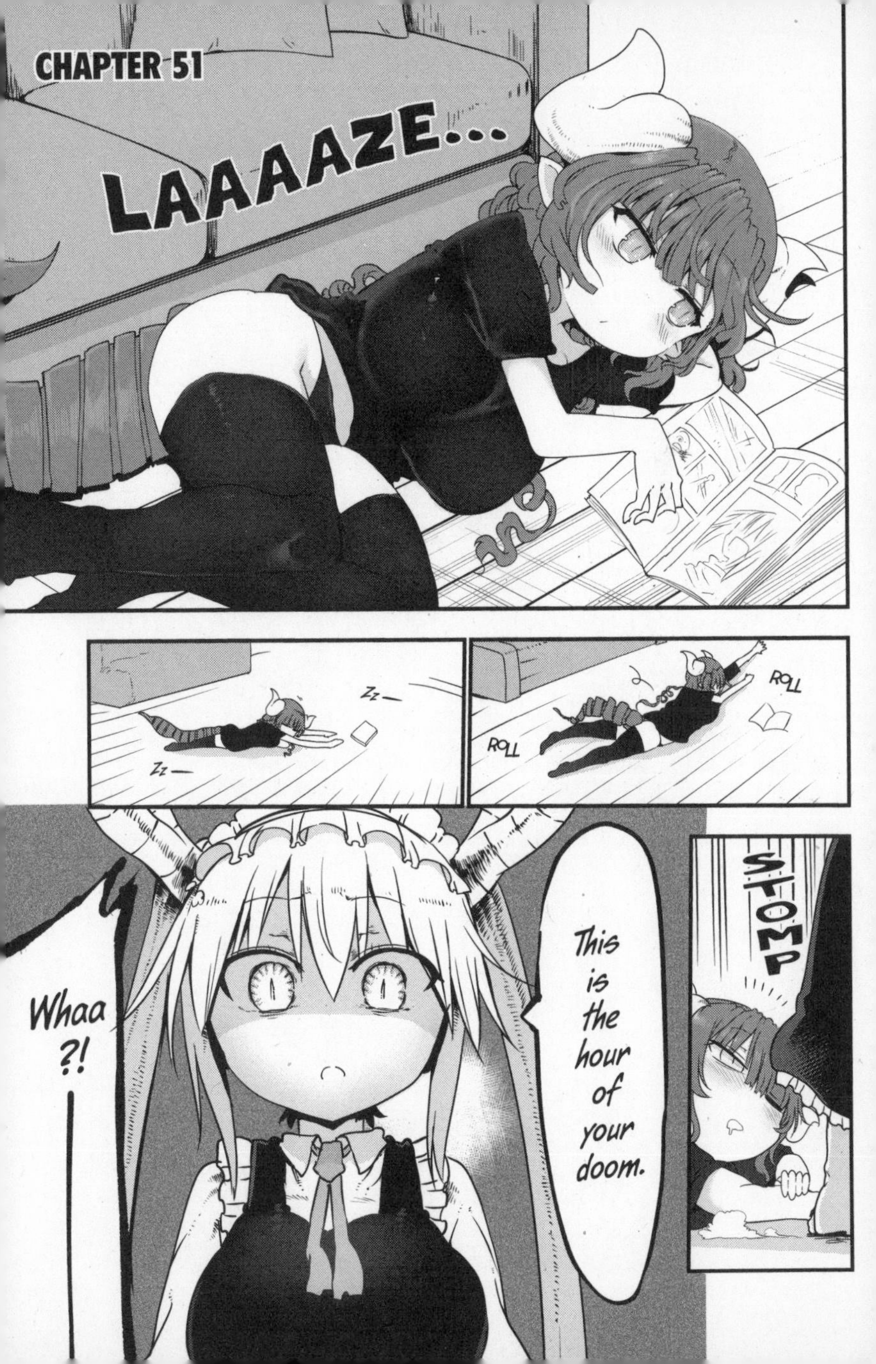
CHAPTER 51
LAAAAZE...
ROLL
ROLL
Zz—
Zz—
STOMP
This is the hour of your doom.
Whaa?!

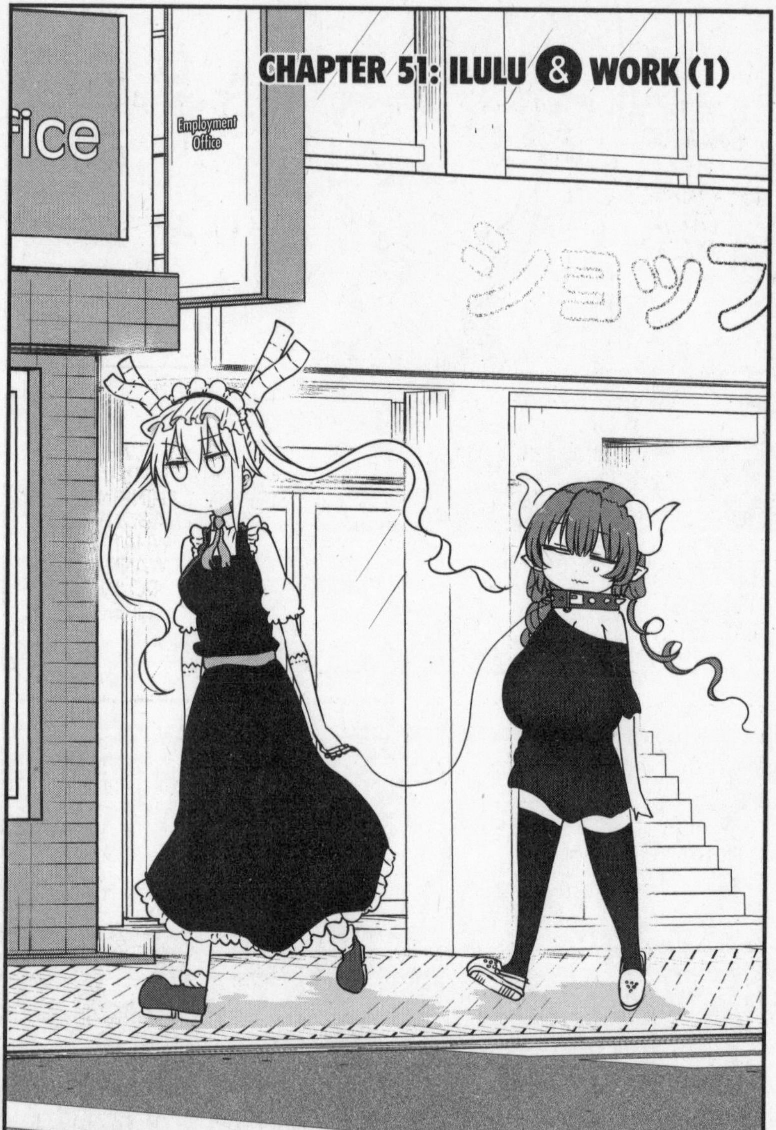
CHAPTER 51: ILULU & WORK (1)
fice
Employment Office
ショッフ

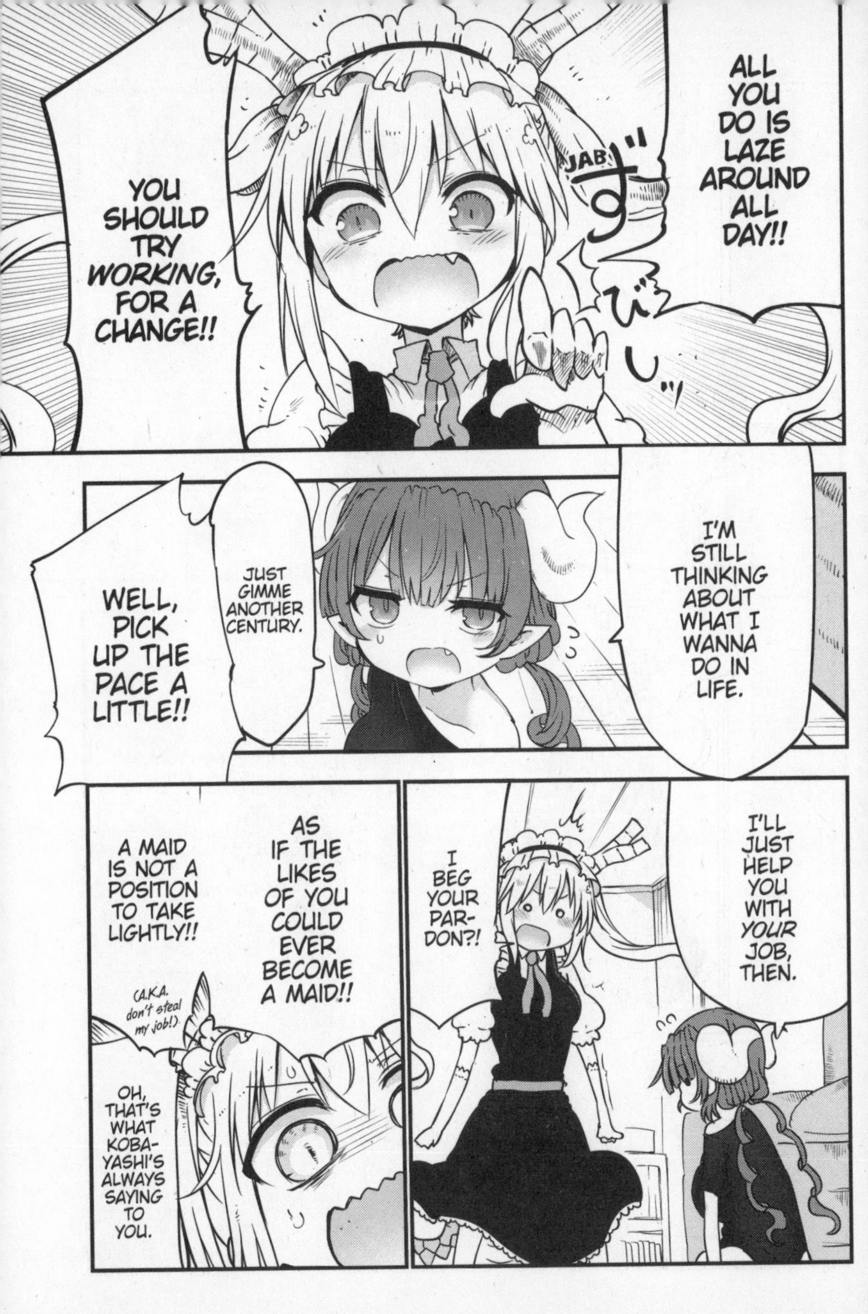
ALL YOU DO IS LAZE AROUND ALL DAY!!
JAB
YOU SHOULD TRY *WORKING*, FOR A CHANGE!!
I'M STILL THINKING ABOUT WHAT I WANNA DO IN LIFE.
JUST GIMME ANOTHER CENTURY.
WELL, PICK UP THE PACE A LITTLE!!
I'LL JUST HELP YOU WITH *YOUR* JOB, THEN.
I BEG YOUR PARDON?!
AS IF THE LIKES OF YOU COULD EVER BECOME A MAID!!
A MAID IS NOT A POSITION TO TAKE LIGHTLY!!
(A.K.A. don't steal my job!)
OH, THAT'S WHAT KOBAYASHI'S ALWAYS SAYING TO YOU.

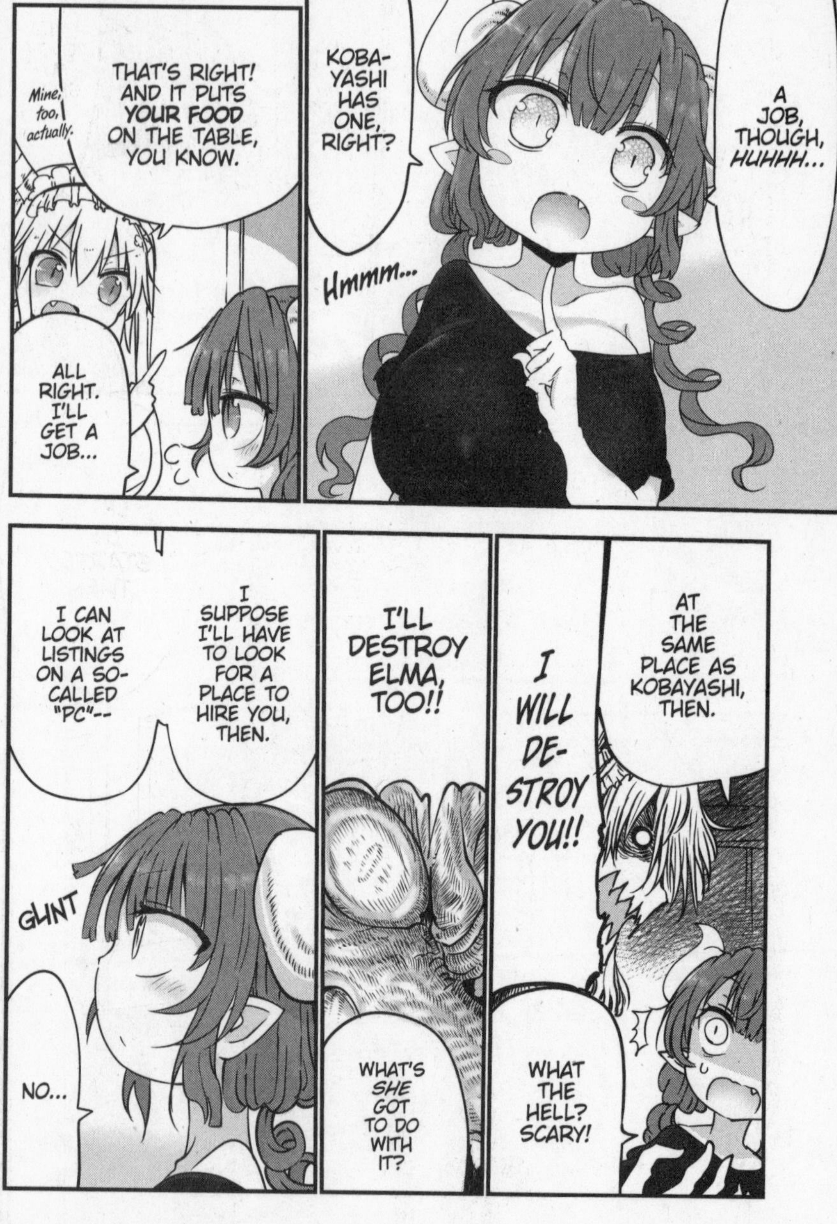
A JOB, THOUGH, HUHHH...
KOBAYASHI HAS ONE, RIGHT?
Hmmm...
THAT'S RIGHT! AND IT PUTS YOUR FOOD ON THE TABLE, YOU KNOW.
Mine, too, actually.
ALL RIGHT. I'LL GET A JOB...
AT THE SAME PLACE AS KOBAYASHI, THEN.
I WILL DESTROY YOU!!
WHAT THE HELL? SCARY!
I'LL DESTROY ELMA, TOO!!
WHAT'S SHE GOT TO DO WITH IT?
I SUPPOSE I'LL HAVE TO LOOK FOR A PLACE TO HIRE YOU, THEN.
I CAN LOOK AT LISTINGS ON A SO-CALLED "PC"--
GLINT
NO...

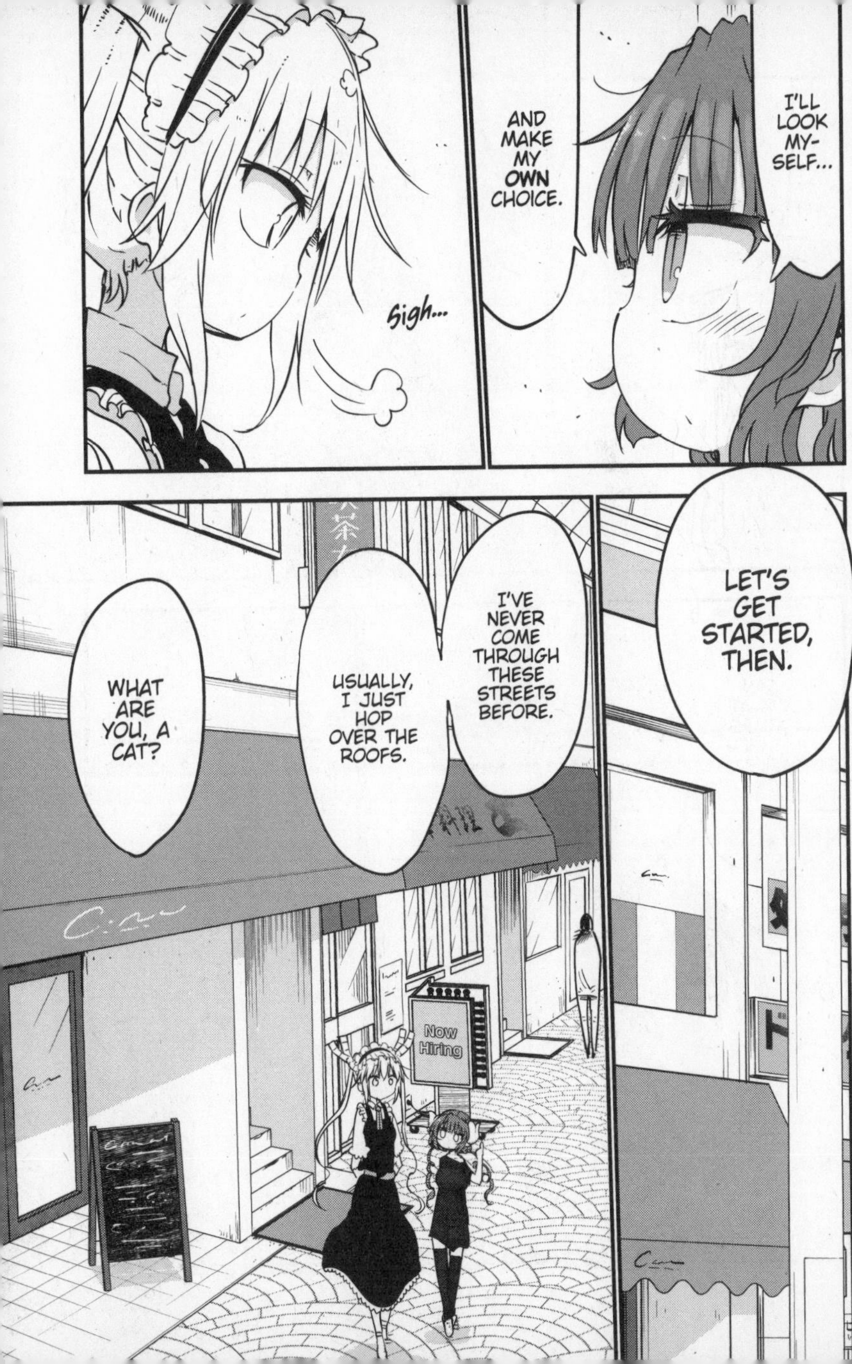
I'LL LOOK MY-SELF...
AND MAKE MY OWN CHOICE.
Sigh...
LET'S GET STARTED, THEN.
I'VE NEVER COME THROUGH THESE STREETS BEFORE.
USUALLY, I JUST HOP OVER THE ROOFS.
WHAT ARE YOU, A CAT?
Now Hiring

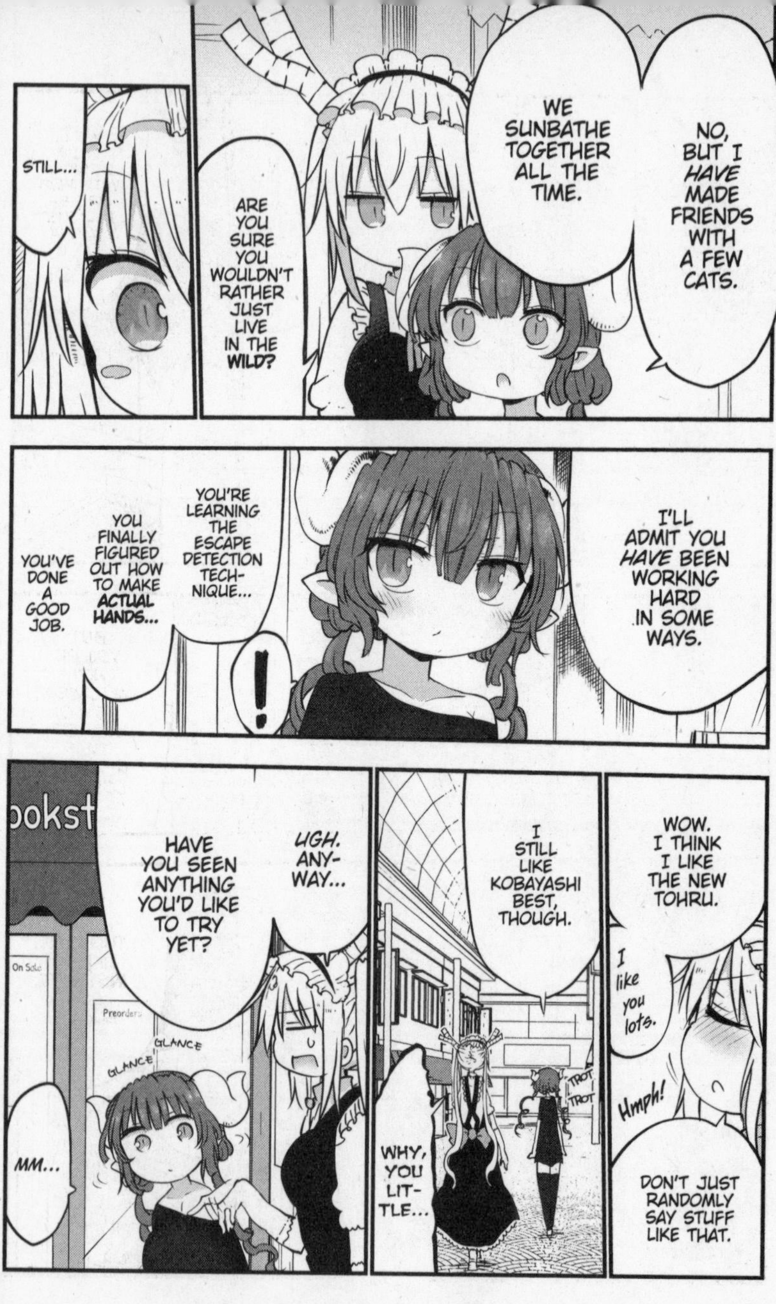
NO, BUT I *HAVE* MADE FRIENDS WITH A FEW CATS.
WE SUNBATHE TOGETHER ALL THE TIME.
ARE YOU SURE YOU WOULDN'T RATHER JUST LIVE IN THE **WILD?**
STILL...
I'LL ADMIT YOU *HAVE* BEEN WORKING HARD IN SOME WAYS.
!
YOU'RE LEARNING THE ESCAPE DETECTION TECH-NIQUE...
YOU FINALLY FIGURED OUT HOW TO MAKE **ACTUAL HANDS...**
YOU'VE DONE A GOOD JOB.
WOW. I THINK I LIKE THE NEW TOHRU.
I like you lots.
Hmph!
DON'T JUST RANDOMLY SAY STUFF LIKE THAT.
I STILL LIKE KOBAYASHI BEST, THOUGH.
TROT TROT
WHY, YOU LIT-TLE...
UGH. ANY-WAY...
HAVE YOU SEEN ANYTHING YOU'D LIKE TO TRY YET?
ookst
On Sale
Preorders
GLANCE GLANCE
MM...

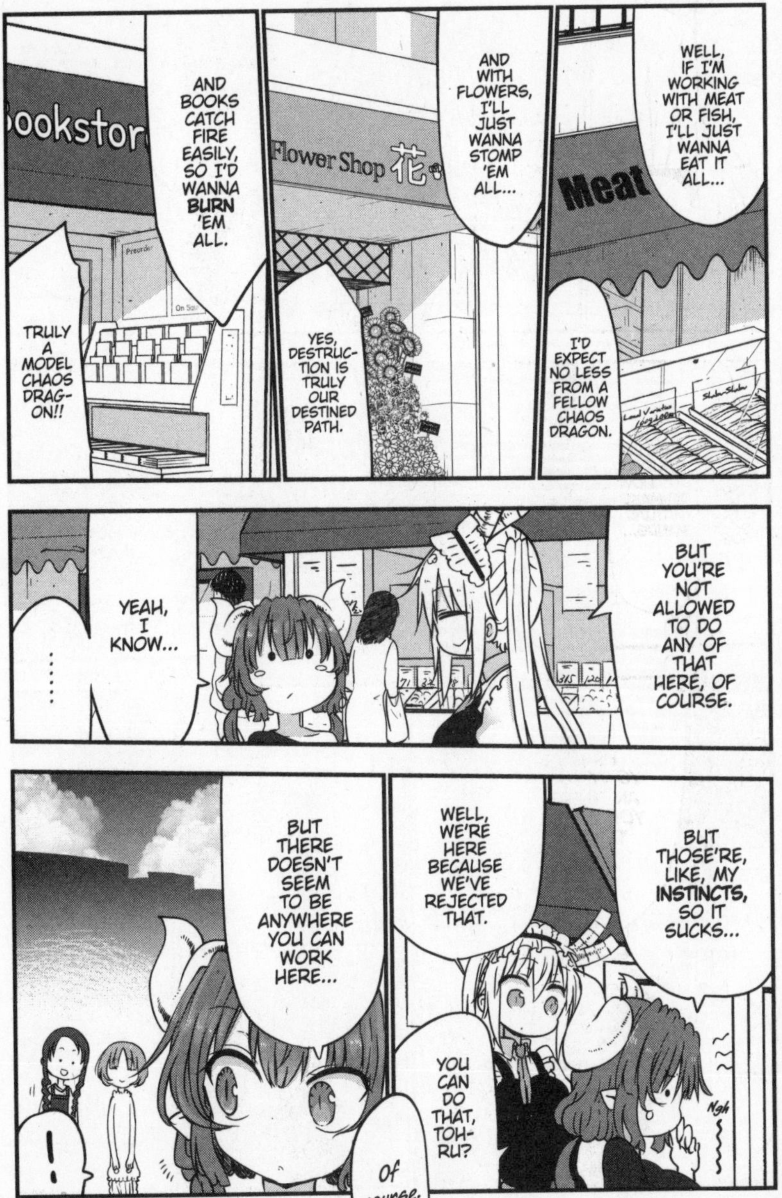
Meat
WELL, IF I'M WORKING WITH MEAT OR FISH, I'LL JUST WANNA EAT IT ALL...
I'D EXPECT NO LESS FROM A FELLOW CHAOS DRAGON.
Flower Shop 花
AND WITH FLOWERS, I'LL JUST WANNA STOMP 'EM ALL...
YES, DESTRUCTION IS TRULY OUR DESTINED PATH.
AND BOOKS CATCH FIRE EASILY, SO I'D WANNA **BURN** 'EM ALL.
TRULY A MODEL CHAOS DRAGON!!
BUT YOU'RE NOT ALLOWED TO DO ANY OF THAT HERE, OF COURSE.
YEAH, I KNOW...
......
BUT THOSE'RE, LIKE, MY **INSTINCTS**, SO IT SUCKS...
WELL, WE'RE HERE BECAUSE WE'VE REJECTED THAT.
Ngh
YOU CAN DO THAT, TOHRU?
Of course.
BUT THERE DOESN'T SEEM TO BE ANYWHERE YOU CAN WORK HERE...
!

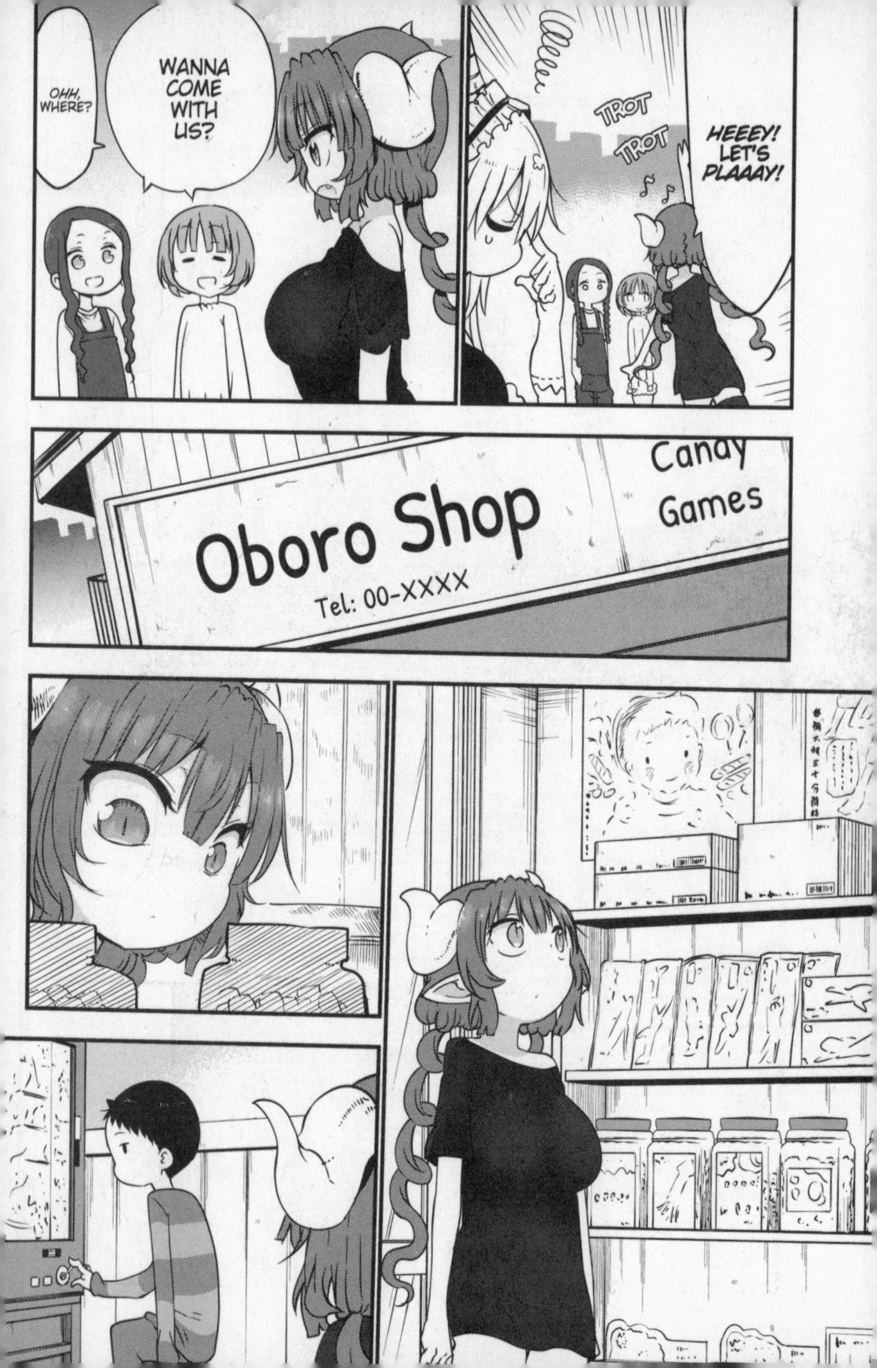
TROT
TROT
HEEEY! LET'S PLAAAY!
WANNA COME WITH US?
OHH, WHERE?
Candy
Games
Oboro Shop
Tel: 00-XXXX

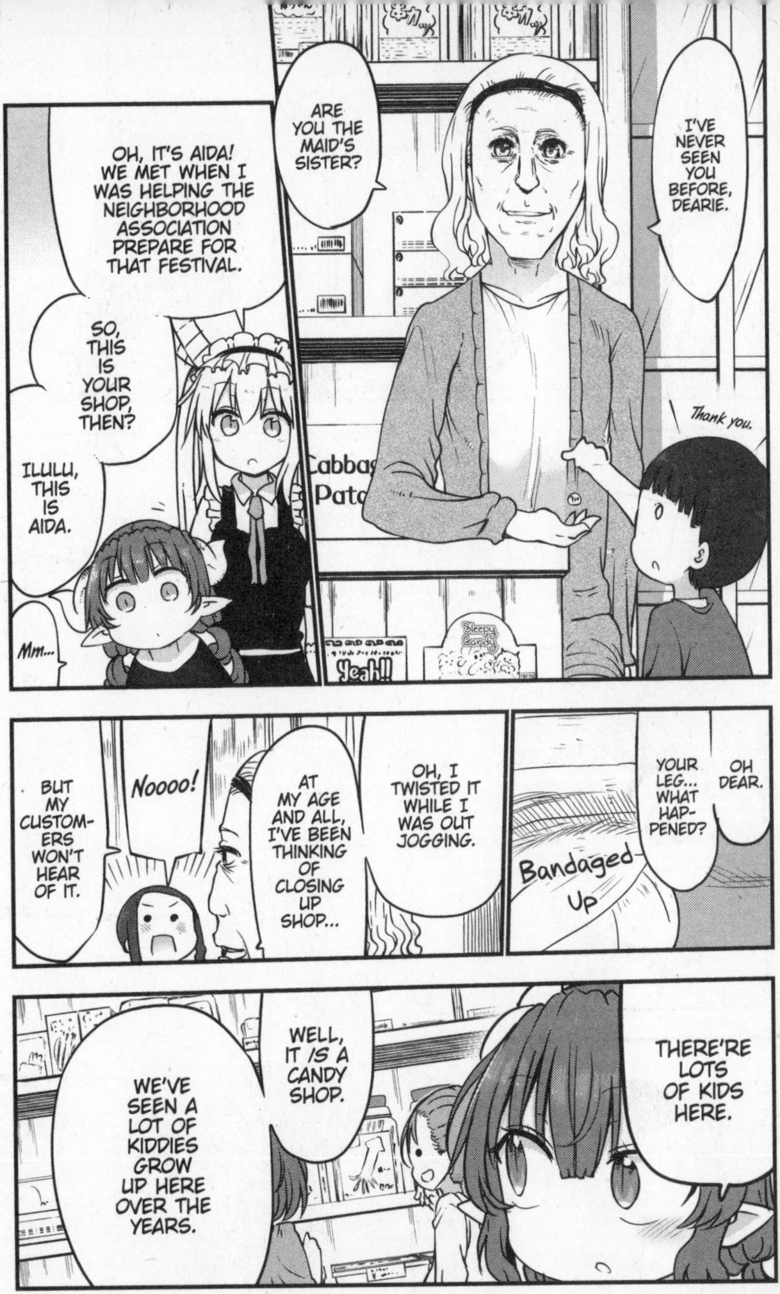
I'VE NEVER SEEN YOU BEFORE, DEARIE.
ARE YOU THE MAID'S SISTER?
Thank you.
OH, IT'S AIDA! WE MET WHEN I WAS HELPING THE NEIGHBORHOOD ASSOCIATION PREPARE FOR THAT FESTIVAL.
SO, THIS IS YOUR SHOP, THEN?
ILULU, THIS IS AIDA.
Mm...
Sleepy Candy
Yeah!!
OH DEAR.
YOUR LEG... WHAT HAPPENED?
Bandaged Up
OH, I TWISTED IT WHILE I WAS OUT JOGGING.
AT MY AGE AND ALL, I'VE BEEN THINKING OF CLOSING UP SHOP...
Noooo!
BUT MY CUSTOMERS WON'T HEAR OF IT.
THERE'RE LOTS OF KIDS HERE.
WELL, IT IS A CANDY SHOP.
WE'VE SEEN A LOT OF KIDDIES GROW UP HERE OVER THE YEARS.

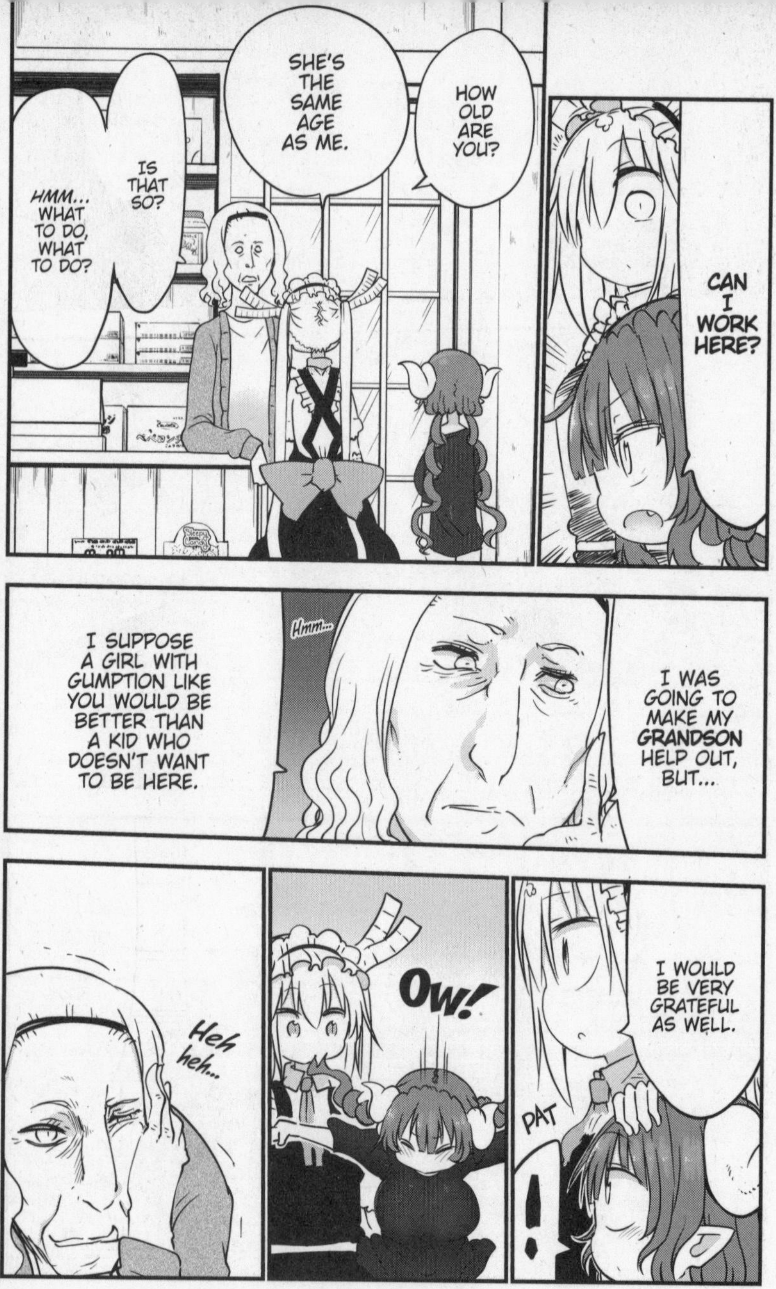
CAN I WORK HERE?
HOW OLD ARE YOU?
SHE'S THE SAME AGE AS ME.
IS THAT SO?
HMM... WHAT TO DO, WHAT TO DO?
I WAS GOING TO MAKE MY GRANDSON HELP OUT, BUT...
Hmm...
I SUPPOSE A GIRL WITH GUMPTION LIKE YOU WOULD BE BETTER THAN A KID WHO DOESN'T WANT TO BE HERE.
I WOULD BE VERY GRATEFUL AS WELL.
PAT
!
OW!
Heh heh...

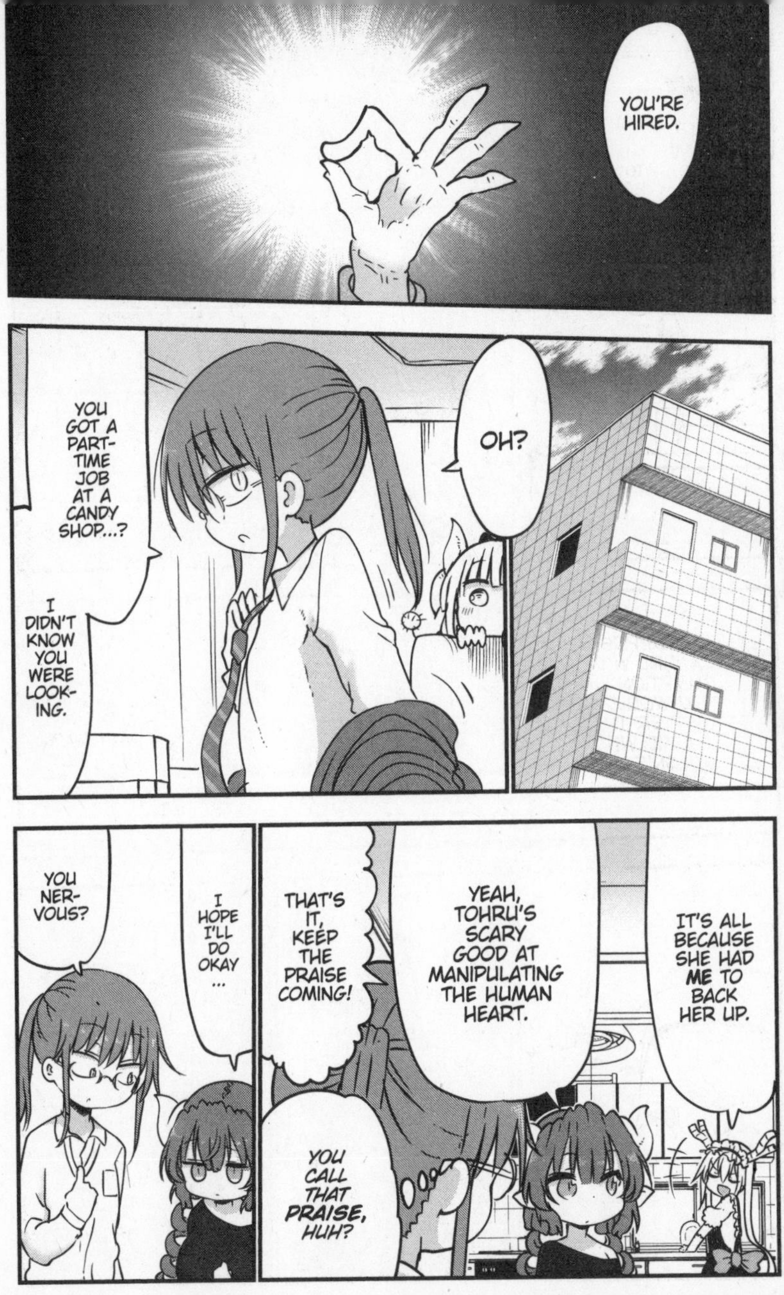
YOU'RE HIRED.
OH?
YOU GOT A PART-TIME JOB AT A CANDY SHOP...?
I DIDN'T KNOW YOU WERE LOOKING.
IT'S ALL BECAUSE SHE HAD **ME** TO BACK HER UP.
YEAH, TOHRU'S SCARY GOOD AT MANIPULATING THE HUMAN HEART.
THAT'S IT, KEEP THE PRAISE COMING!
YOU CALL THAT ***PRAISE***, HUH?
I HOPE I'LL DO OKAY ...
YOU NERVOUS?

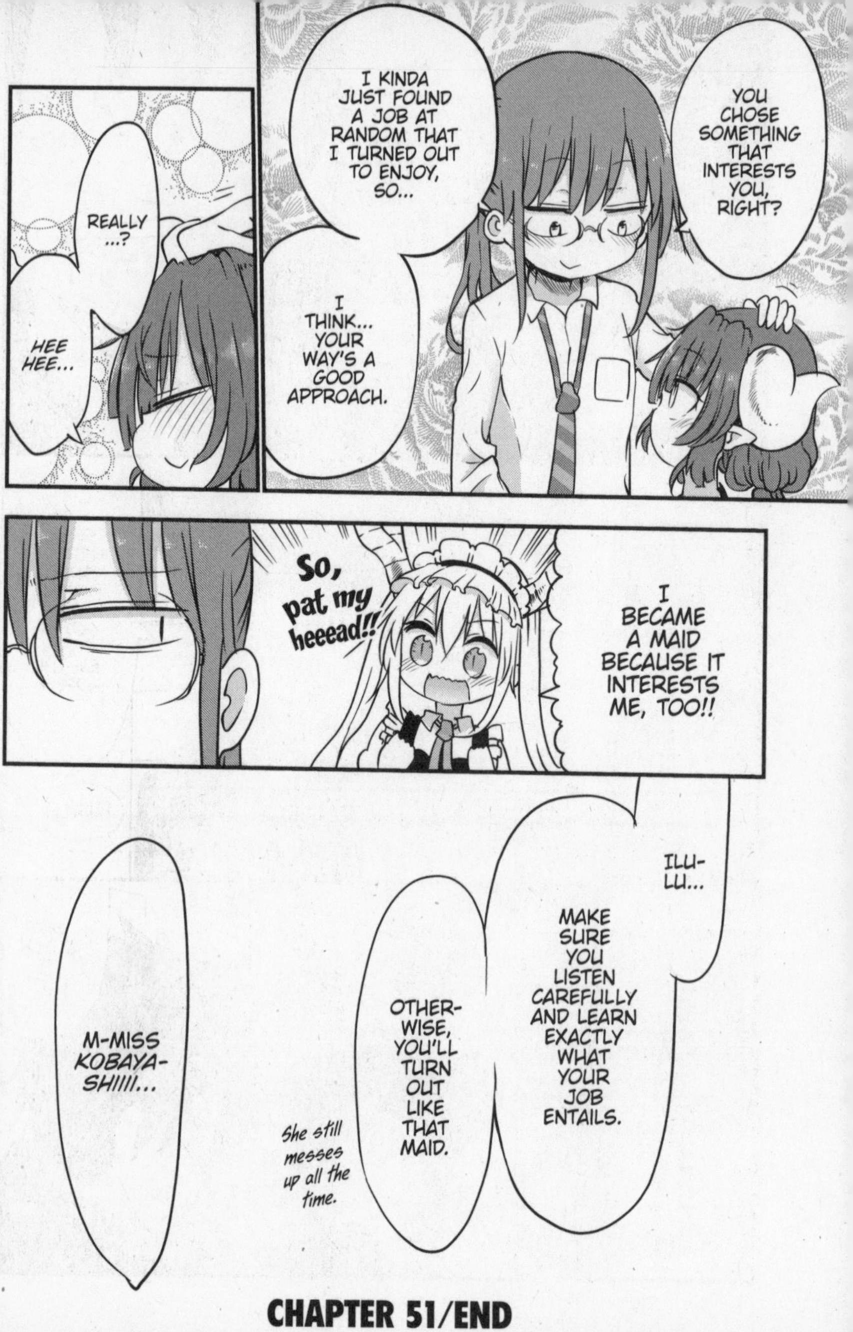
YOU CHOSE SOMETHING THAT INTERESTS YOU, RIGHT?
I KINDA JUST FOUND A JOB AT RANDOM THAT I TURNED OUT TO ENJOY, SO...
I THINK... YOUR WAY'S A GOOD APPROACH.
REALLY ...?
HEE HEE...
I BECAME A MAID BECAUSE IT INTERESTS ME, TOO!!
So, pat my heeeead!!
ILU-LU...
MAKE SURE YOU LISTEN CAREFULLY AND LEARN EXACTLY WHAT YOUR JOB ENTAILS.
OTHER-WISE, YOU'LL TURN OUT LIKE THAT MAID.
She still messes up all the time.
M-MISS KOBAYA-SHIIII...

CHAPTER 51/END

CHAPTER 52

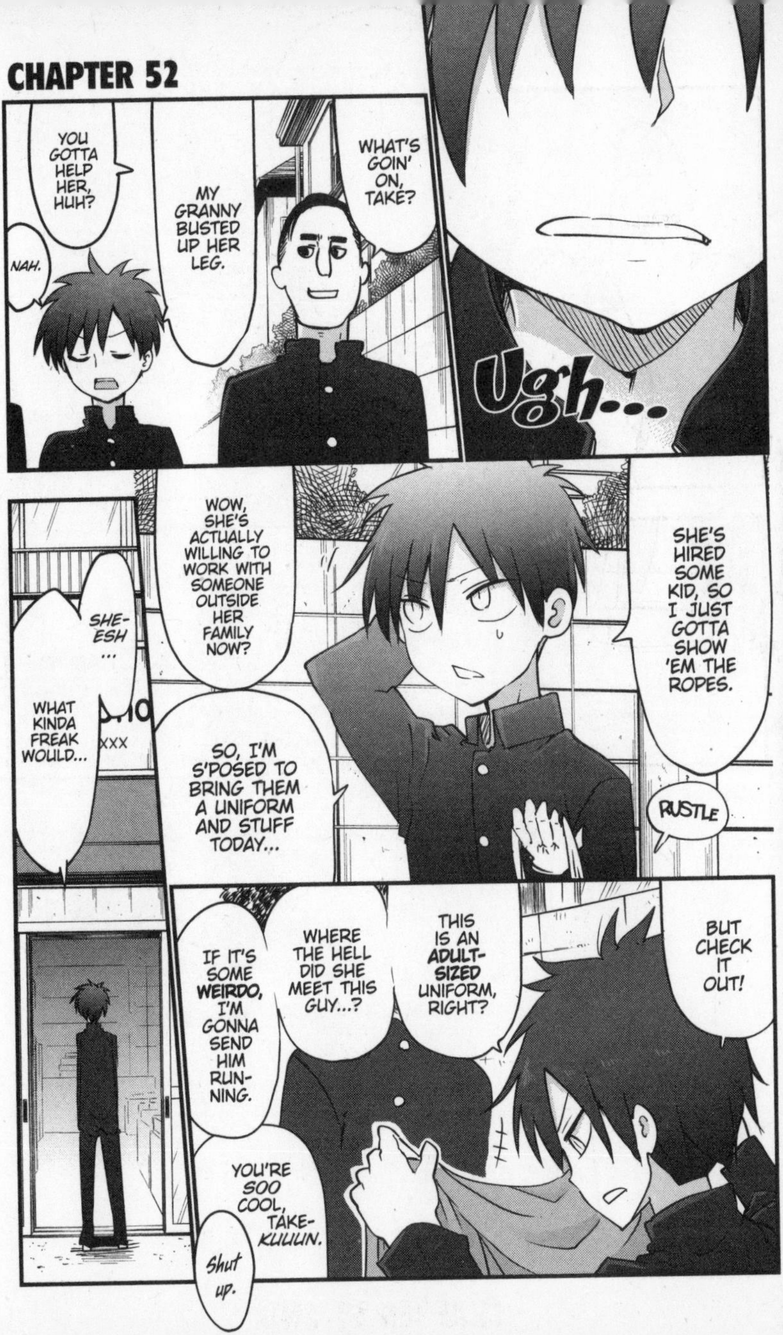
Ugh...
WHAT'S GOIN' ON, TAKE?
MY GRANNY BUSTED UP HER LEG.
YOU GOTTA HELP HER, HUH?
NAH.
SHE'S HIRED SOME KID, SO I JUST GOTTA SHOW 'EM THE ROPES.
RUSTLE
WOW, SHE'S ACTUALLY WILLING TO WORK WITH SOMEONE OUTSIDE HER FAMILY NOW?
SO, I'M S'POSED TO BRING THEM A UNIFORM AND STUFF TODAY...
SHE-ESH...
WHAT KINDA FREAK WOULD...
BUT CHECK IT OUT!
THIS IS AN **ADULT-SIZED** UNIFORM, RIGHT?
WHERE THE HELL DID SHE MEET THIS GUY...?
IF IT'S SOME **WEIRDO,** I'M GONNA SEND HIM RUN-NING.
YOU'RE SOO COOL, TAKE-KUUUN.
Shut up.

CHAPTER 52: ILULU & WORK (2)

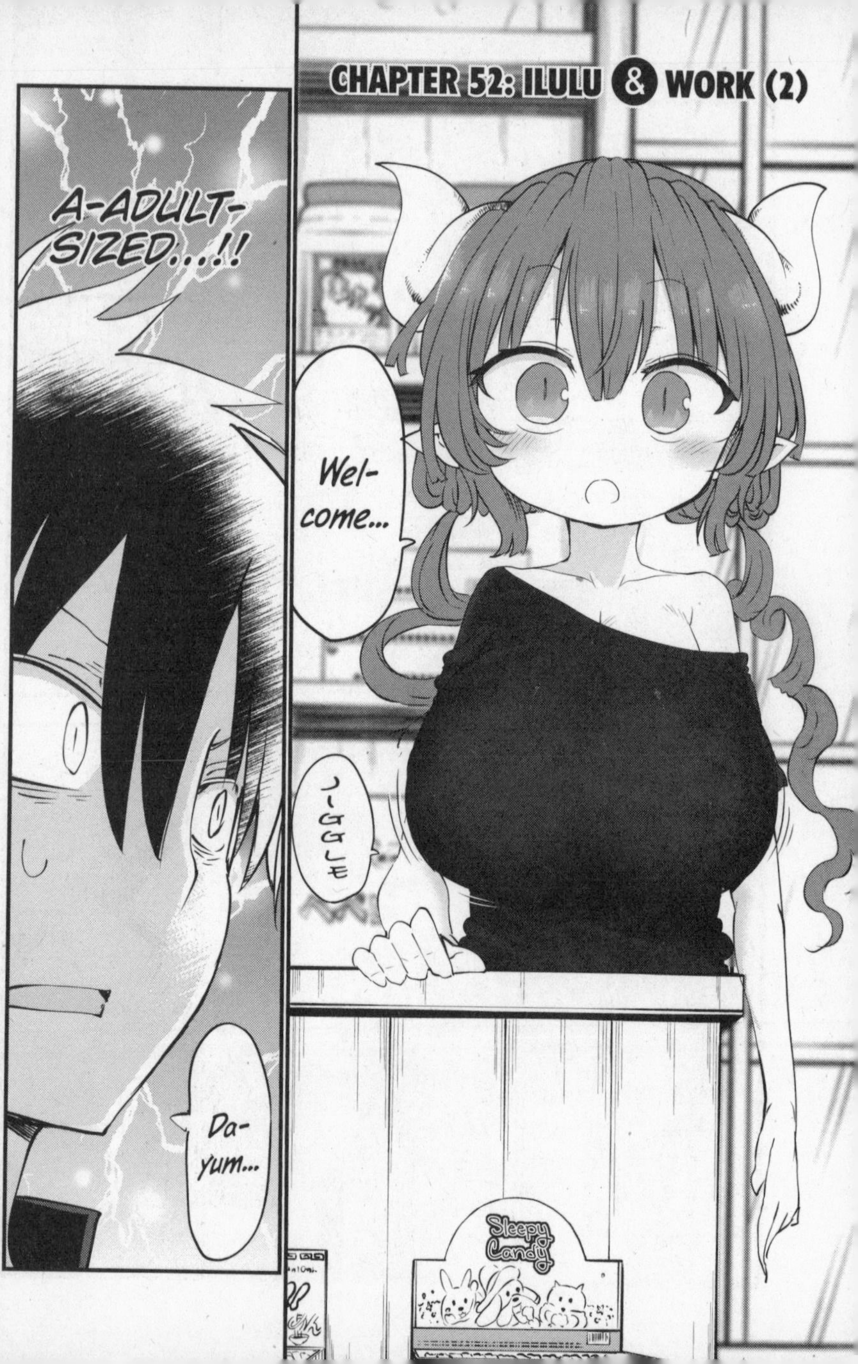
Wel-come...
JIGGLE
A-ADULT-SIZED...!!
Da-yum...
Sleepy Candy

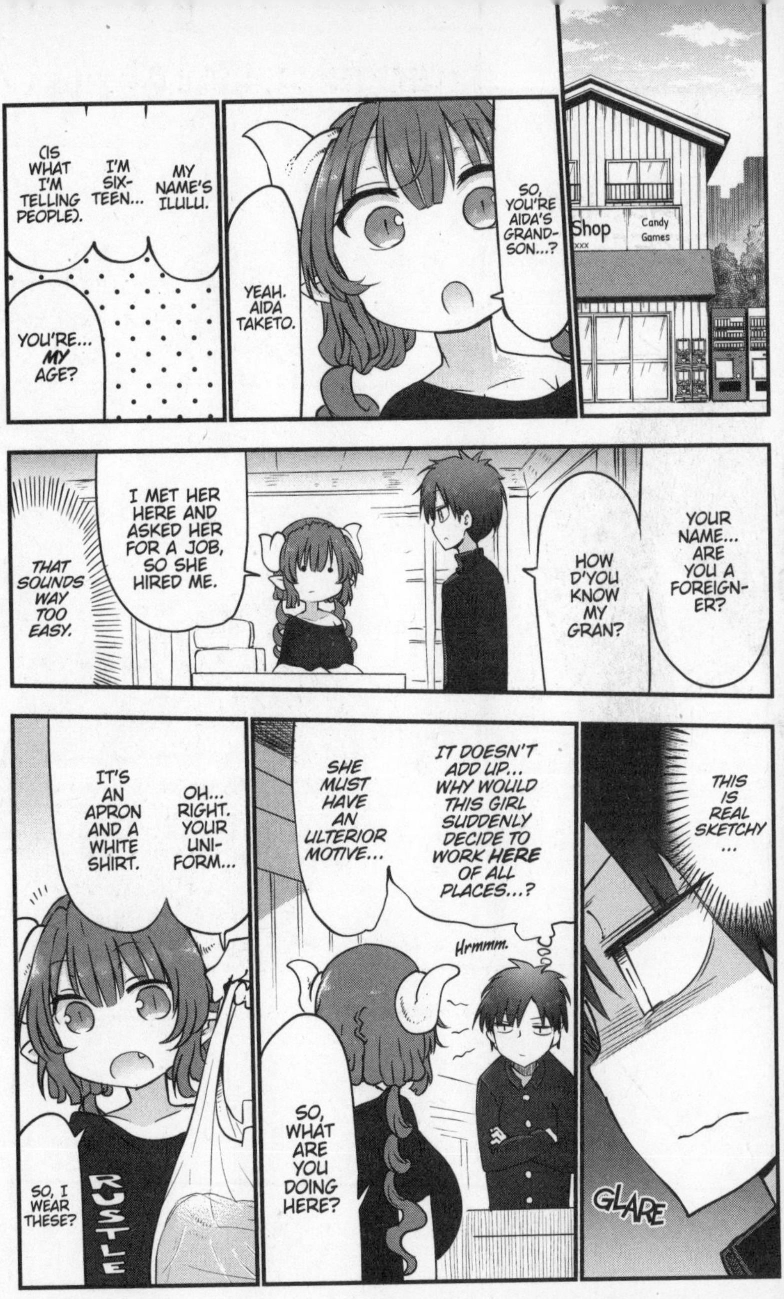
Shop
Candy
Games
SO, YOU'RE AIDA'S GRANDSON...?
YEAH. AIDA TAKETO.
MY NAME'S ILULU.
I'M SIXTEEN...
(IS WHAT I'M TELLING PEOPLE).
YOU'RE... MY AGE?
YOUR NAME... ARE YOU A FOREIGNER?
HOW D'YOU KNOW MY GRAN?
I MET HER HERE AND ASKED HER FOR A JOB, SO SHE HIRED ME.
THAT SOUNDS WAY TOO EASY.
THIS IS REAL SKETCHY...
GLARE
IT DOESN'T ADD UP... WHY WOULD THIS GIRL SUDDENLY DECIDE TO WORK HERE OF ALL PLACES...?
SHE MUST HAVE AN ULTERIOR MOTIVE...
Hrmmm.
SO, WHAT ARE YOU DOING HERE?
OH... RIGHT. YOUR UNIFORM...
IT'S AN APRON AND A WHITE SHIRT.
SO, I WEAR THESE?
RUSTLE

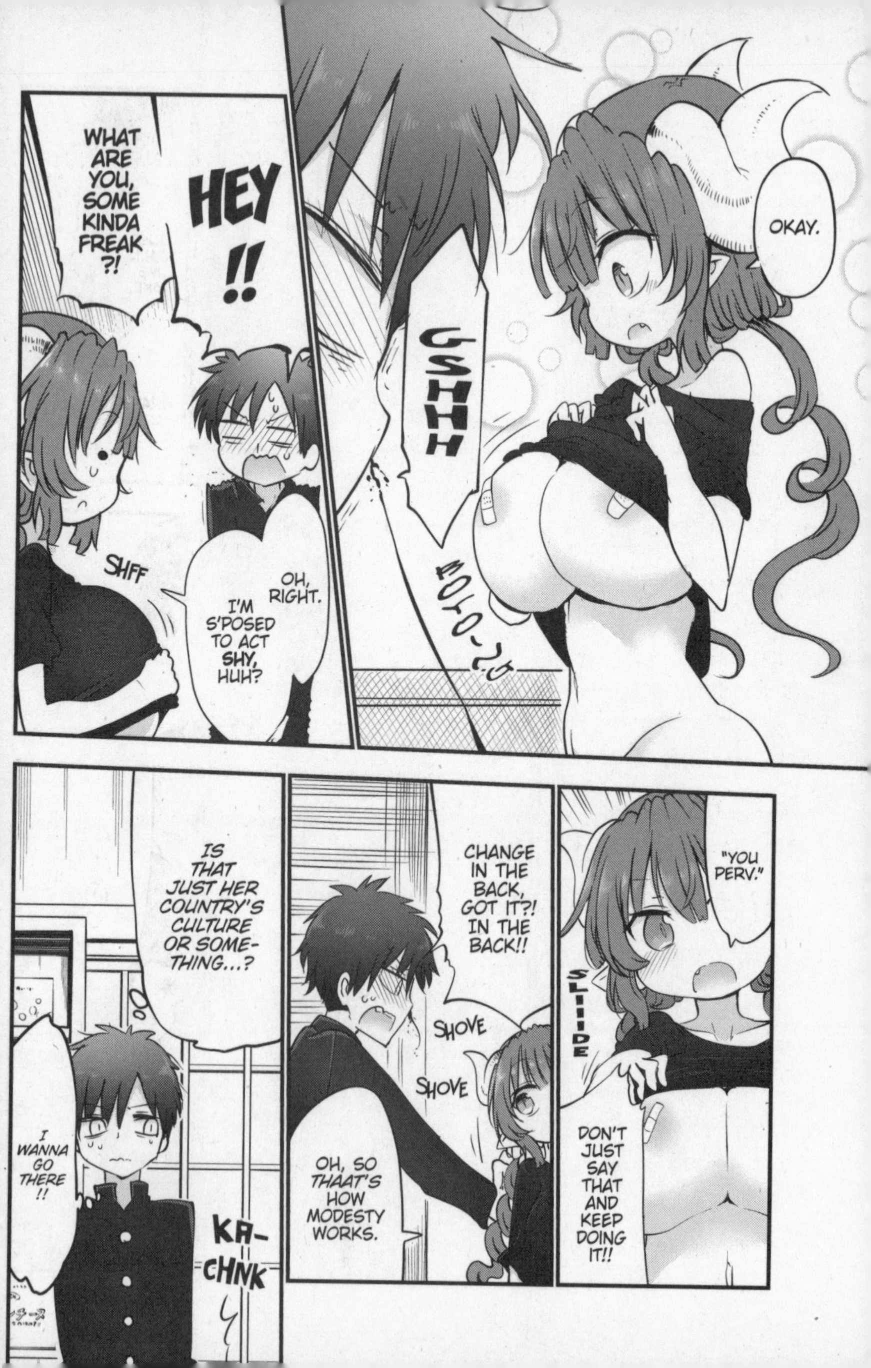
OKAY.
GSHHH
BOYOING
HEY!!
WHAT ARE YOU, SOME KINDA FREAK?!
SHFF
OH, RIGHT. I'M S'POSED TO ACT SHY, HUH?
"YOU PERV."
SLIIDE
DON'T JUST SAY THAT AND KEEP DOING IT!!
CHANGE IN THE BACK, GOT IT?! IN THE BACK!!
SHOVE
SHOVE
OH, SO THAAT'S HOW MODESTY WORKS.
IS THAT JUST HER COUNTRY'S CULTURE OR SOMETHING...?
I WANNA GO THERE!!
KA-CHNK

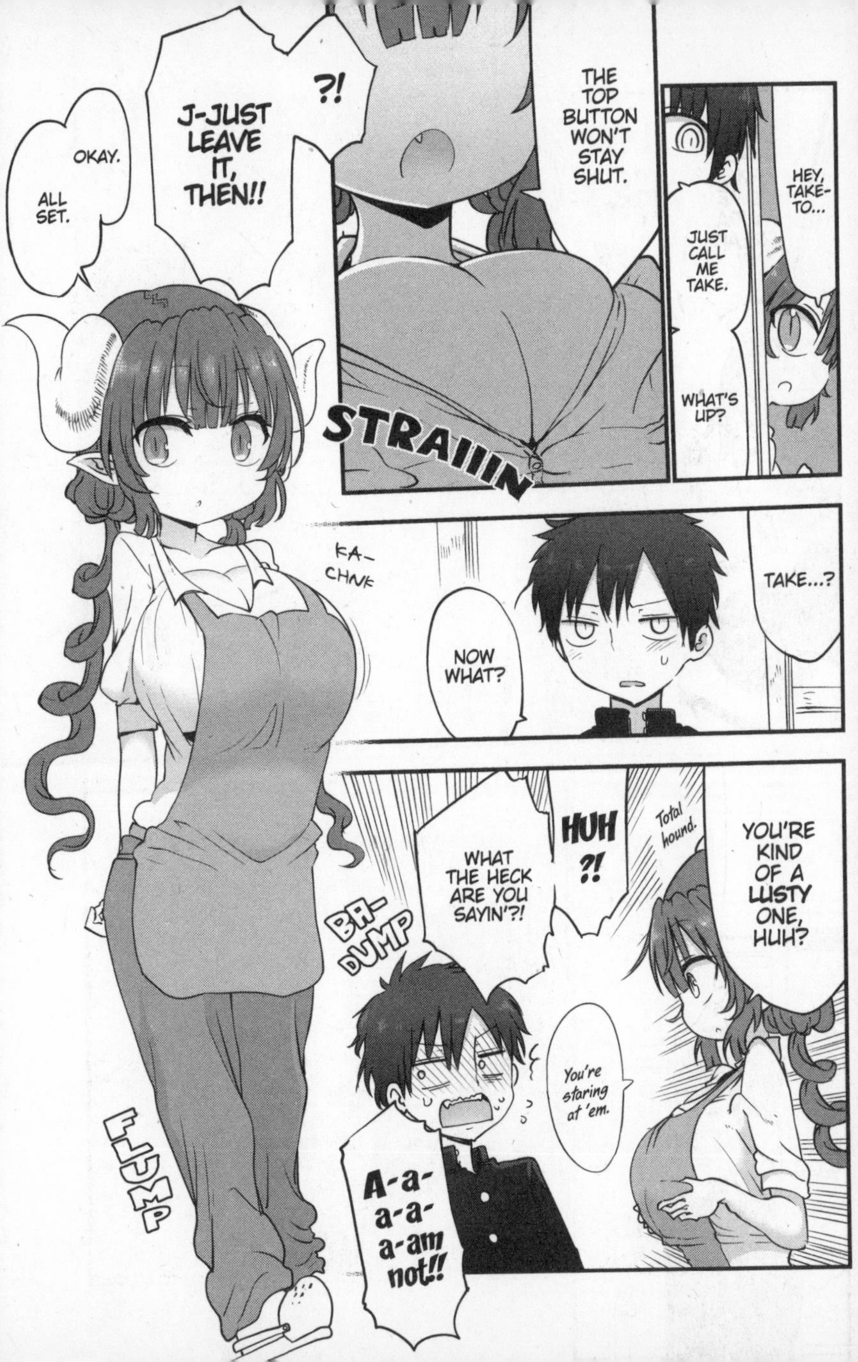

HEY, TAKE-TO...
JUST CALL ME TAKE.
WHAT'S UP?
THE TOP BUTTON WON'T STAY SHUT.
?!
STRAIIIN
J-JUST LEAVE IT, THEN!!
OKAY. ALL SET.
FLUMP
TAKE...?
NOW WHAT?
KA-CHNK
YOU'RE KIND OF A LUSTY ONE, HUH?
Total hound.
HUH ?!
WHAT THE HECK ARE YOU SAYIN'?!
BA-DUMP
You're staring at 'em.
A-a-a-a-a-a-am not!!

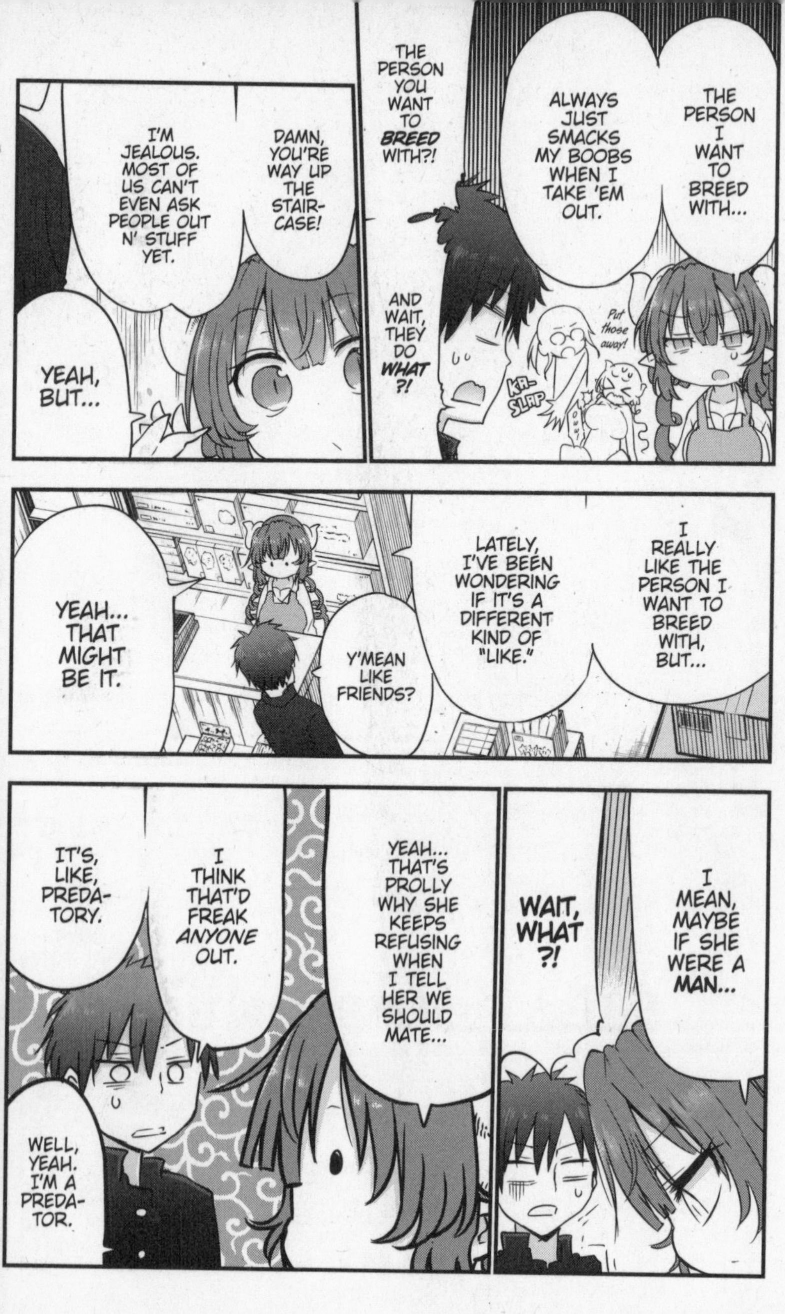
THE PERSON I WANT TO BREED WITH...
ALWAYS JUST SMACKS MY BOOBS WHEN I TAKE 'EM OUT.
THE PERSON YOU WANT TO *BREED* WITH?!
Put those away!
KA-SLAP
AND WAIT, THEY DO *WHAT* ?!
DAMN, YOU'RE WAY UP THE STAIR-CASE!
I'M JEALOUS. MOST OF US CAN'T EVEN ASK PEOPLE OUT N' STUFF YET.
YEAH, BUT...
I REALLY LIKE THE PERSON I WANT TO BREED WITH, BUT...
LATELY, I'VE BEEN WONDERING IF IT'S A DIFFERENT KIND OF "LIKE."
Y'MEAN LIKE FRIENDS?
YEAH... THAT MIGHT BE IT.
I MEAN, MAYBE IF SHE WERE A *MAN*...
WAIT, WHAT ?!
YEAH... THAT'S PROLLY WHY SHE KEEPS REFUSING WHEN I TELL HER WE SHOULD MATE...
I THINK THAT'D FREAK *ANYONE* OUT.
IT'S, LIKE, PREDA-TORY.
WELL, YEAH. I'M A PREDA-TOR.

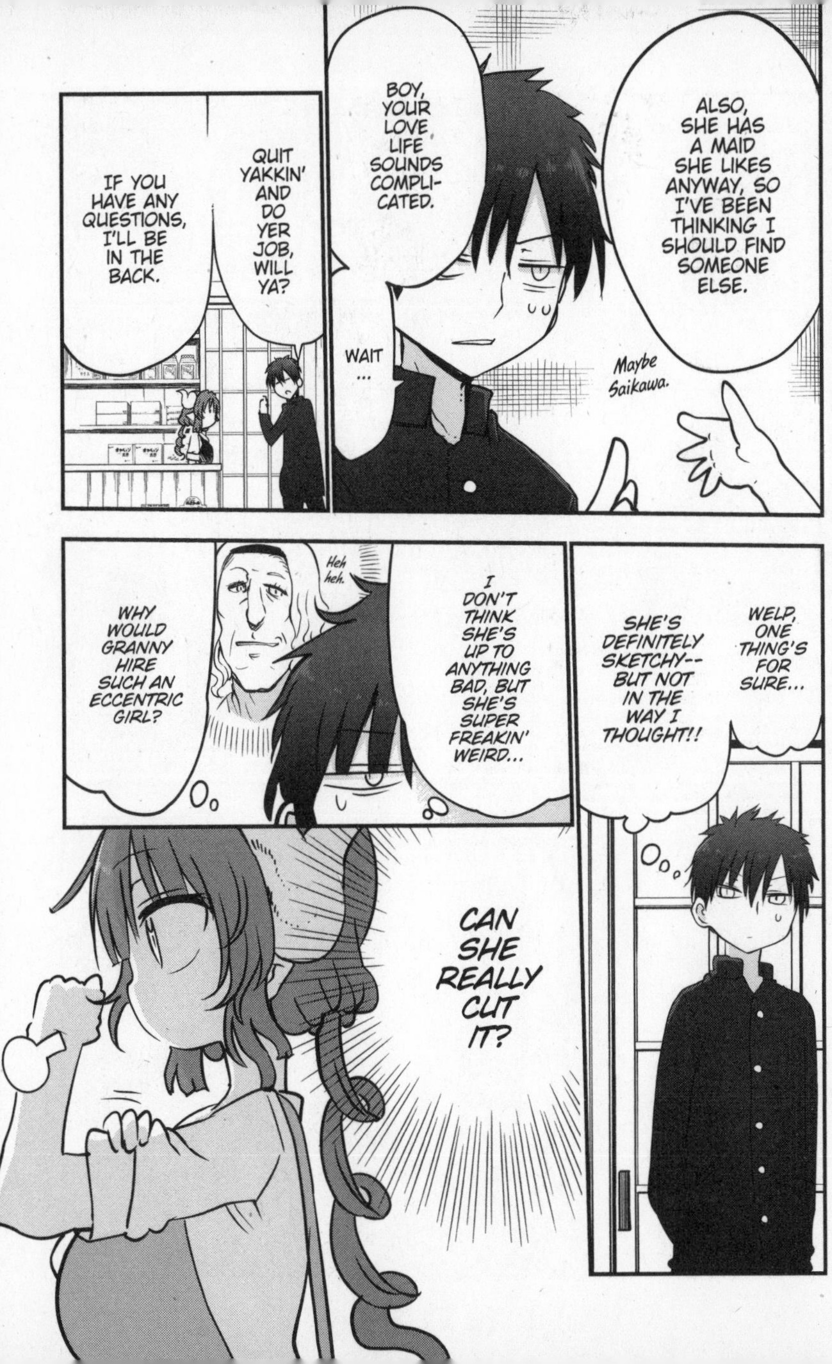
ALSO, SHE HAS A MAID SHE LIKES ANYWAY, SO I'VE BEEN THINKING I SHOULD FIND SOMEONE ELSE.
Maybe Saikawa.
BOY, YOUR LOVE LIFE SOUNDS COMPLICATED.
WAIT ...
QUIT YAKKIN' AND DO YER JOB, WILL YA?
IF YOU HAVE ANY QUESTIONS, I'LL BE IN THE BACK.
WELP, ONE THING'S FOR SURE...
SHE'S DEFINITELY SKETCHY-- BUT NOT IN THE WAY I THOUGHT!!
Heh heh.
I DON'T THINK SHE'S UP TO ANYTHING BAD, BUT SHE'S SUPER FREAKIN' WEIRD...
WHY WOULD GRANNY HIRE SUCH AN ECCENTRIC GIRL?
CAN SHE REALLY CUT IT?

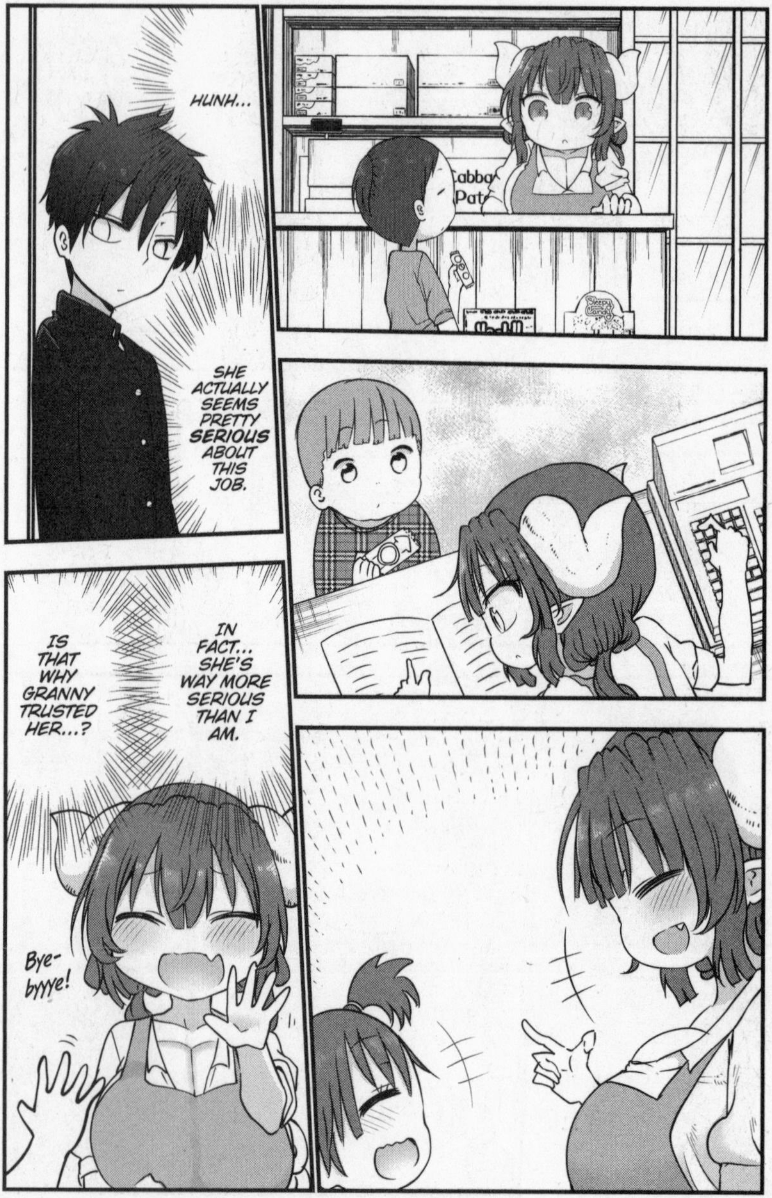
HUNH...
SHE ACTUALLY SEEMS PRETTY SERIOUS ABOUT THIS JOB.
IN FACT... SHE'S WAY MORE SERIOUS THAN I AM.
IS THAT WHY GRANNY TRUSTED HER...?
Bye-byyye!

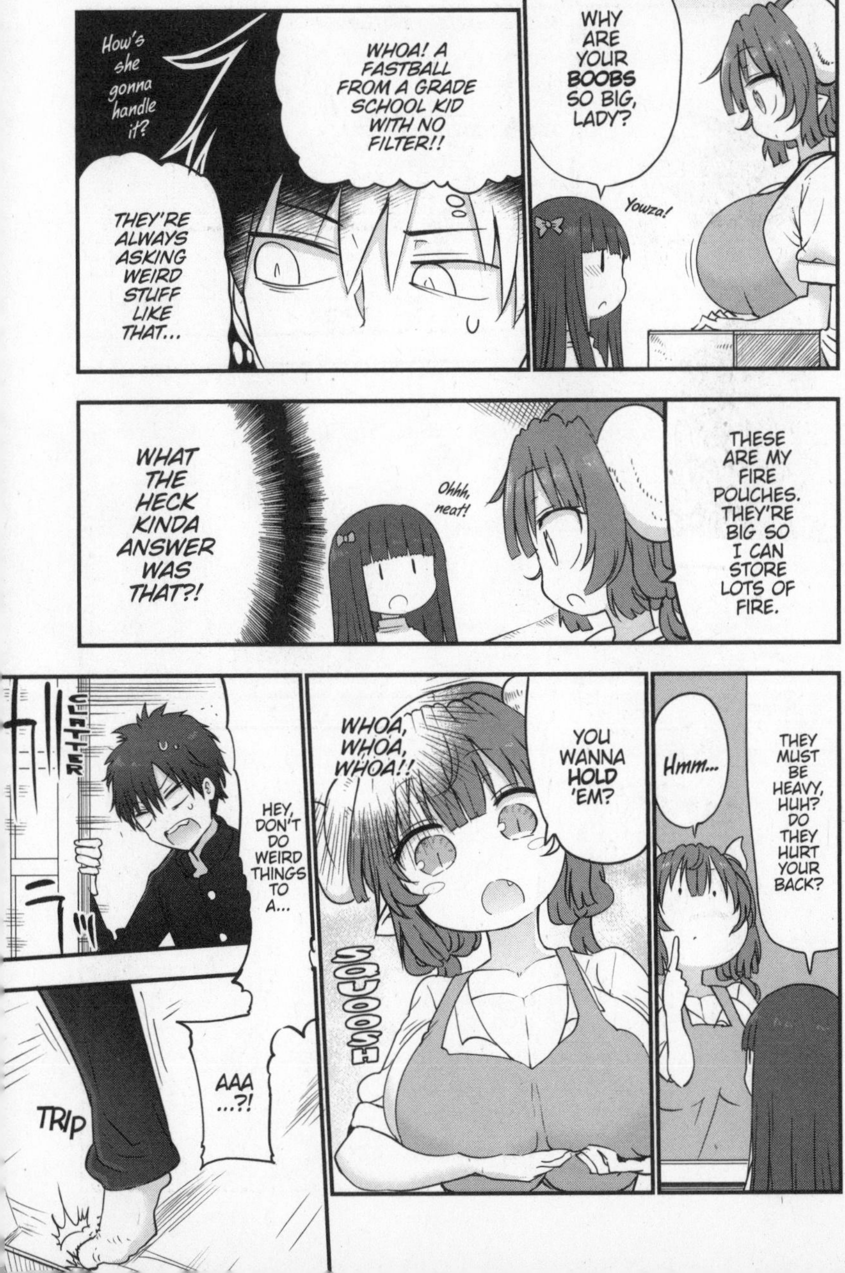
WHY ARE YOUR BOOBS SO BIG, LADY?
Yowza!
WHOA! A FASTBALL FROM A GRADE SCHOOL KID WITH NO FILTER!!
How's she gonna handle it?
THEY'RE ALWAYS ASKING WEIRD STUFF LIKE THAT...
THESE ARE MY FIRE POUCHES. THEY'RE BIG SO I CAN STORE LOTS OF FIRE.
Ohhh, neat!
WHAT THE HECK KINDA ANSWER WAS THAT?!
THEY MUST BE HEAVY, HUH? DO THEY HURT YOUR BACK?
Hmm...
YOU WANNA HOLD 'EM?
WHOA, WHOA, WHOA!!
SQUOOSH
CLATTER
HEY, DON'T DO WEIRD THINGS TO A...
AAA ...?!
TRIP

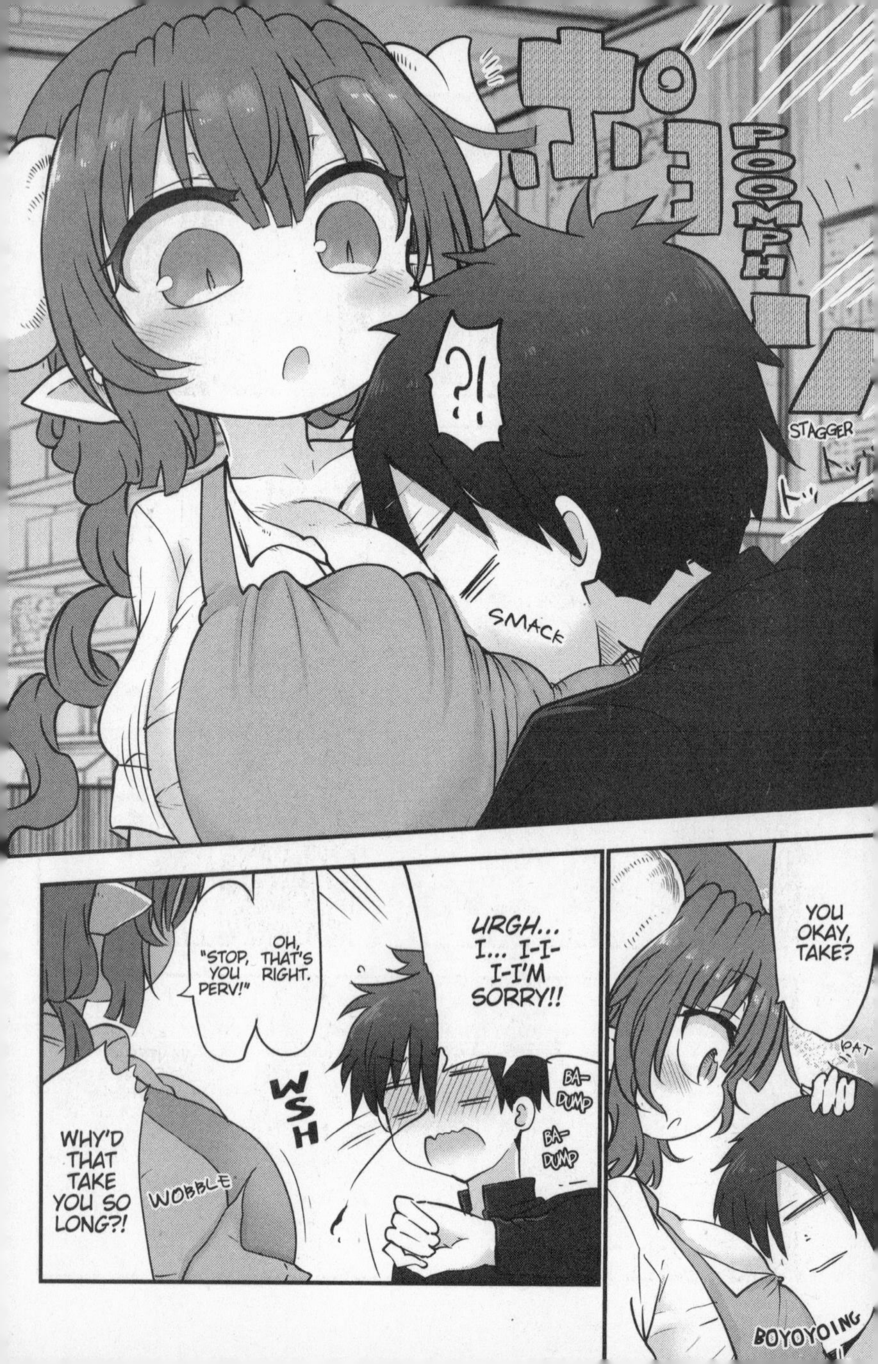
POOOMPH
?!
STAGGER
SMACK
YOU OKAY, TAKE?
PAT
BOYOYOING
URGH... I... I-I-I-I'M SORRY!!
BA-DUMP
BA-DUMP
WSH
OH, THAT'S RIGHT.
"STOP, YOU PERV!"
WHY'D THAT TAKE YOU SO LONG?!
WOBBLE

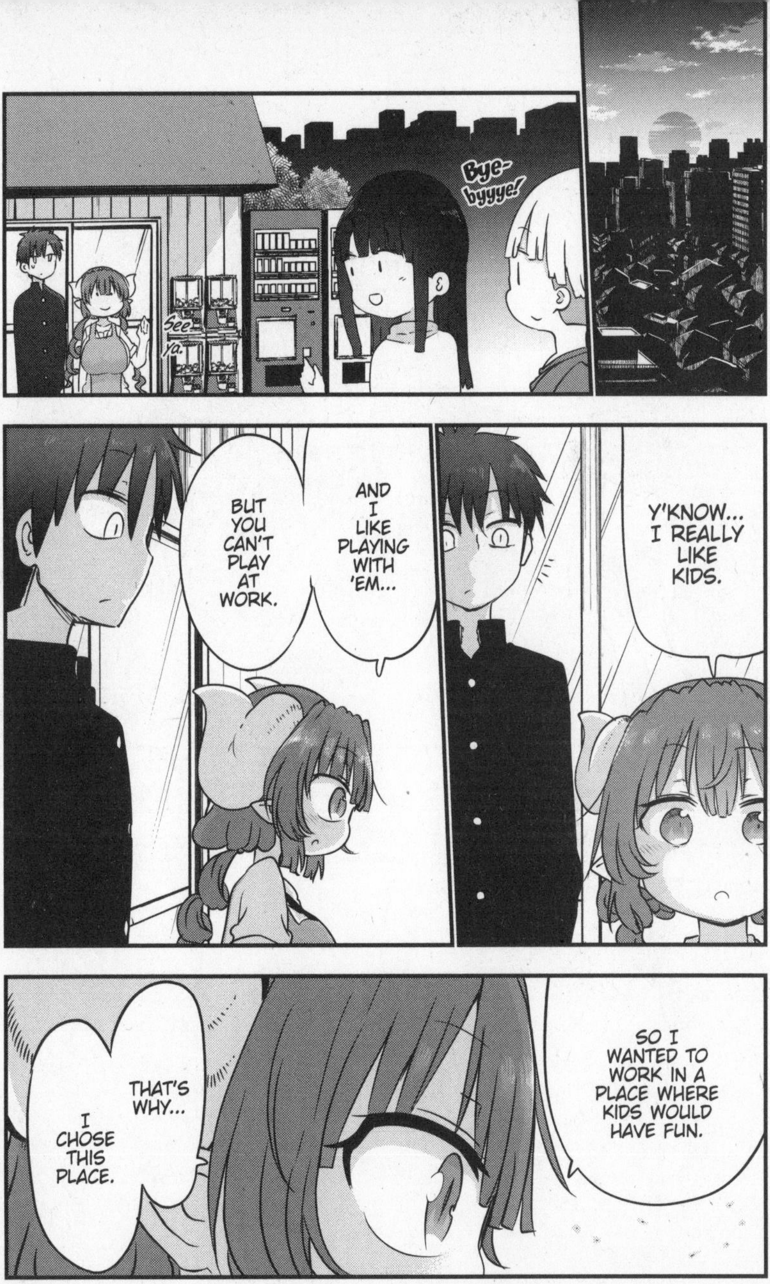
Bye-byyye!
See-ya.
Y'KNOW... I REALLY LIKE KIDS.
AND I LIKE PLAYING WITH 'EM...
BUT YOU CAN'T PLAY AT WORK.
SO I WANTED TO WORK IN A PLACE WHERE KIDS WOULD HAVE FUN.
THAT'S WHY...
I CHOSE THIS PLACE.

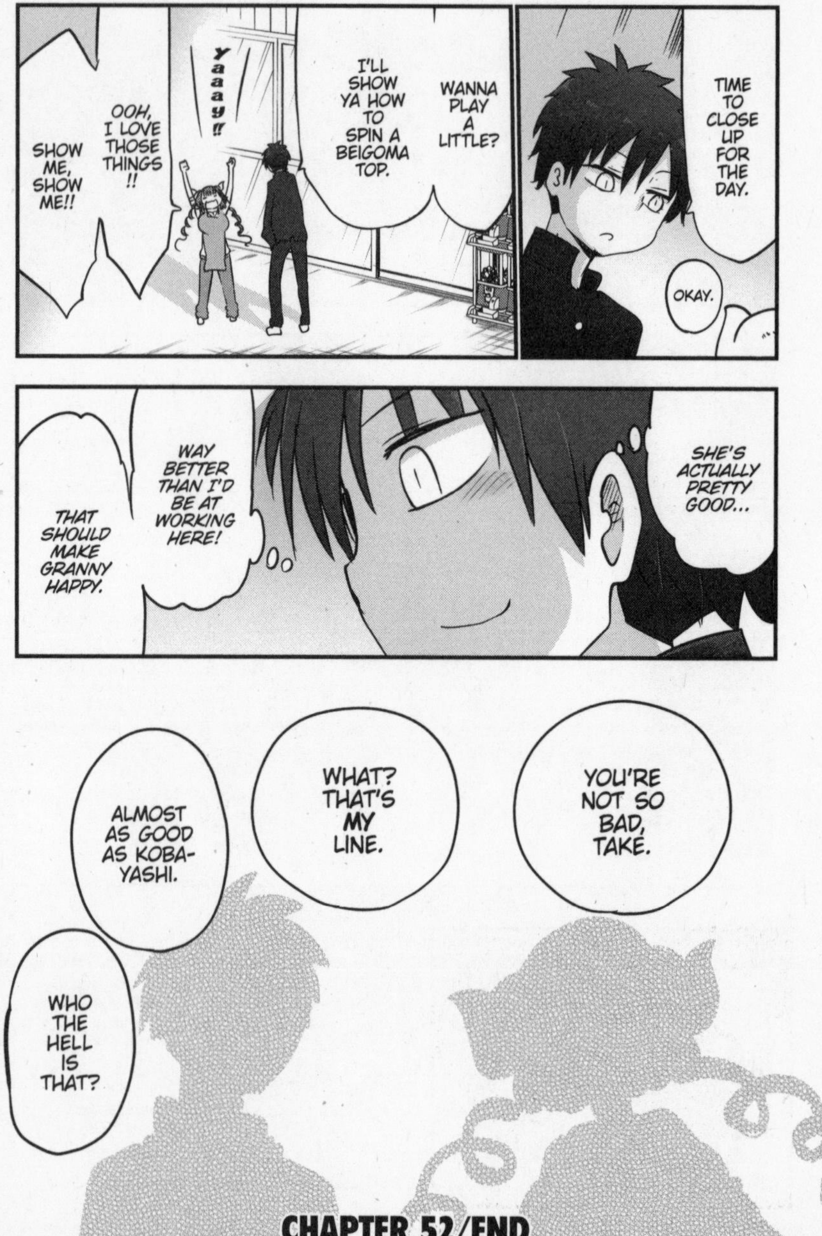
TIME TO CLOSE UP FOR THE DAY.
OKAY.
WANNA PLAY A LITTLE?
I'LL SHOW YA HOW TO SPIN A BEIGOMA TOP.
Yaaaay!!
OOH, I LOVE THOSE THINGS!!
SHOW ME, SHOW ME!!
SHE'S ACTUALLY PRETTY GOOD...
WAY BETTER THAN I'D BE AT WORKING HERE!
THAT SHOULD MAKE GRANNY HAPPY.
YOU'RE NOT SO BAD, TAKE.
WHAT? THAT'S MY LINE.
ALMOST AS GOOD AS KOBA-YASHI.
WHO THE HELL IS THAT?
CHAPTER 52/END

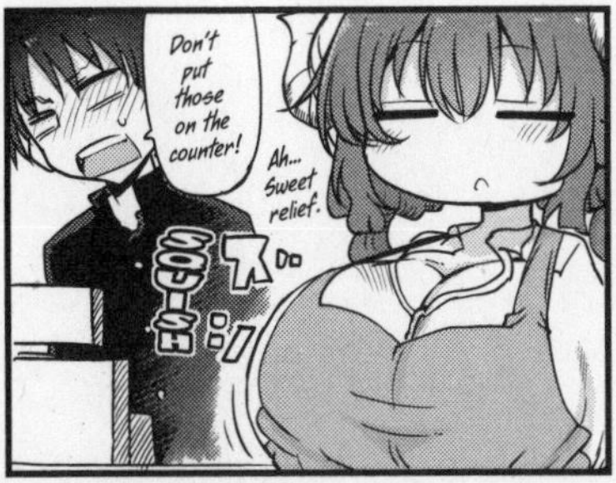
Don't put those on the counter!
Ah... Sweet relief.
SQUISH

Miss Kobayashi's
Dragon Maid

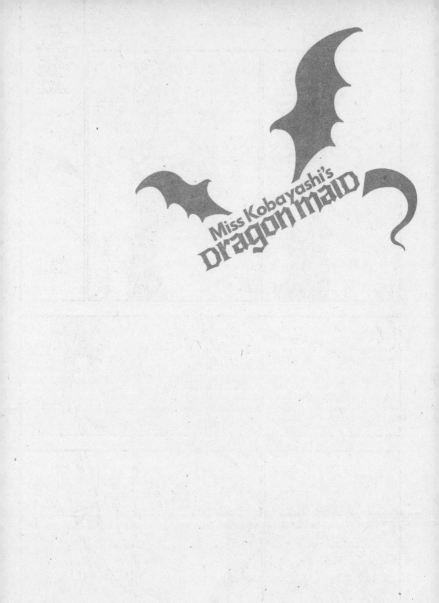

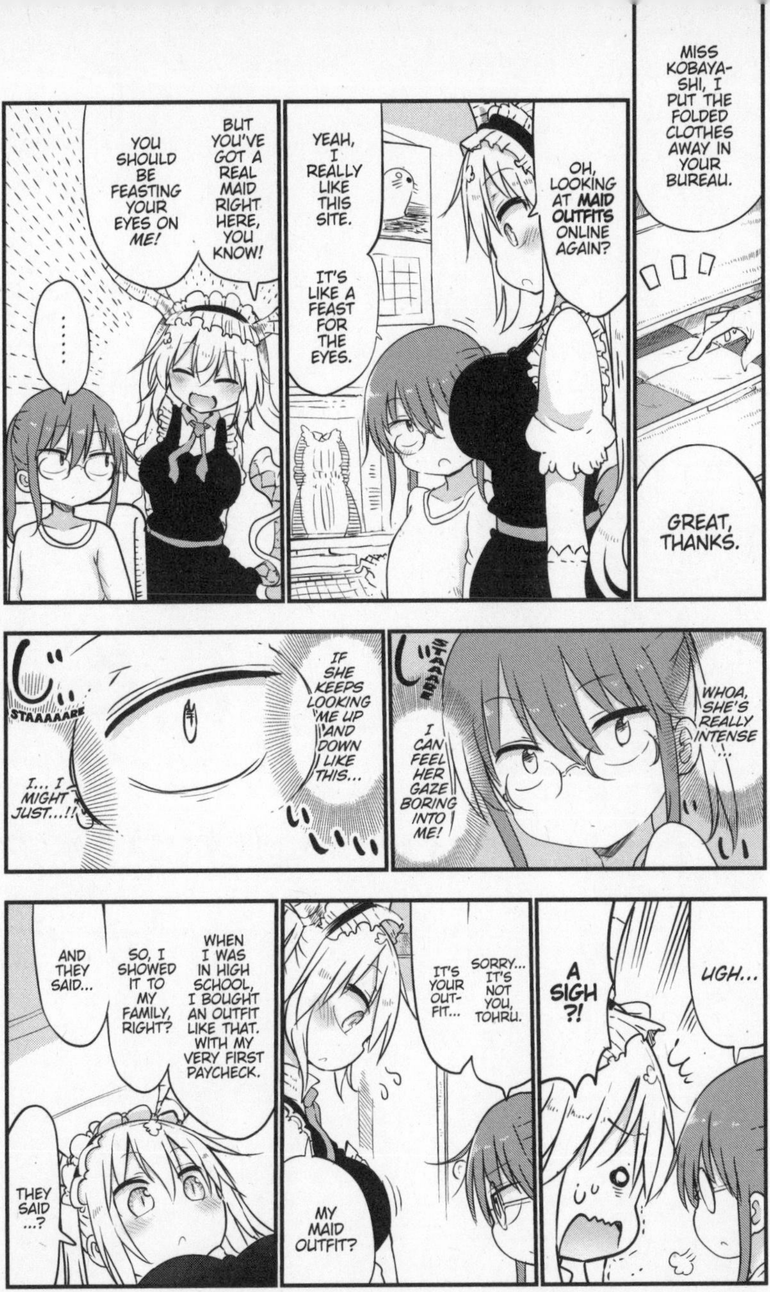
MISS KOBAYASHI, I PUT THE FOLDED CLOTHES AWAY IN YOUR BUREAU.
GREAT, THANKS.
OH, LOOKING AT **MAID OUTFITS** ONLINE AGAIN?
YEAH, I REALLY LIKE THIS SITE.
IT'S LIKE A FEAST FOR THE EYES.
BUT YOU'VE GOT A REAL MAID RIGHT HERE, YOU KNOW!
YOU SHOULD BE FEASTING YOUR EYES ON *ME!*
......
STAAAARE
WHOA, SHE'S REALLY INTENSE...
I CAN FEEL HER GAZE BORING INTO ME!
IF SHE KEEPS LOOKING ME UP AND DOWN LIKE THIS...
STAAAAARE
I... I MIGHT JUST...!!
UGH...
A SIGH?!
SORRY... IT'S NOT YOU, TOHRU.
IT'S YOUR OUTFIT...
MY MAID OUTFIT?
WHEN I WAS IN HIGH SCHOOL, I BOUGHT AN OUTFIT LIKE THAT. WITH MY VERY FIRST PAYCHECK.
SO, I SHOWED IT TO MY FAMILY, RIGHT?
AND THEY SAID...
THEY SAID...?

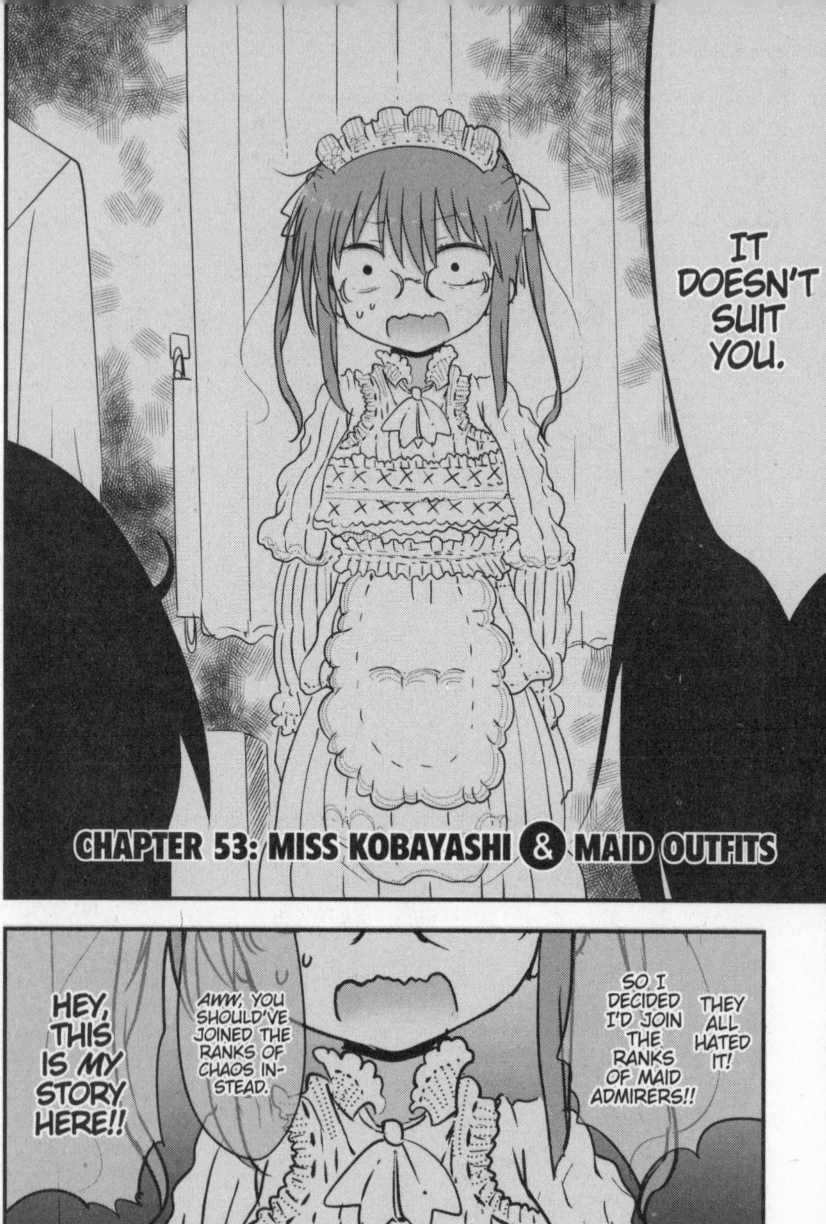
IT DOESN'T SUIT YOU.
CHAPTER 53: MISS KOBAYASHI & MAID OUTFITS
THEY ALL HATED IT!
SO I DECIDED I'D JOIN THE RANKS OF MAID ADMIRERS!!
AWW, YOU SHOULD'VE JOINED THE RANKS OF CHAOS IN-STEAD.
HEY, THIS IS *MY* STORY HERE!!

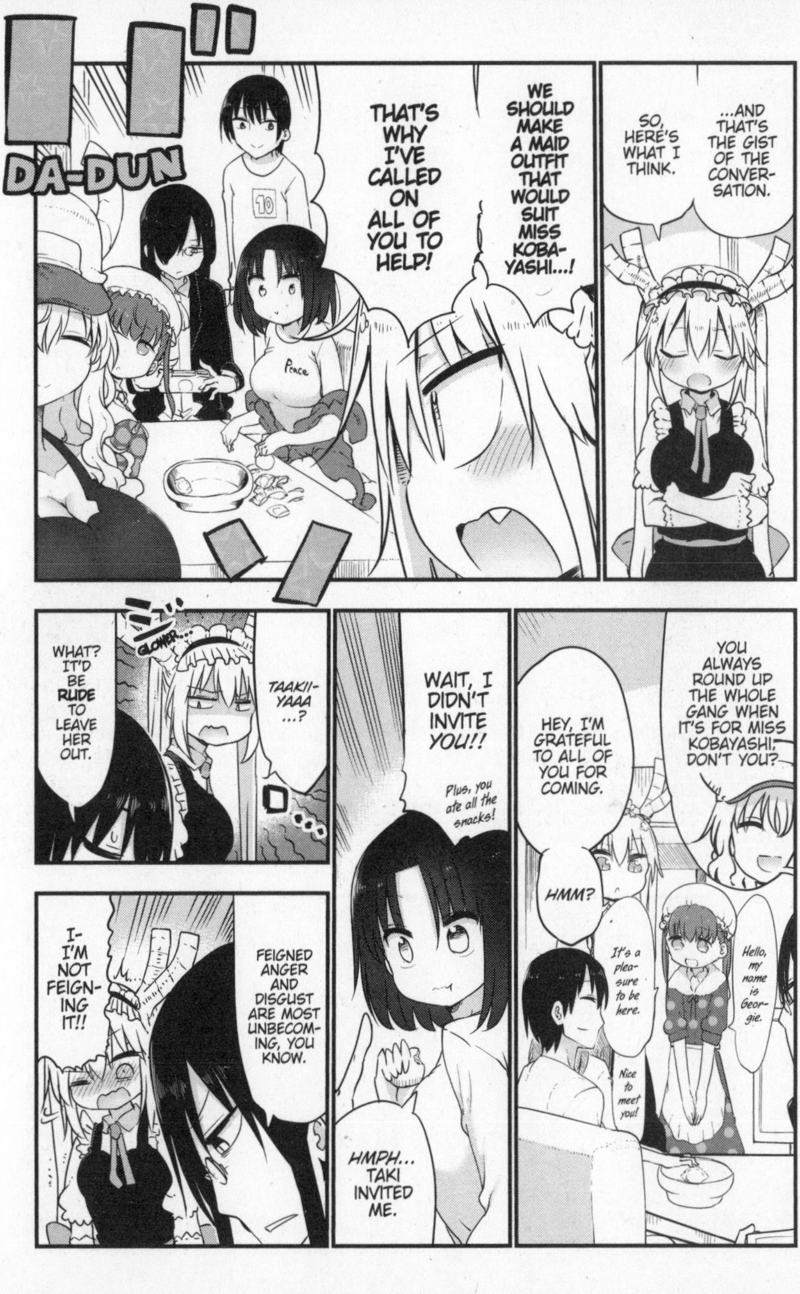
...AND THAT'S THE GIST OF THE CONVERSATION.
SO, HERE'S WHAT I THINK.
WE SHOULD MAKE A MAID OUTFIT THAT WOULD SUIT MISS KOBAYASHI...!
THAT'S WHY I'VE CALLED ON ALL OF YOU TO HELP!
DA-DUN
YOU ALWAYS ROUND UP THE WHOLE GANG WHEN IT'S FOR MISS KOBAYASHI, DON'T YOU?
HEY, I'M GRATEFUL TO ALL OF YOU FOR COMING.
HMM?
Hello, my name is Georgie.
It's a pleasure to be here.
Nice to meet you!
WAIT, I DIDN'T INVITE YOU!!
Plus, you ate all the snacks!
HMPH... TAKI INVITED ME.
TAAKII-YAAA...?
GLOWER...
WHAT? IT'D BE RUDE TO LEAVE HER OUT.
FEIGNED ANGER AND DISGUST ARE MOST UNBECOMING, YOU KNOW.
I-I'M NOT FEIGNING IT!!

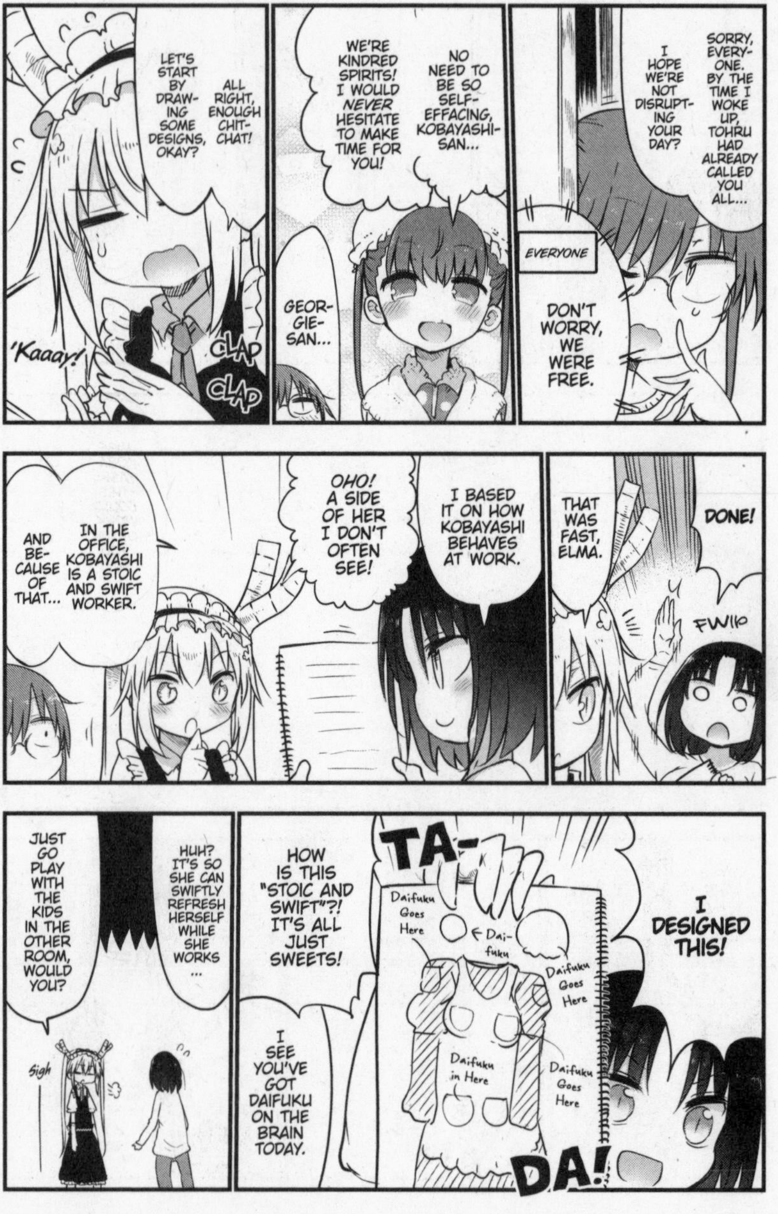
SORRY, EVERYONE. BY THE TIME I WOKE UP, TOHRU HAD ALREADY CALLED YOU ALL...
I HOPE WE'RE NOT DISRUPTING YOUR DAY?
EVERYONE
DON'T WORRY, WE WERE FREE.
NO NEED TO BE SO SELF-EFFACING, KOBAYASHI-SAN...
WE'RE KINDRED SPIRITS! I WOULD *NEVER* HESITATE TO MAKE TIME FOR YOU!
GEORGIE-SAN...
ALL RIGHT, ENOUGH CHIT-CHAT!
LET'S START BY DRAWING SOME DESIGNS, OKAY?
CLAP
CLAP
'Kaaay!
DONE!
FWIP
THAT WAS FAST, ELMA.
I BASED IT ON HOW KOBAYASHI BEHAVES AT WORK.
OHO! A SIDE OF HER I DON'T OFTEN SEE!
IN THE OFFICE, KOBAYASHI IS A STOIC AND SWIFT WORKER.
AND BECAUSE OF THAT...
TA-
I DESIGNED THIS!
Daifuku Goes Here
← Daifuku
Daifuku Goes Here
Daifuku in Here
Daifuku Goes Here
DA!
HOW IS THIS "STOIC AND SWIFT"?! IT'S ALL JUST SWEETS!
I SEE YOU'VE GOT DAIFUKU ON THE BRAIN TODAY.
HUH? IT'S SO SHE CAN SWIFTLY REFRESH HERSELF WHILE SHE WORKS...
JUST GO PLAY WITH THE KIDS IN THE OTHER ROOM, WOULD YOU?
Sigh

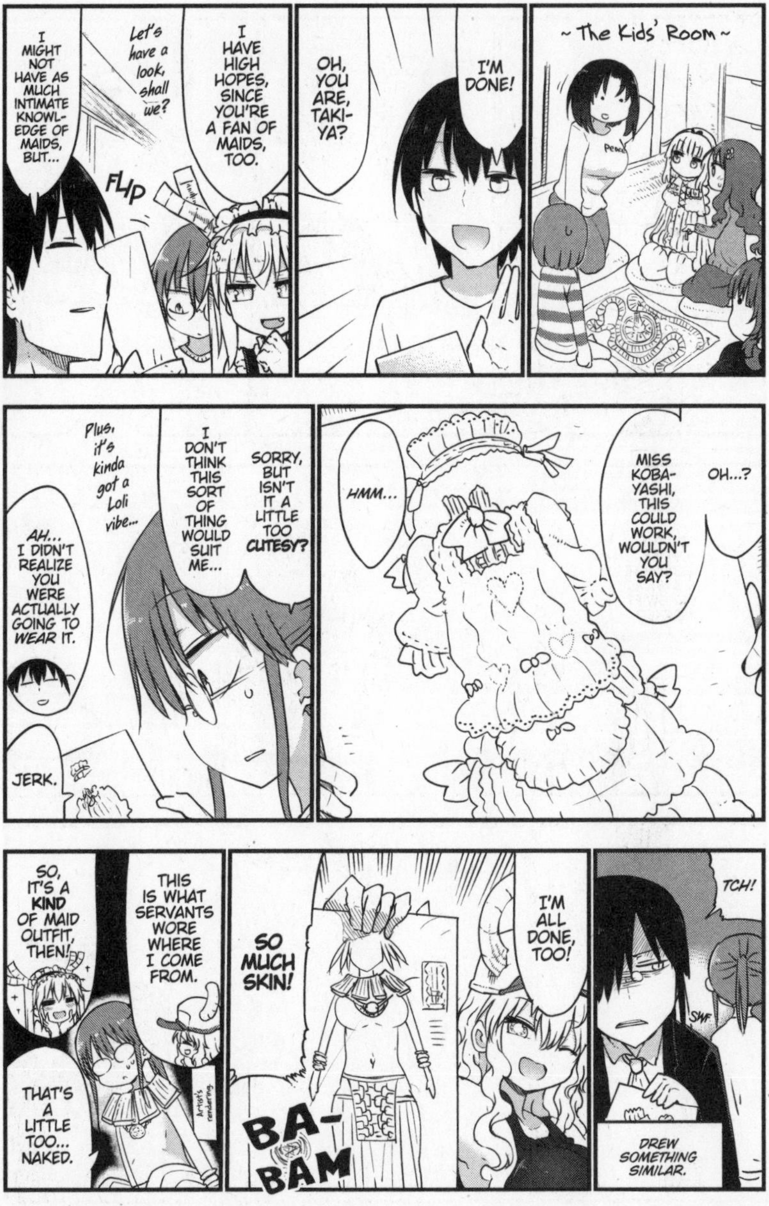
~The Kids' Room~
I'M DONE!
OH, YOU ARE, TAKIYA?
I HAVE HIGH HOPES, SINCE YOU'RE A FAN OF MAIDS, TOO.
Let's have a look, shall we?
I MIGHT NOT HAVE AS MUCH INTIMATE KNOWLEDGE OF MAIDS, BUT...
FLIP
MISS KOBAYASHI, THIS COULD WORK, WOULDN'T YOU SAY?
OH...?
HMM...
SORRY, BUT ISN'T IT A LITTLE TOO CUTESY?
I DON'T THINK THIS SORT OF THING WOULD SUIT ME...
Plus, it's kinda got a Loli vibe...
AH... I DIDN'T REALIZE YOU WERE ACTUALLY GOING TO WEAR IT.
JERK.
TCH!
SWF
DREW SOMETHING SIMILAR.
I'M ALL DONE, TOO!
SO MUCH SKIN!
BA-BAM
THIS IS WHAT SERVANTS WORE WHERE I COME FROM.
SO, IT'S A KIND OF MAID OUTFIT, THEN!
Artist's rendering.
THAT'S A LITTLE TOO... NAKED.

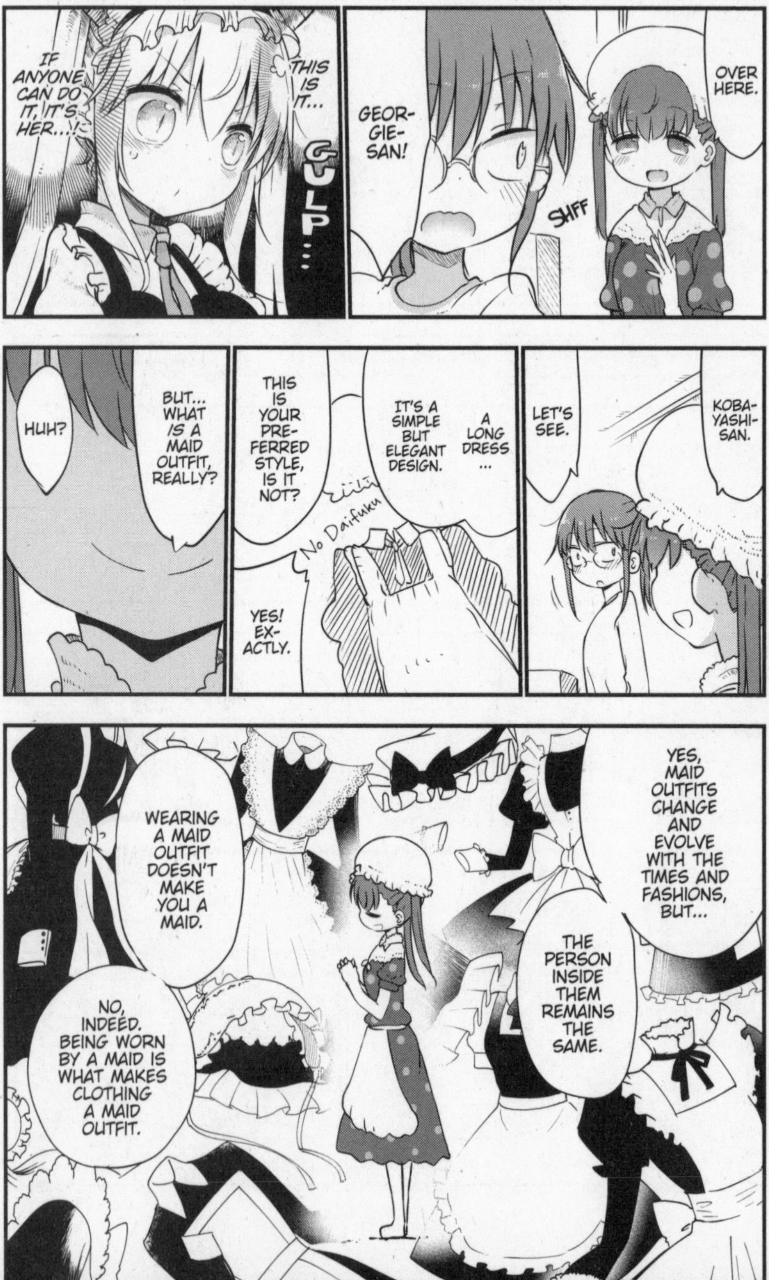
OVER HERE.
GEORGIE-SAN!
SHFF
THIS IS IT...
IF ANYONE CAN DO IT, IT'S HER...!
GULP...
KOBAYASHI-SAN.
LET'S SEE.
A LONG DRESS...
IT'S A SIMPLE BUT ELEGANT DESIGN.
THIS IS YOUR PREFERRED STYLE, IS IT NOT?
No Daifuku
YES! EXACTLY.
BUT... WHAT IS A MAID OUTFIT, REALLY?
HUH?
YES, MAID OUTFITS CHANGE AND EVOLVE WITH THE TIMES AND FASHIONS, BUT...
THE PERSON INSIDE THEM REMAINS THE SAME.
WEARING A MAID OUTFIT DOESN'T MAKE YOU A MAID.
NO, INDEED. BEING WORN BY A MAID IS WHAT MAKES CLOTHING A MAID OUTFIT.

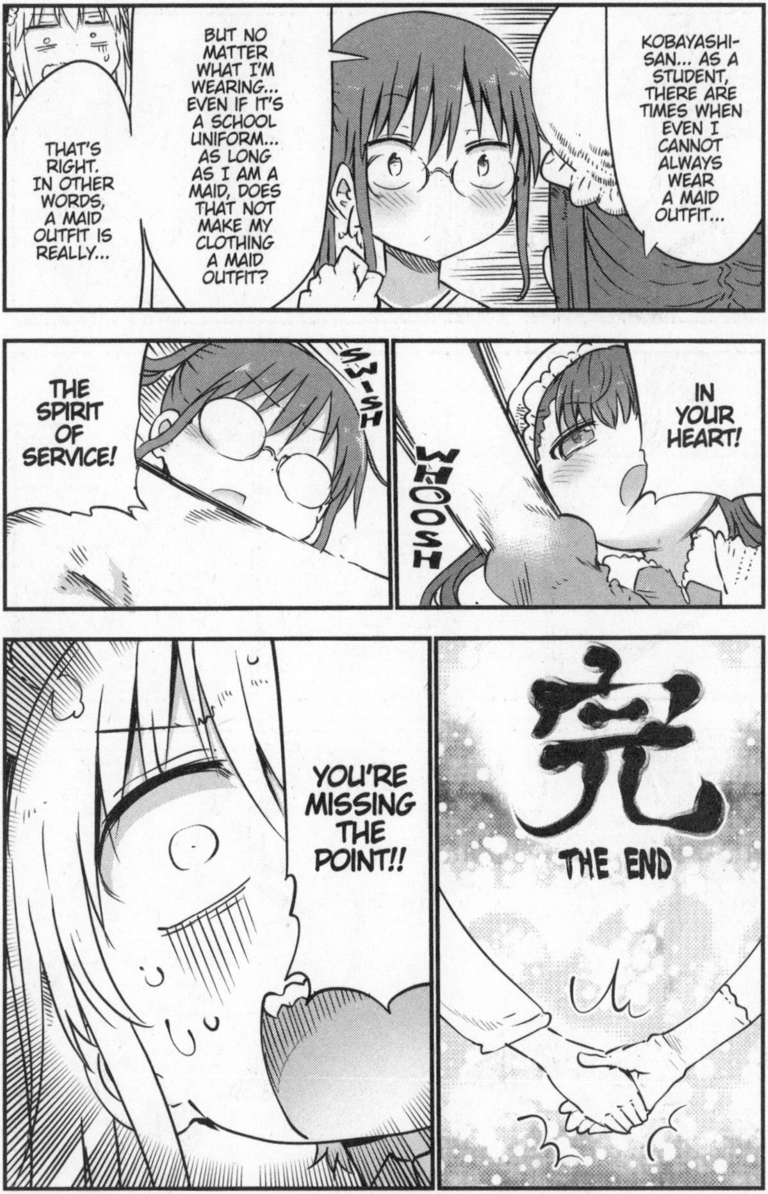
KOBAYASHI-SAN... AS A STUDENT, THERE ARE TIMES WHEN EVEN I CANNOT ALWAYS WEAR A MAID OUTFIT...
BUT NO MATTER WHAT I'M WEARING... EVEN IF IT'S A SCHOOL UNIFORM... AS LONG AS I AM A MAID, DOES THAT NOT MAKE MY CLOTHING A MAID OUTFIT?
THAT'S RIGHT. IN OTHER WORDS, A MAID OUTFIT IS REALLY...
IN YOUR HEART!
WHOOSH
SWISH
THE SPIRIT OF SERVICE!
完
THE END
YOU'RE MISSING THE POINT!!

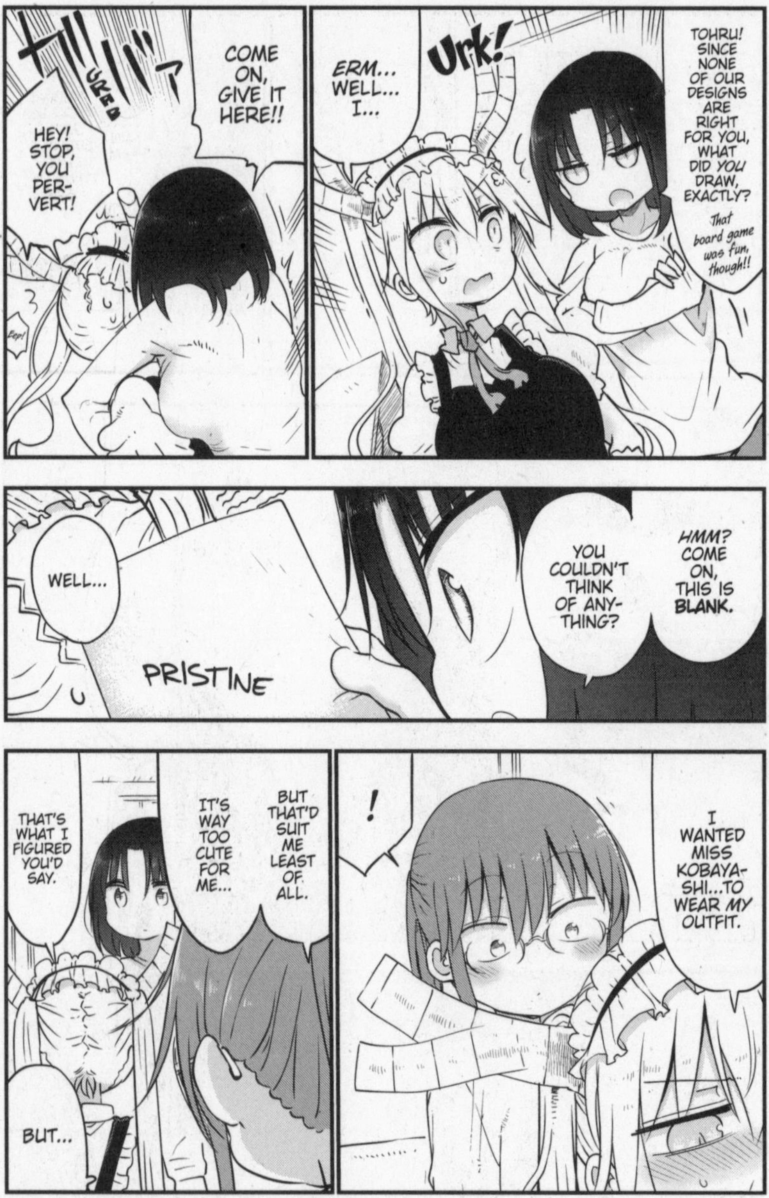
TOHRU! SINCE NONE OF OUR DESIGNS ARE RIGHT FOR YOU, WHAT DID YOU DRAW, EXACTLY?
That board game was fun, though!!
Urk!
ERM... WELL... I...
COME ON, GIVE IT HERE!!
GRAB
HEY! STOP, YOU PER-VERT!
Eep!
HMM? COME ON, THIS IS BLANK.
YOU COULDN'T THINK OF ANY-THING?
WELL...
PRISTINE
I WANTED MISS KOBAYA-SHI...TO WEAR MY OUTFIT.
!
......
BUT THAT'D SUIT ME LEAST OF ALL.
IT'S WAY TOO CUTE FOR ME...
THAT'S WHAT I FIGURED YOU'D SAY.
BUT...

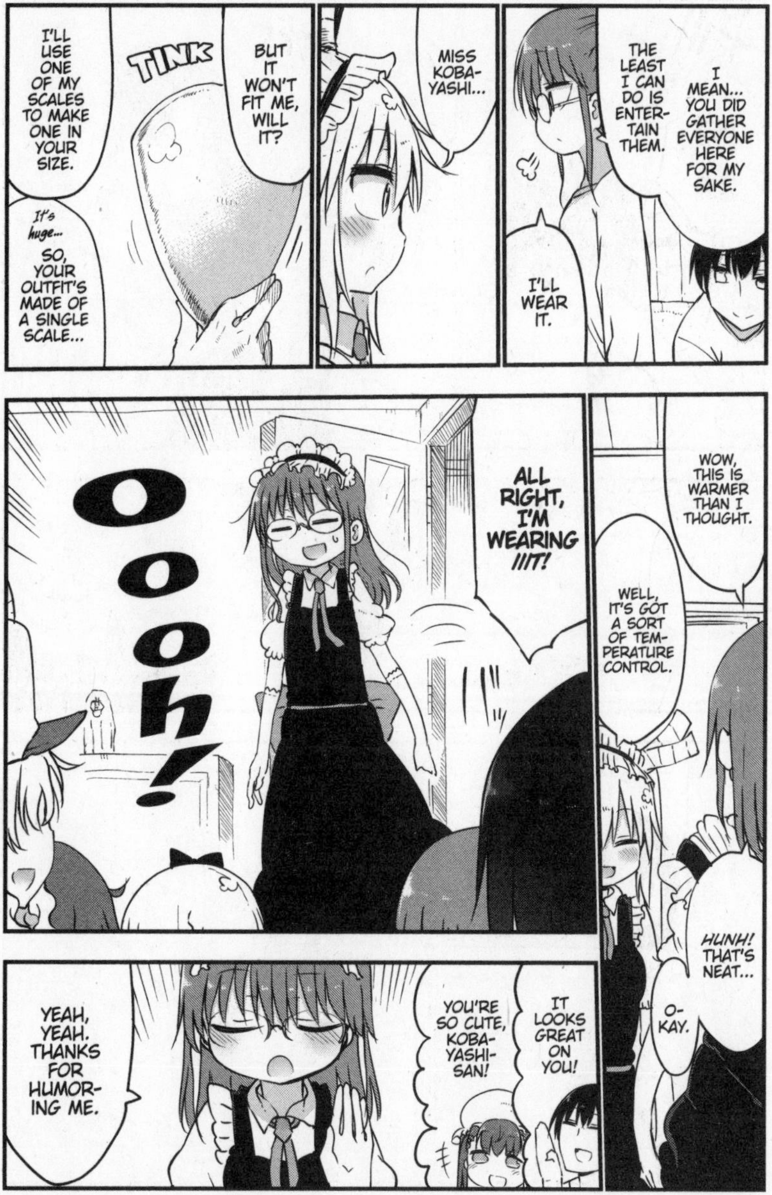
I MEAN... YOU DID GATHER EVERYONE HERE FOR MY SAKE.
THE LEAST I CAN DO IS ENTERTAIN THEM.
I'LL WEAR IT.
MISS KOBAYASHI...
BUT IT WON'T FIT ME, WILL IT?
TINK
I'LL USE ONE OF MY SCALES TO MAKE ONE IN YOUR SIZE.
It's huge...
SO, YOUR OUTFIT'S MADE OF A SINGLE SCALE...
WOW, THIS IS WARMER THAN I THOUGHT.
WELL, IT'S GOT A SORT OF TEMPERATURE CONTROL.
HUNH! THAT'S NEAT...
O-KAY.
ALL RIGHT, I'M WEARING IIIT!
Oooh!
IT LOOKS GREAT ON YOU!
YOU'RE SO CUTE, KOBAYASHI-SAN!
YEAH, YEAH. THANKS FOR HUMORING ME.

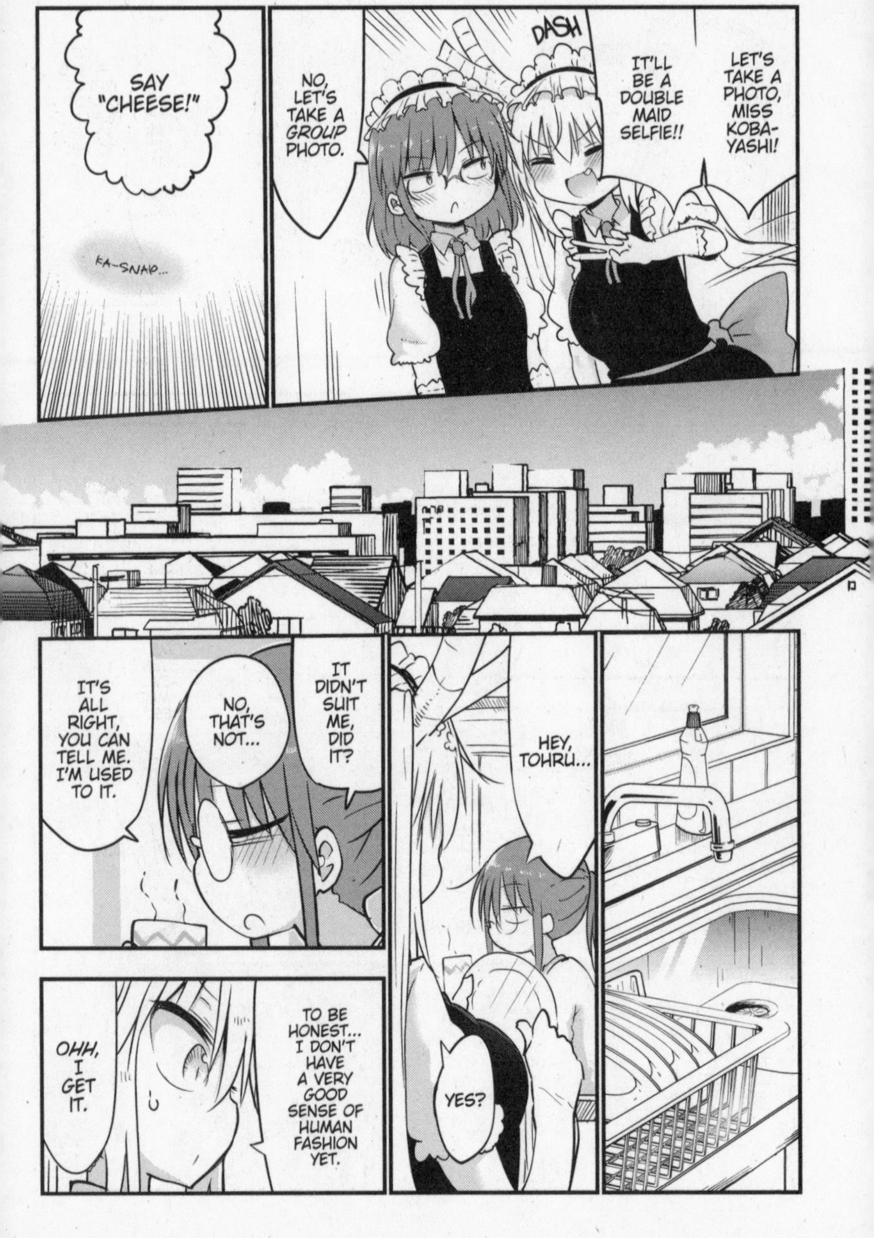
LET'S TAKE A PHOTO, MISS KOBAYASHI!
DASH
IT'LL BE A DOUBLE MAID SELFIE!!
NO, LET'S TAKE A *GROUP* PHOTO.
SAY "CHEESE!"
KA-SNAP...
HEY, TOHRU...
YES?
IT DIDN'T SUIT ME, DID IT?
NO, THAT'S NOT...
IT'S ALL RIGHT, YOU CAN TELL ME. I'M USED TO IT.
TO BE HONEST... I DON'T HAVE A VERY GOOD SENSE OF HUMAN FASHION YET.
OHH, I GET IT.

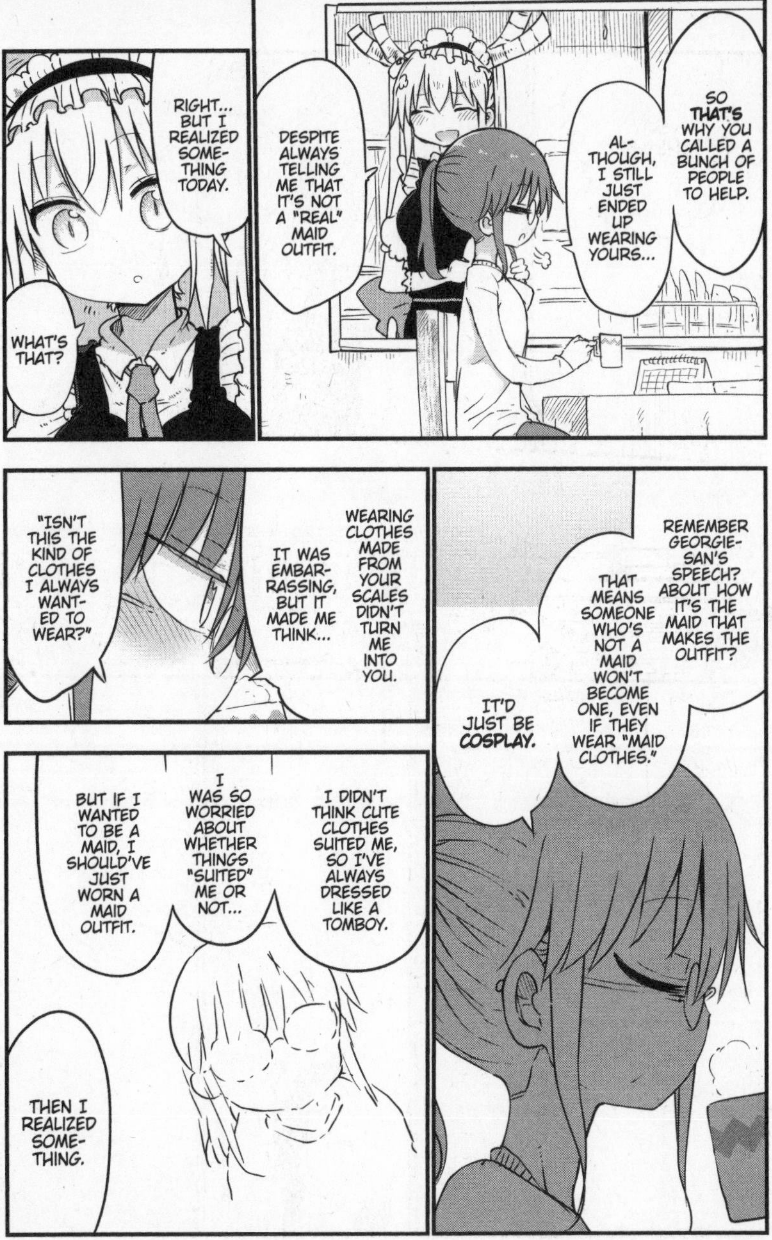
SO THAT'S WHY YOU CALLED A BUNCH OF PEOPLE TO HELP.
ALTHOUGH, I STILL JUST ENDED UP WEARING YOURS...
DESPITE ALWAYS TELLING ME THAT IT'S NOT A "REAL" MAID OUTFIT.
RIGHT... BUT I REALIZED SOMETHING TODAY.
WHAT'S THAT?
REMEMBER GEORGIE-SAN'S SPEECH? ABOUT HOW IT'S THE MAID THAT MAKES THE OUTFIT?
THAT MEANS SOMEONE WHO'S NOT A MAID WON'T BECOME ONE, EVEN IF THEY WEAR "MAID CLOTHES."
IT'D JUST BE COSPLAY.
WEARING CLOTHES MADE FROM YOUR SCALES DIDN'T TURN ME INTO YOU.
IT WAS EMBARRASSING, BUT IT MADE ME THINK...
"ISN'T THIS THE KIND OF CLOTHES I ALWAYS WANTED TO WEAR?"
I DIDN'T THINK CUTE CLOTHES SUITED ME, SO I'VE ALWAYS DRESSED LIKE A TOMBOY.
I WAS SO WORRIED ABOUT WHETHER THINGS "SUITED" ME OR NOT...
BUT IF I WANTED TO BE A MAID, I SHOULD'VE JUST WORN A MAID OUTFIT.
THEN I REALIZED SOMETHING.

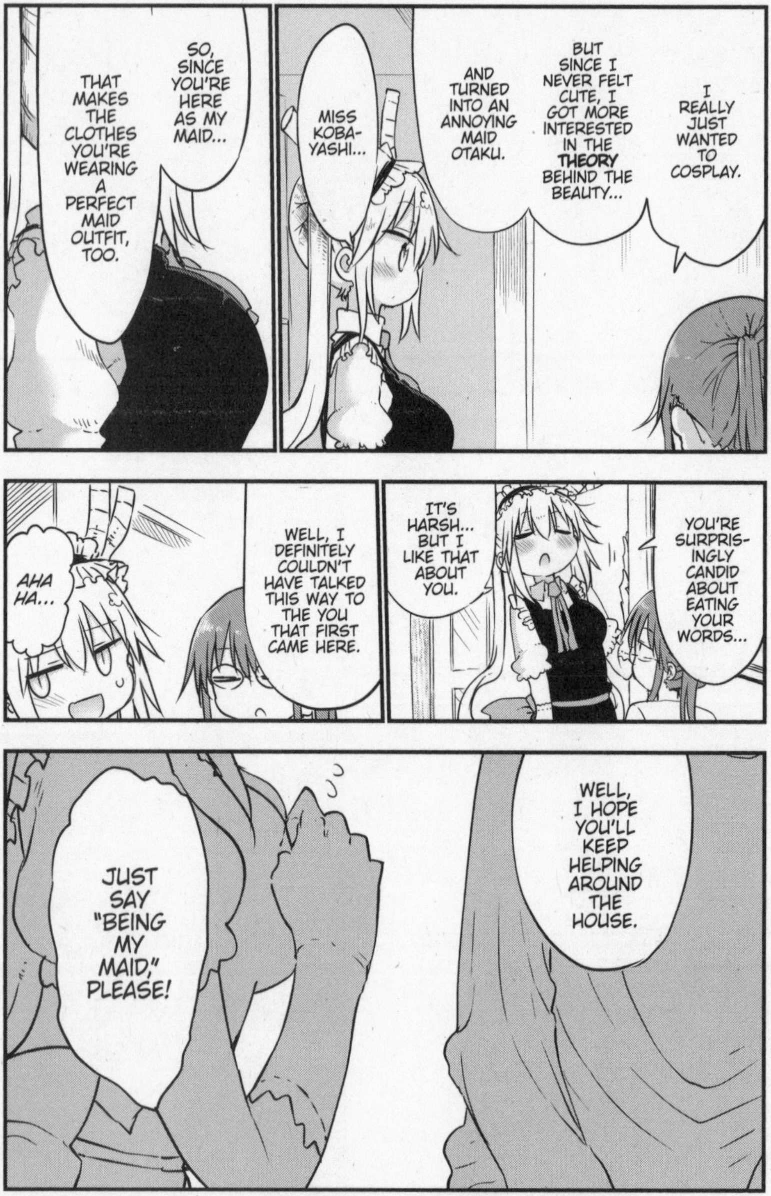
I REALLY JUST WANTED TO COSPLAY.
BUT SINCE I NEVER FELT CUTE, I GOT MORE INTERESTED IN THE **THEORY** BEHIND THE BEAUTY...
AND TURNED INTO AN ANNOYING MAID OTAKU.
MISS KOBAYASHI...
SO, SINCE YOU'RE HERE AS MY MAID...
THAT MAKES THE CLOTHES YOU'RE WEARING A PERFECT MAID OUTFIT, TOO.
YOU'RE SURPRISINGLY CANDID ABOUT EATING YOUR WORDS...
IT'S HARSH... BUT I LIKE THAT ABOUT YOU.
WELL, I DEFINITELY COULDN'T HAVE TALKED THIS WAY TO THE YOU THAT FIRST CAME HERE.
AHA HA...
WELL, I HOPE YOU'LL KEEP HELPING AROUND THE HOUSE.
JUST SAY "BEING MY MAID," PLEASE!

CHAPTER 53/END

Magical
Girl Style

Miss Kobayashi's Dragon Maid

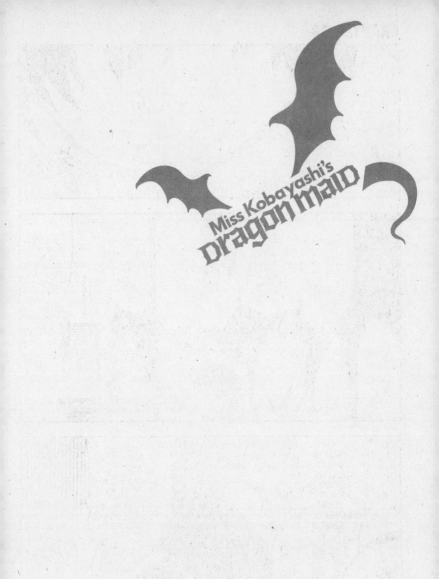

CHAPTER 54

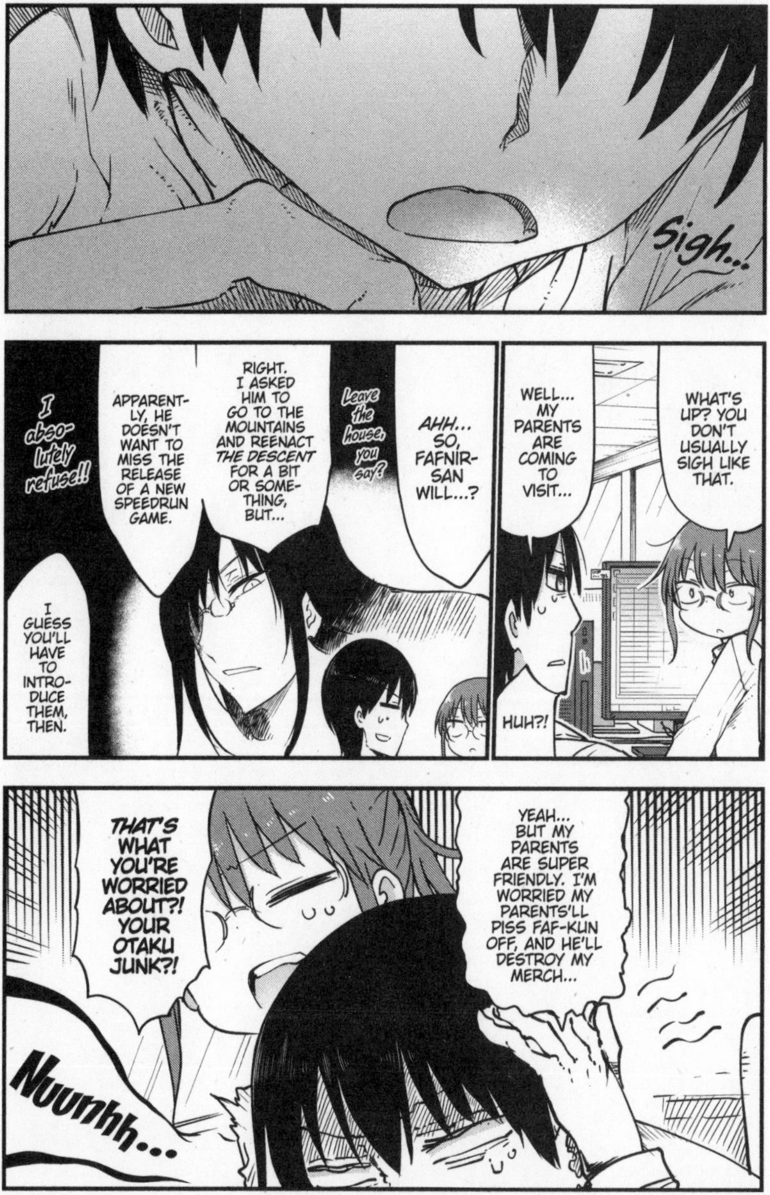
Sigh...
WHAT'S UP? YOU DON'T USUALLY SIGH LIKE THAT.
WELL... MY PARENTS ARE COMING TO VISIT...
HUH?!
AHH... SO, FAFNIR-SAN WILL...?
Leave the house, you say?
RIGHT. I ASKED HIM TO GO TO THE MOUNTAINS AND REENACT THE DESCENT FOR A BIT OR SOMETHING, BUT...
APPARENTLY, HE DOESN'T WANT TO MISS THE RELEASE OF A NEW SPEEDRUN GAME.
I absolutely refuse!!
I GUESS YOU'LL HAVE TO INTRODUCE THEM, THEN.
YEAH... BUT MY PARENTS ARE SUPER FRIENDLY. I'M WORRIED MY PARENTS'LL PISS FAF-KUN OFF, AND HE'LL DESTROY MY MERCH...
THAT'S WHAT YOU'RE WORRIED ABOUT?! YOUR OTAKU JUNK?!
Nuuunhh...

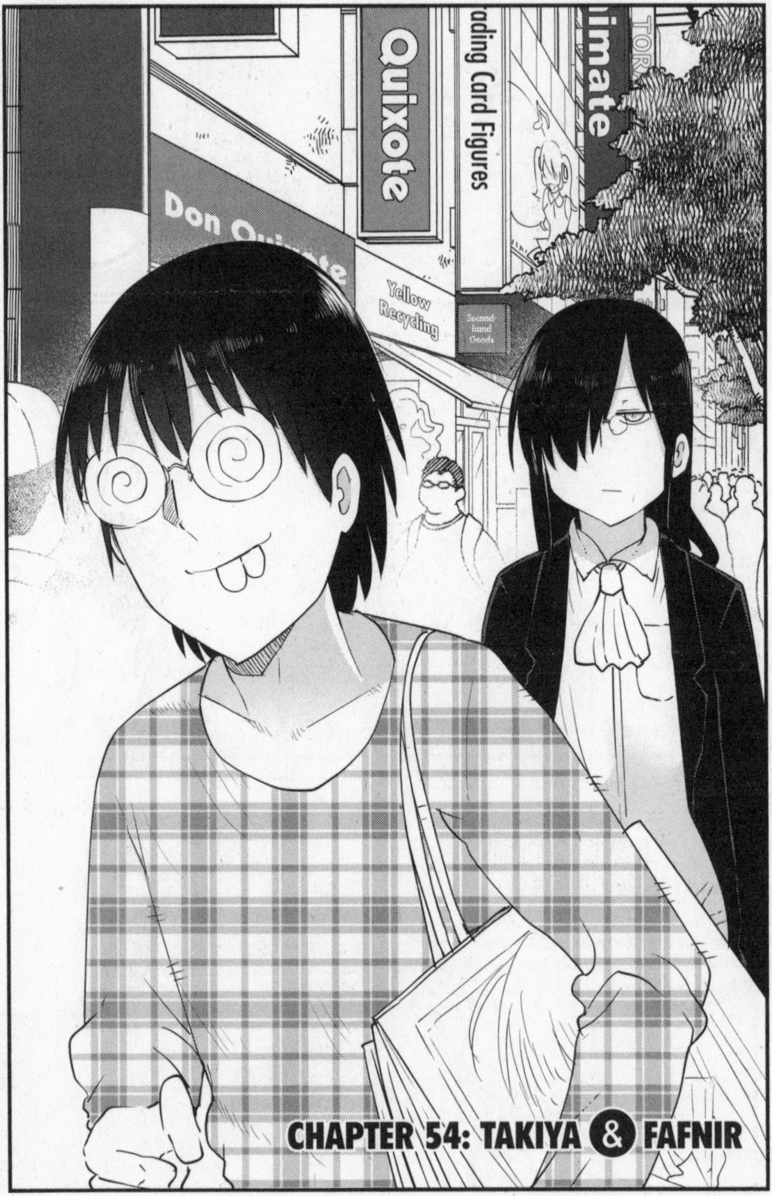
Quixote
Trading Card Figures
Yellow Recycling
Second-hand Goods
CHAPTER 54: TAKIYA & FAFNIR

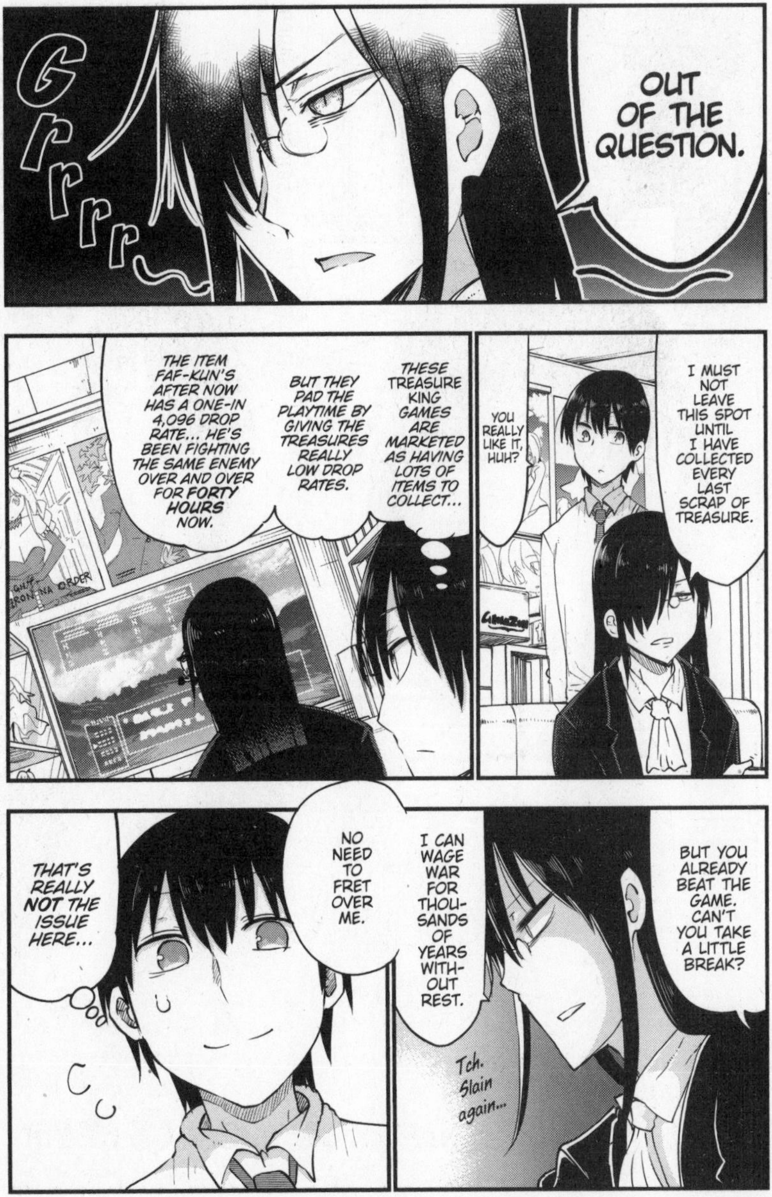
OUT OF THE QUESTION.
Grrrr
I MUST NOT LEAVE THIS SPOT UNTIL I HAVE COLLECTED EVERY LAST SCRAP OF TREASURE.
YOU REALLY LIKE IT, HUH?
THESE TREASURE KING GAMES ARE MARKETED AS HAVING LOTS OF ITEMS TO COLLECT...
BUT THEY PAD THE PLAYTIME BY GIVING THE TREASURES REALLY LOW DROP RATES.
THE ITEM FAF-KUN'S AFTER NOW HAS A ONE-IN 4,096 DROP RATE... HE'S BEEN FIGHTING THE SAME ENEMY OVER AND OVER FOR **FORTY HOURS** NOW.
BUT YOU ALREADY BEAT THE GAME. CAN'T YOU TAKE A LITTLE BREAK?
I CAN WAGE WAR FOR THOUSANDS OF YEARS WITHOUT REST.
NO NEED TO FRET OVER ME.
Tch. Slain again...
THAT'S REALLY **NOT** THE ISSUE HERE...

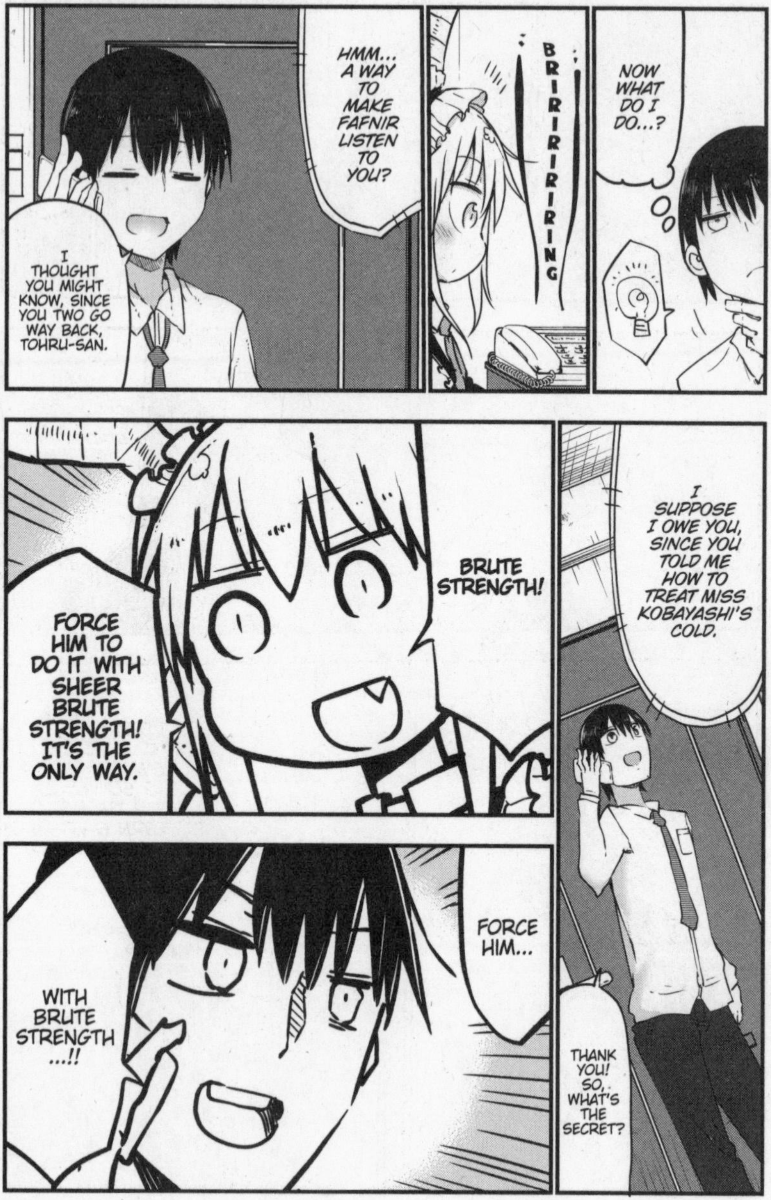
NOW WHAT DO I DO...?
BRIRIRIRIRING
HMM... A WAY TO MAKE FAFNIR LISTEN TO YOU?
I THOUGHT YOU MIGHT KNOW, SINCE YOU TWO GO WAY BACK, TOHRU-SAN.
I SUPPOSE I OWE YOU, SINCE YOU TOLD ME HOW TO TREAT MISS KOBAYASHI'S COLD.
THANK YOU! SO, WHAT'S THE SECRET?
BRUTE STRENGTH!
FORCE HIM TO DO IT WITH SHEER BRUTE STRENGTH! IT'S THE ONLY WAY.
FORCE HIM...
WITH BRUTE STRENGTH ...!!

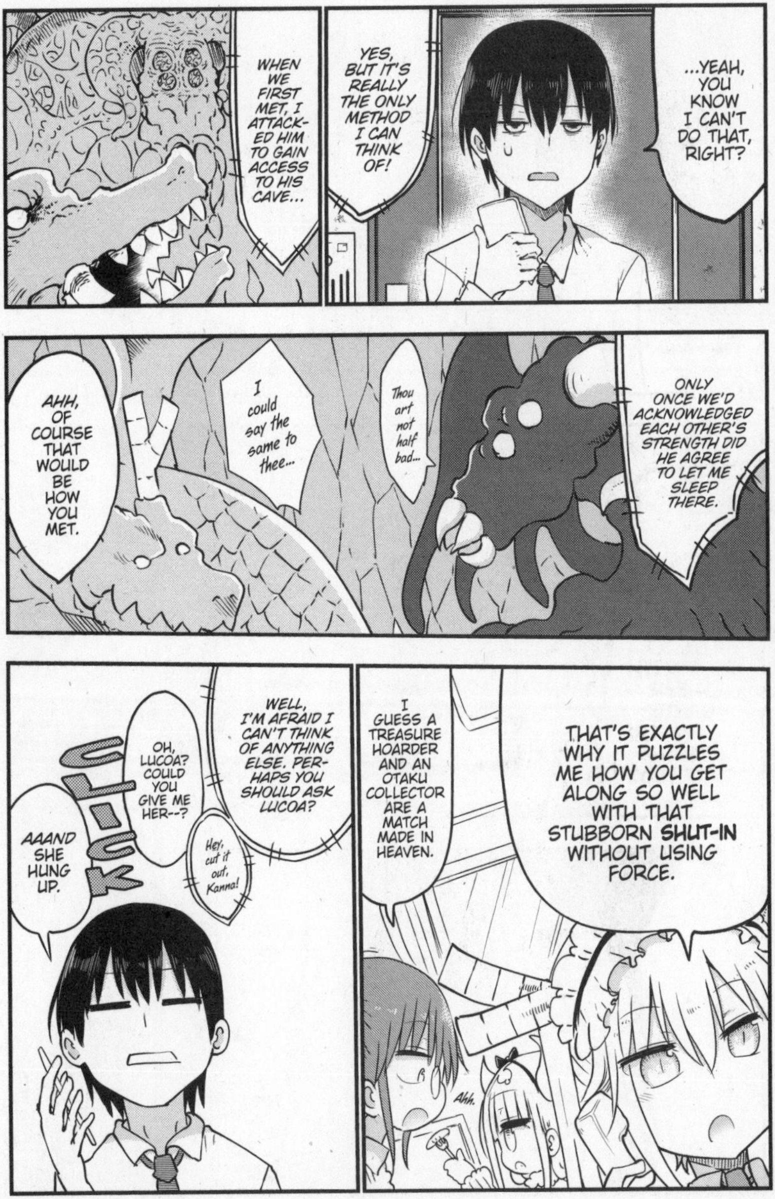
...YEAH, YOU KNOW I CAN'T DO THAT, RIGHT?
YES, BUT IT'S REALLY THE ONLY METHOD I CAN THINK OF!
WHEN WE FIRST MET, I ATTACK-ED HIM TO GAIN ACCESS TO HIS CAVE...
ONLY ONCE WE'D ACKNOWLEDGED EACH OTHER'S STRENGTH DID HE AGREE TO LET ME SLEEP THERE.
Thou art not half bad...
I could say the same to thee...
AHH, OF COURSE THAT WOULD BE HOW YOU MET.
THAT'S EXACTLY WHY IT PUZZLES ME HOW YOU GET ALONG SO WELL WITH THAT STUBBORN SHUT-IN WITHOUT USING FORCE.
I GUESS A TREASURE HOARDER AND AN OTAKU COLLECTOR ARE A MATCH MADE IN HEAVEN.
Ahh.
WELL, I'M AFRAID I CAN'T THINK OF ANYTHING ELSE. PER-HAPS YOU SHOULD ASK LUCOA?
Hey, cut it out, Kanna!
OH, LUCOA? COULD YOU GIVE ME HER--?
CLICK
AAAND SHE HUNG UP.

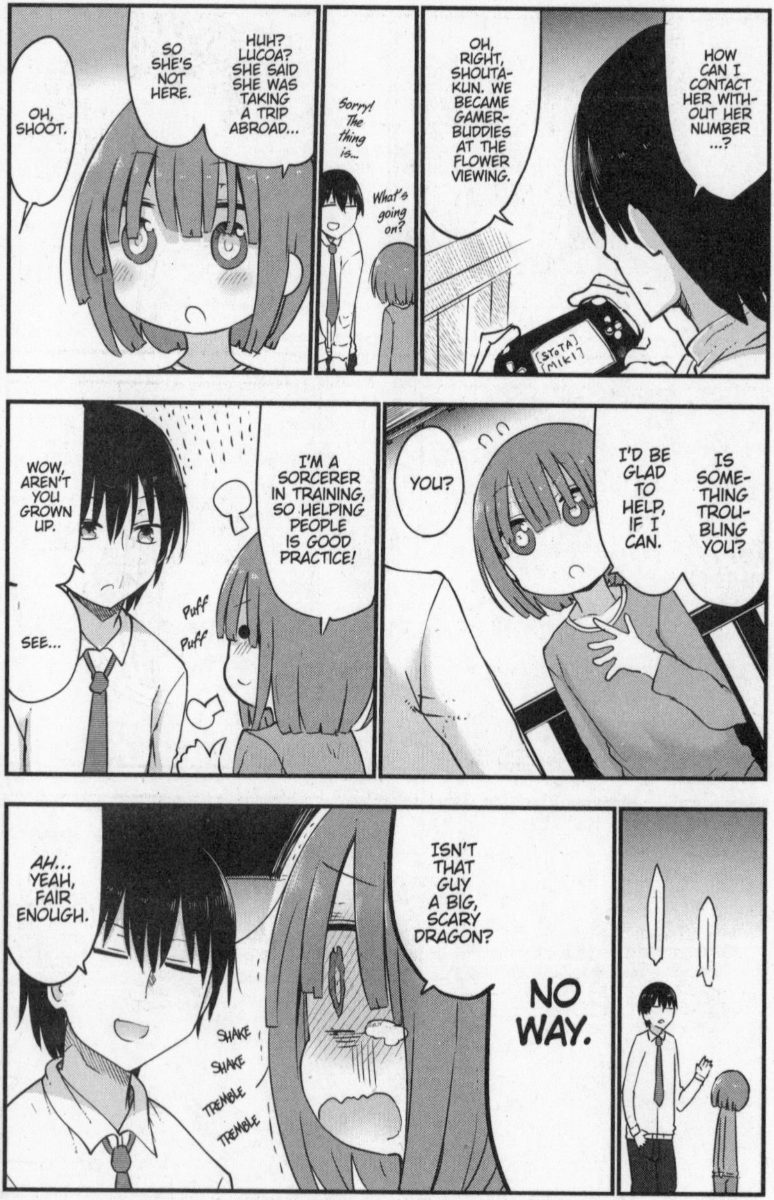
HOW CAN I CONTACT HER WITHOUT HER NUMBER ...?
OH, RIGHT, SHOUTA-KUN. WE BECAME GAMER-BUDDIES AT THE FLOWER VIEWING.
[SHOTA]
[MIKI]
Sorry! The thing is...
What's going on?
HUH? LUCOA? SHE SAID SHE WAS TAKING A TRIP ABROAD...
SO SHE'S NOT HERE.
OH, SHOOT.
IS SOMETHING TROUBLING YOU?
I'D BE GLAD TO HELP, IF I CAN.
YOU?
I'M A SORCERER IN TRAINING, SO HELPING PEOPLE IS GOOD PRACTICE!
Puff
Puff
WOW, AREN'T YOU GROWN UP.
SEE...
NO WAY.
ISN'T THAT GUY A BIG, SCARY DRAGON?
SHAKE
SHAKE
TREMBLE
TREMBLE
AH... YEAH, FAIR ENOUGH.

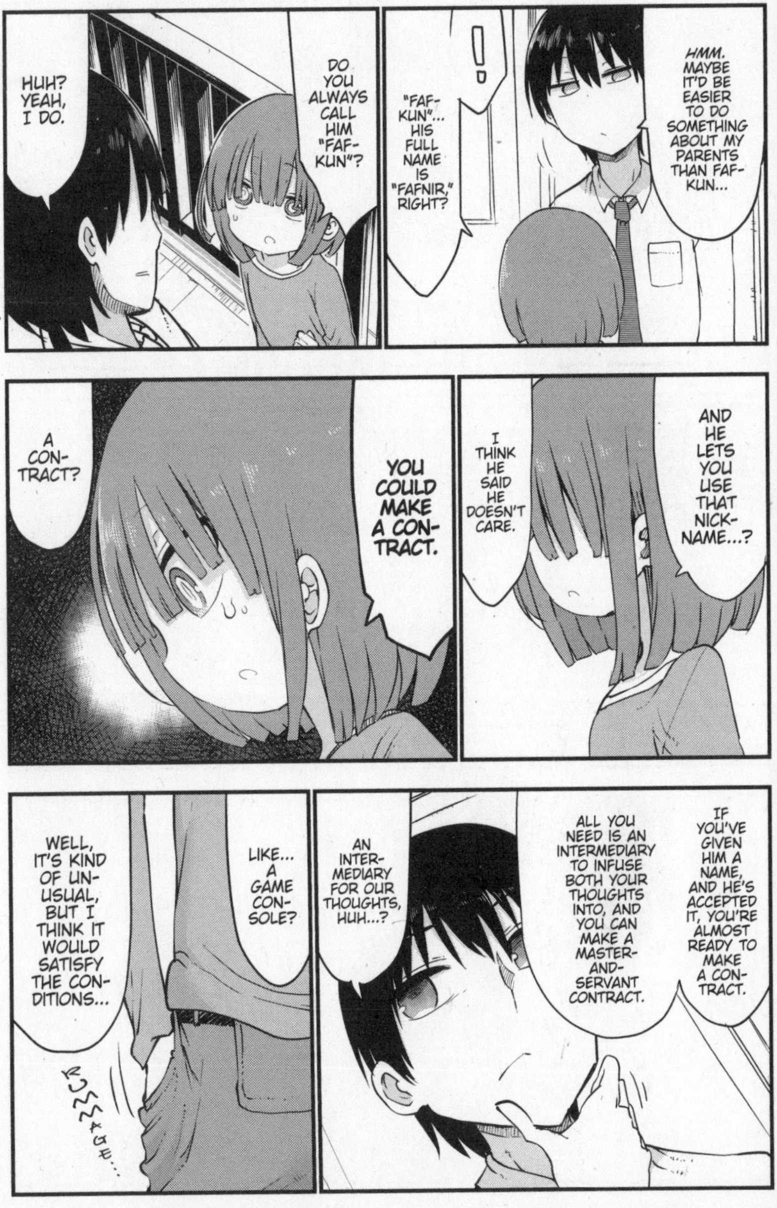
HMM. MAYBE IT'D BE EASIER TO DO SOMETHING ABOUT MY PARENTS THAN FAF-KUN...
!
"FAF-KUN"... HIS FULL NAME IS "FAFNIR," RIGHT?
DO YOU ALWAYS CALL HIM "FAF-KUN"?
HUH? YEAH, I DO.
AND HE LETS YOU USE THAT NICKNAME...?
I THINK HE SAID HE DOESN'T CARE.
YOU COULD MAKE A CONTRACT.
A CONTRACT?
IF YOU'VE GIVEN HIM A NAME, AND HE'S ACCEPTED IT, YOU'RE ALMOST READY TO MAKE A CONTRACT.
ALL YOU NEED IS AN INTERMEDIARY TO INFUSE BOTH YOUR THOUGHTS INTO, AND YOU CAN MAKE A MASTER-AND-SERVANT CONTRACT.
AN INTERMEDIARY FOR OUR THOUGHTS, HUH...?
LIKE... A GAME CONSOLE?
WELL, IT'S KIND OF UNUSUAL, BUT I THINK IT WOULD SATISFY THE CONDITIONS...
RUMMAGE...

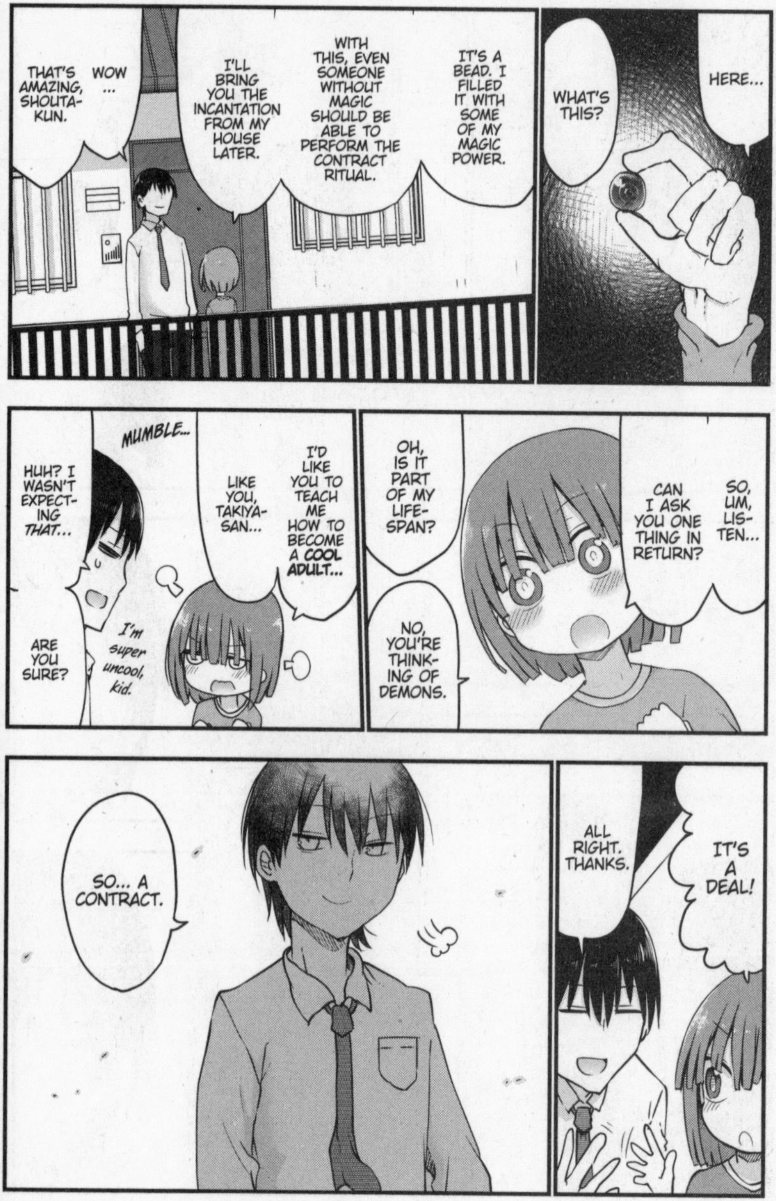
HERE...
WHAT'S THIS?
IT'S A BEAD. I FILLED IT WITH SOME OF MY MAGIC POWER.
WITH THIS, EVEN SOMEONE WITHOUT MAGIC SHOULD BE ABLE TO PERFORM THE CONTRACT RITUAL.
I'LL BRING YOU THE INCANTATION FROM MY HOUSE LATER.
WOW...
THAT'S AMAZING, SHOUTA-KUN.
SO, UM, LISTEN...
CAN I ASK YOU ONE THING IN RETURN?
OH, IS IT PART OF MY LIFESPAN?
NO, YOU'RE THINKING OF DEMONS.
I'D LIKE YOU TO TEACH ME HOW TO BECOME A COOL ADULT...
LIKE YOU, TAKIYA-SAN...
MUMBLE...
HUH? I WASN'T EXPECTING THAT...
I'm super uncool, kid.
ARE YOU SURE?
IT'S A DEAL!
ALL RIGHT. THANKS.
SO... A CONTRACT.

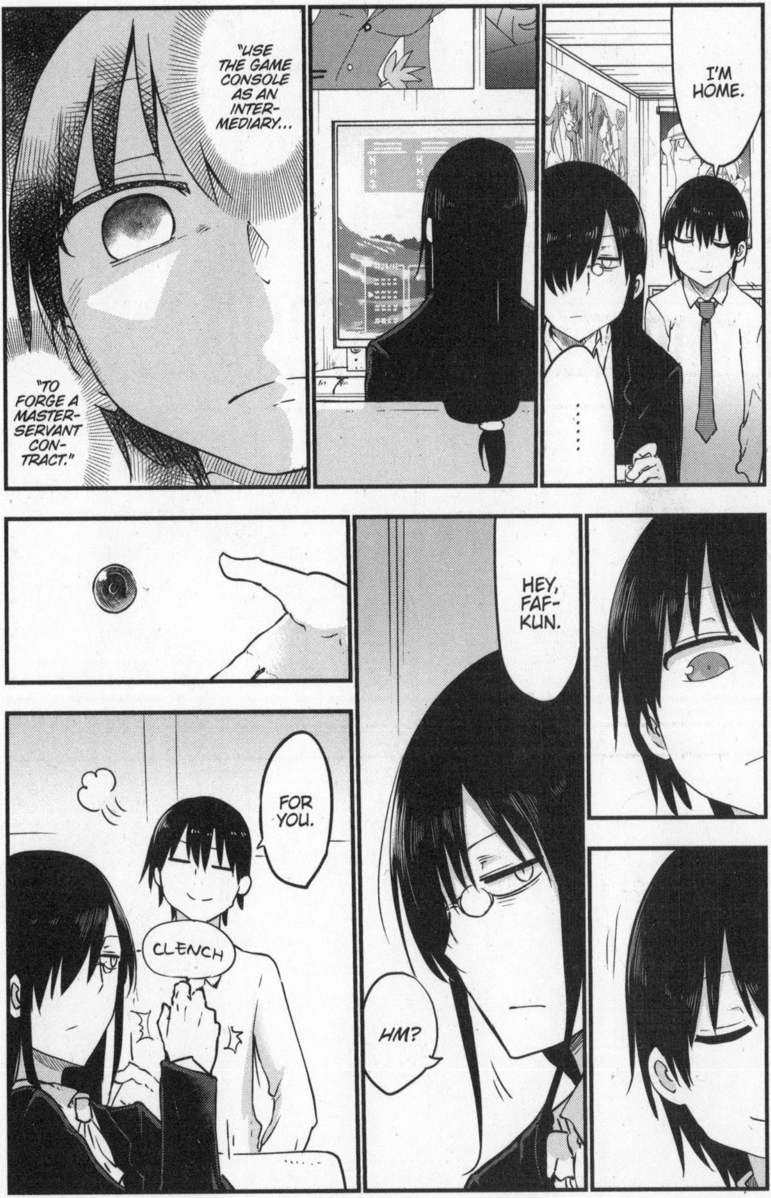
I'M HOME.
......
"USE THE GAME CONSOLE AS AN INTER-MEDIARY...
"TO FORGE A MASTER-SERVANT CON-TRACT."
HEY, FAF-KUN.
HM?
FOR YOU.
CLENCH

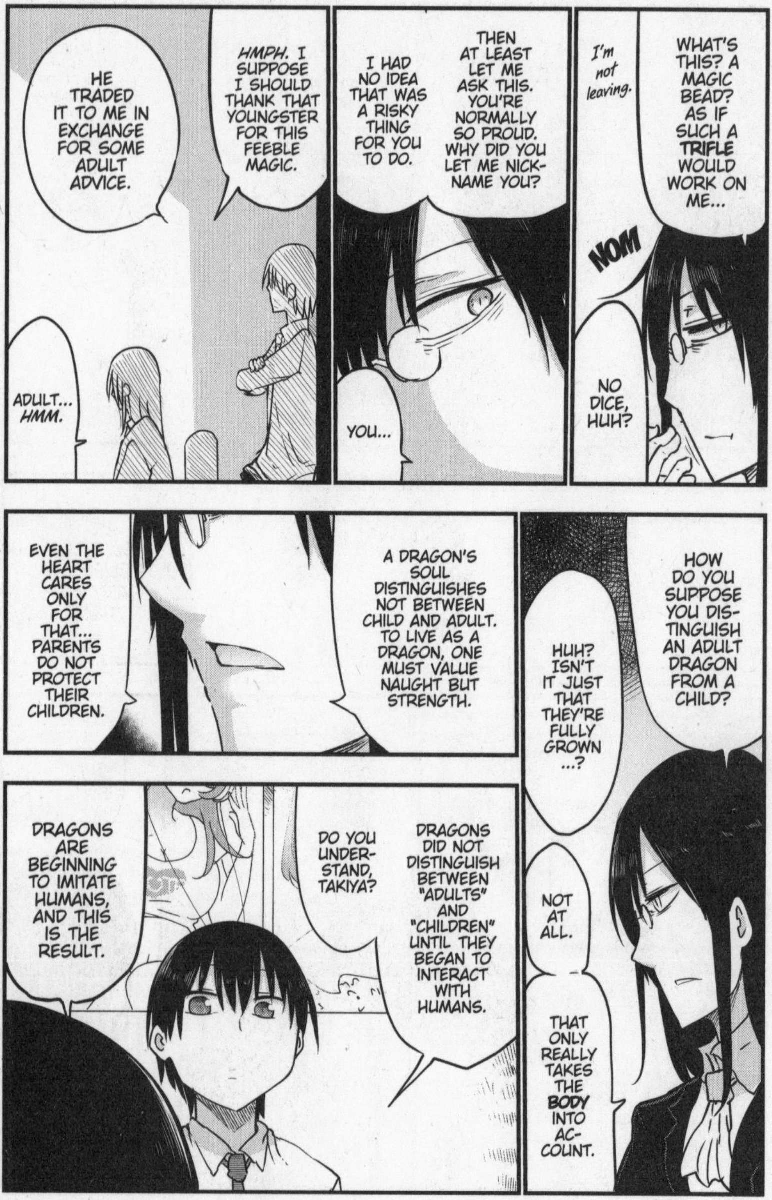
WHAT'S THIS? A MAGIC BEAD? AS IF SUCH A TRIFLE WOULD WORK ON ME...
I'm not leaving.
NOM
NO DICE, HUH?
THEN AT LEAST LET ME ASK THIS. YOU'RE NORMALLY SO PROUD. WHY DID YOU LET ME NICK-NAME YOU?
I HAD NO IDEA THAT WAS A RISKY THING FOR YOU TO DO.
YOU...
HMPH. I SUPPOSE I SHOULD THANK THAT YOUNGSTER FOR THIS FEEBLE MAGIC.
HE TRADED IT TO ME IN EXCHANGE FOR SOME ADULT ADVICE.
ADULT... HMM.
HOW DO YOU SUPPOSE YOU DIS-TINGUISH AN ADULT DRAGON FROM A CHILD?
HUH? ISN'T IT JUST THAT THEY'RE FULLY GROWN ...?
NOT AT ALL.
THAT ONLY REALLY TAKES THE BODY INTO AC-COUNT.
A DRAGON'S SOUL DISTINGUISHES NOT BETWEEN CHILD AND ADULT. TO LIVE AS A DRAGON, ONE MUST VALUE NAUGHT BUT STRENGTH.
EVEN THE HEART CARES ONLY FOR THAT... PARENTS DO NOT PROTECT THEIR CHILDREN.
DRAGONS DID NOT DISTINGUISH BETWEEN "ADULTS" AND "CHILDREN" UNTIL THEY BEGAN TO INTERACT WITH HUMANS.
DO YOU UNDER-STAND, TAKIYA?
DRAGONS ARE BEGINNING TO IMITATE HUMANS, AND THIS IS THE RESULT.

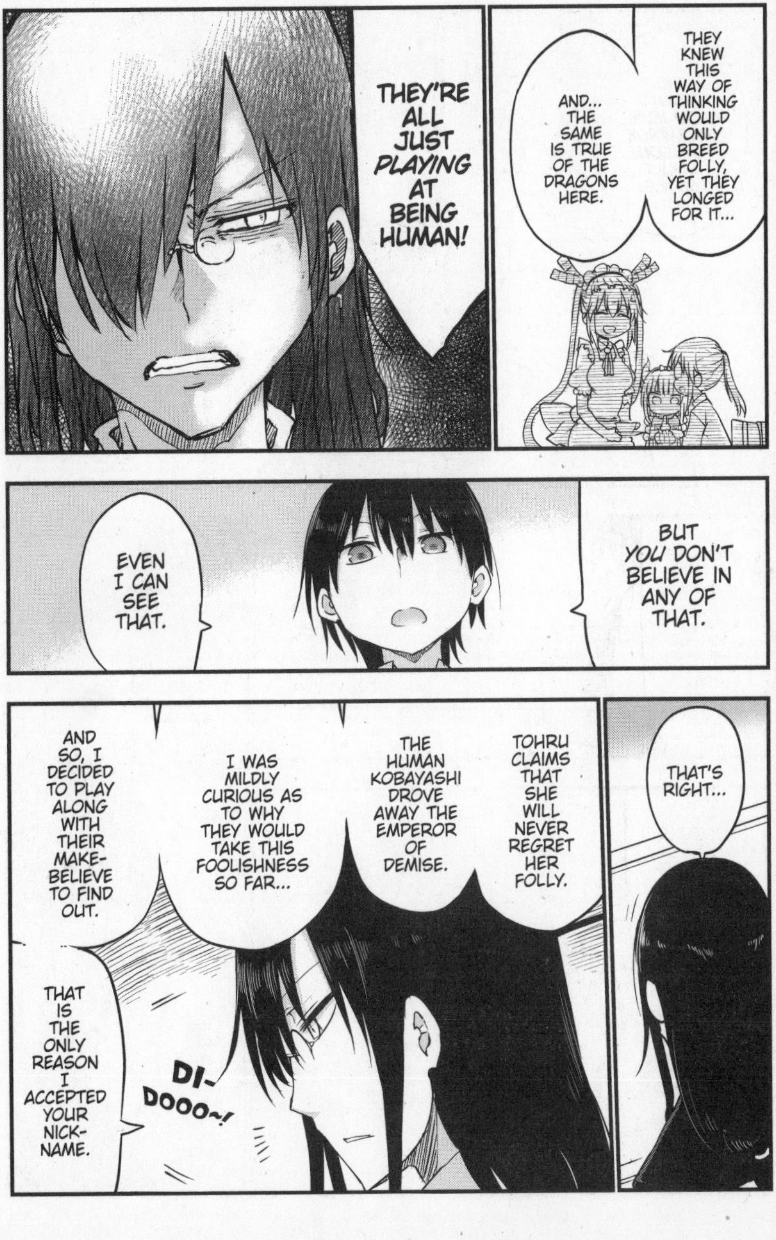
THEY KNEW THIS WAY OF THINKING WOULD ONLY BREED FOLLY, YET THEY LONGED FOR IT...
AND... THE SAME IS TRUE OF THE DRAGONS HERE.
THEY'RE ALL JUST *PLAYING* AT BEING HUMAN!
BUT *YOU* DON'T BELIEVE IN ANY OF THAT.
EVEN I CAN SEE THAT.
THAT'S RIGHT...
TOHRU CLAIMS THAT SHE WILL NEVER REGRET HER FOLLY.
THE HUMAN KOBAYASHI DROVE AWAY THE EMPEROR OF DEMISE.
I WAS MILDLY CURIOUS AS TO WHY THEY WOULD TAKE THIS FOOLISHNESS SO FAR...
AND SO, I DECIDED TO PLAY ALONG WITH THEIR MAKE-BELIEVE TO FIND OUT.
THAT IS THE ONLY REASON I ACCEPTED YOUR NICK-NAME.
DI-DOOO~!

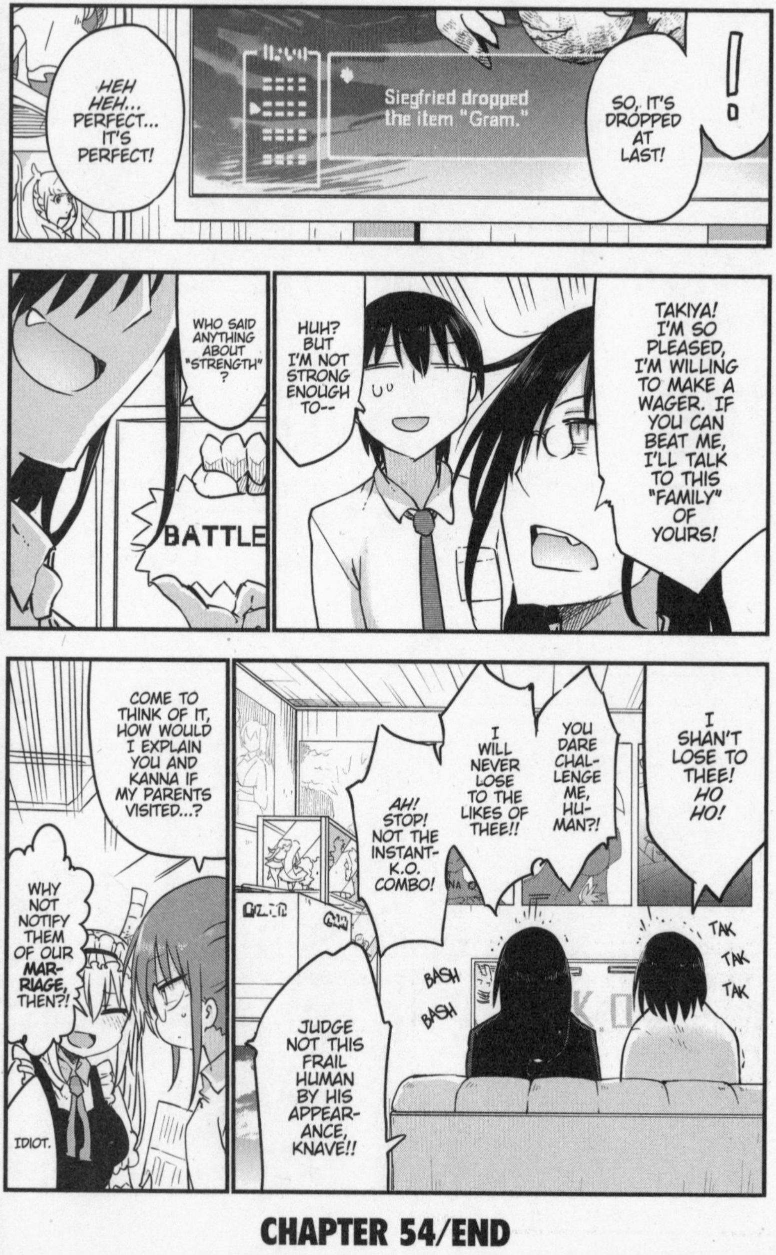
!
SO, IT'S DROPPED AT LAST!
Siegfried dropped the item "Gram."
HEH HEH... PERFECT... IT'S PERFECT!
TAKIYA! I'M SO PLEASED, I'M WILLING TO MAKE A WAGER. IF YOU CAN BEAT ME, I'LL TALK TO THIS "FAMILY" OF YOURS!
HUH? BUT I'M NOT STRONG ENOUGH TO--
WHO SAID ANYTHING ABOUT "STRENGTH"?
BATTLE
I SHAN'T LOSE TO THEE! HO HO!
YOU DARE CHAL-LENGE ME, HU-MAN?!
I WILL NEVER LOSE TO THE LIKES OF THEE!!
AH! STOP! NOT THE INSTANT-K.O. COMBO!
TAK TAK TAK
BASH BASH
JUDGE NOT THIS FRAIL HUMAN BY HIS APPEAR-ANCE, KNAVE!!
COME TO THINK OF IT, HOW WOULD I EXPLAIN YOU AND KANNA IF MY PARENTS VISITED...?
WHY NOT NOTIFY THEM OF OUR MAR-RIAGE, THEN?!
IDIOT.

CHAPTER 54/END

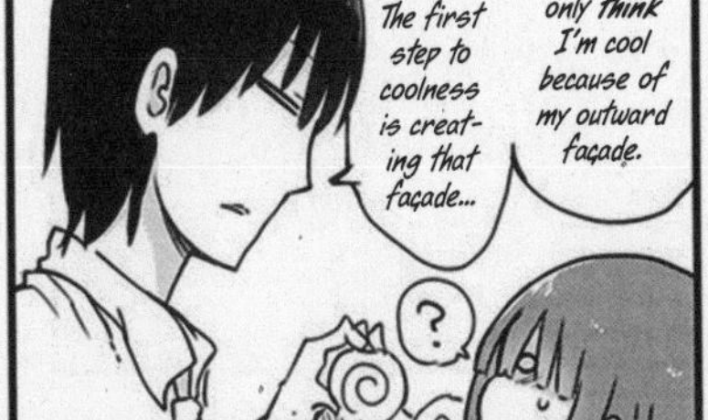
See, you only *think* I'm cool because of my outward façade.
The first step to coolness is creat-ing that façade...
?

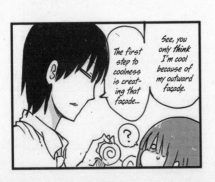

Miss Kobayashi's Dragon Maid

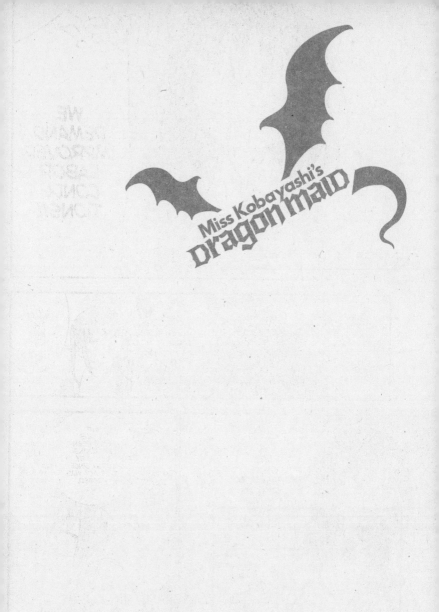

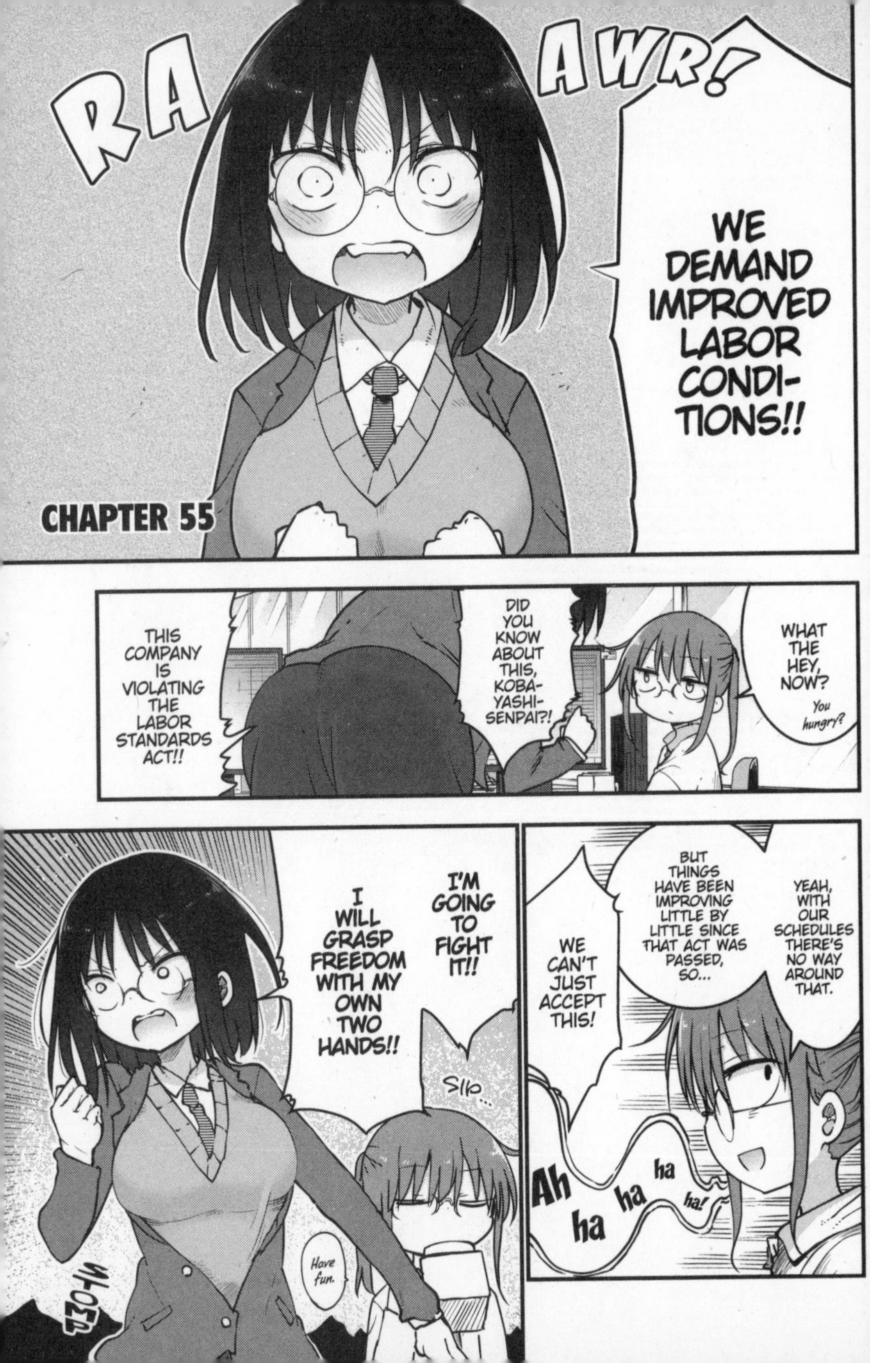
RA AWR!
WE DEMAND IMPROVED LABOR CONDITIONS!!
CHAPTER 55
WHAT THE HEY, NOW?
You hungry?
DID YOU KNOW ABOUT THIS, KOBAYASHI-SENPAI?!
THIS COMPANY IS VIOLATING THE LABOR STANDARDS ACT!!
YEAH, WITH OUR SCHEDULES THERE'S NO WAY AROUND THAT.
BUT THINGS HAVE BEEN IMPROVING LITTLE BY LITTLE SINCE THAT ACT WAS PASSED, SO...
WE CAN'T JUST ACCEPT THIS!
Ah ha ha ha ha!~
I'M GOING TO FIGHT IT!!
I WILL GRASP FREEDOM WITH MY OWN TWO HANDS!!
Have fun.

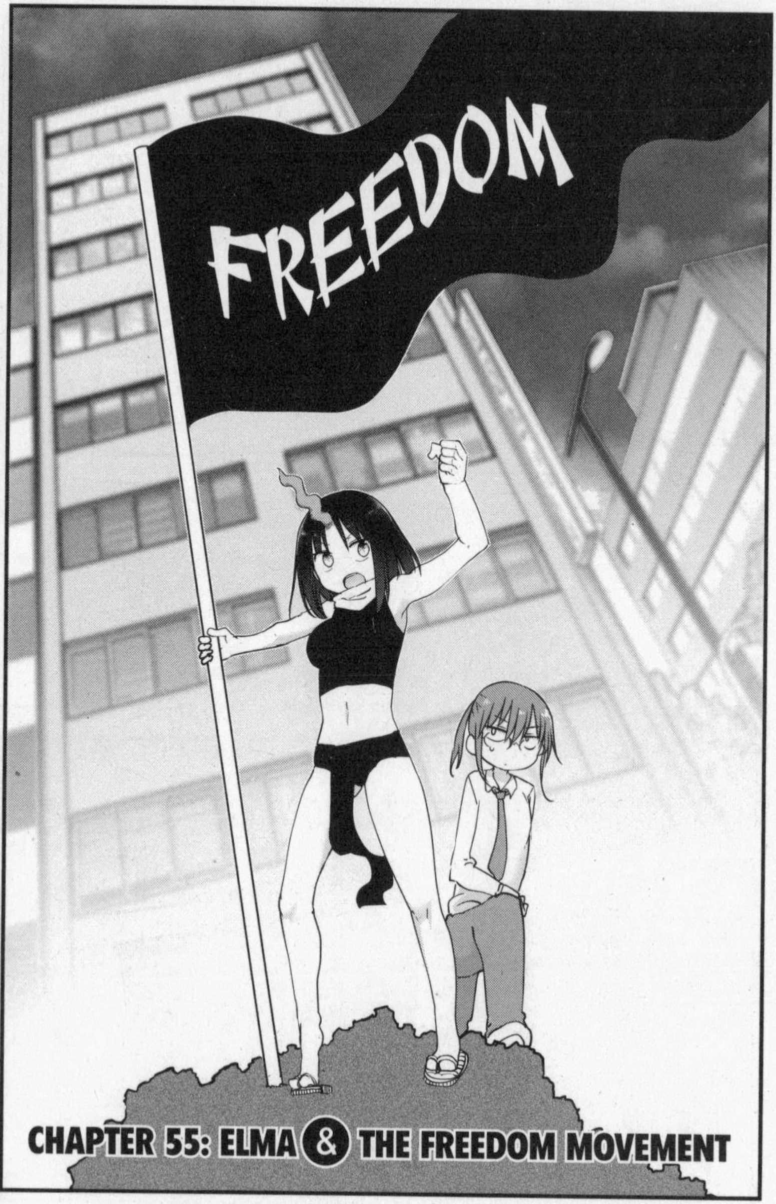
FREEDOM

CHAPTER 55: ELMA & THE FREEDOM MOVEMENT

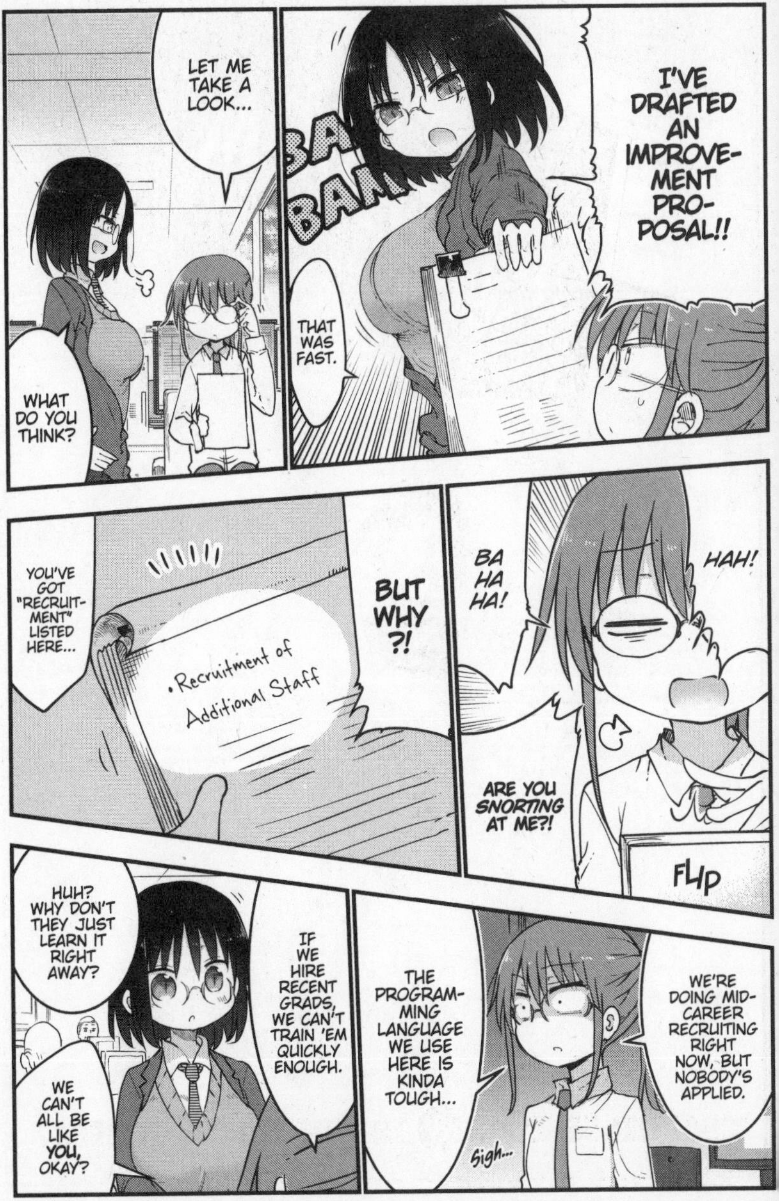
I'VE DRAFTED AN IMPROVEMENT PROPOSAL!!
BA BAM
THAT WAS FAST.
LET ME TAKE A LOOK...
WHAT DO YOU THINK?
HAH!
BA HA HA!
ARE YOU SNORTING AT ME?!
FLIP
BUT WHY?!
YOU'VE GOT "RECRUITMENT" LISTED HERE...
• Recruitment of Additional Staff
WE'RE DOING MID-CAREER RECRUITING RIGHT NOW, BUT NOBODY'S APPLIED.
THE PROGRAMMING LANGUAGE WE USE HERE IS KINDA TOUGH...
Sigh...
IF WE HIRE RECENT GRADS, WE CAN'T TRAIN 'EM QUICKLY ENOUGH.
HUH? WHY DON'T THEY JUST LEARN IT RIGHT AWAY?
WE CAN'T ALL BE LIKE YOU, OKAY?

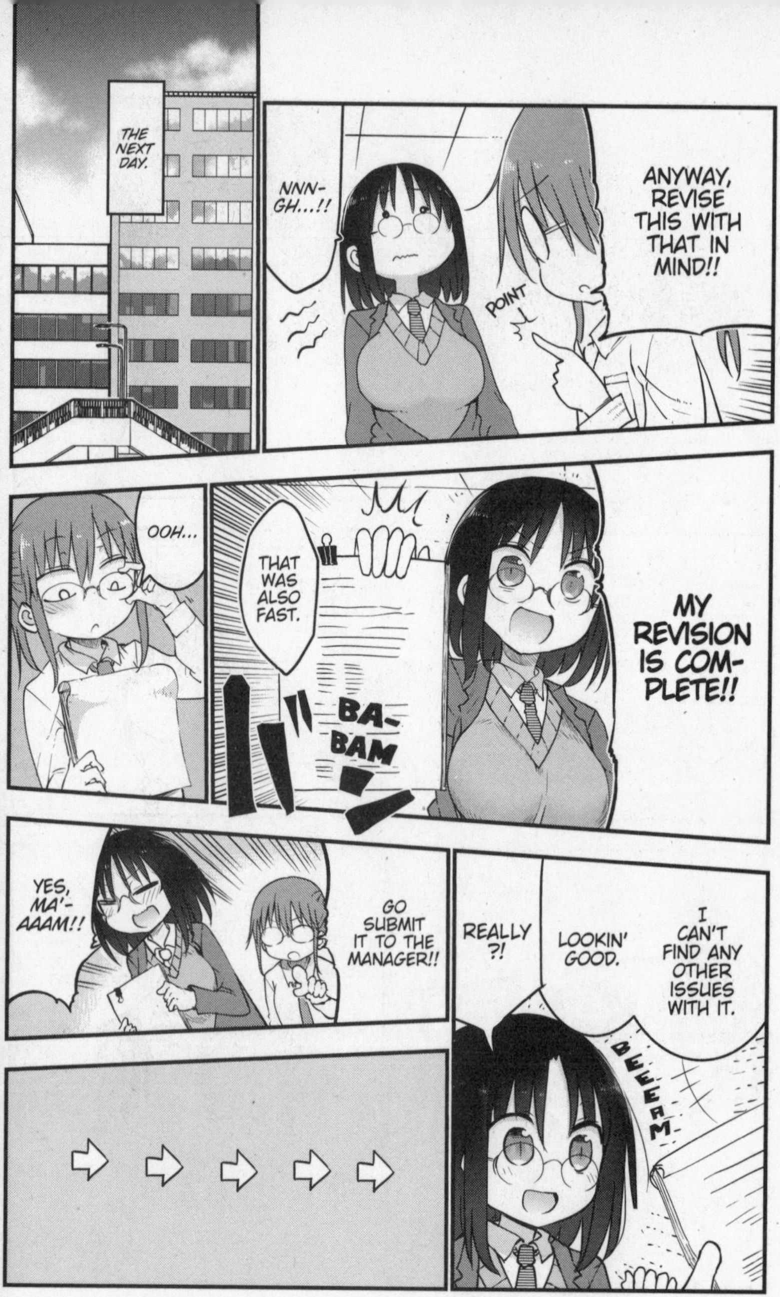
ANYWAY, REVISE THIS WITH THAT IN MIND!!
POINT
NNN-GH...!!
THE NEXT DAY.
MY REVISION IS COMPLETE!!
THAT WAS ALSO FAST.
BA-BAM
OOH...
I CAN'T FIND ANY OTHER ISSUES WITH IT.
LOOKIN' GOOD.
REALLY?!
BEEEAM
GO SUBMIT IT TO THE MANAGER!!
YES, MA'-AAAM!!

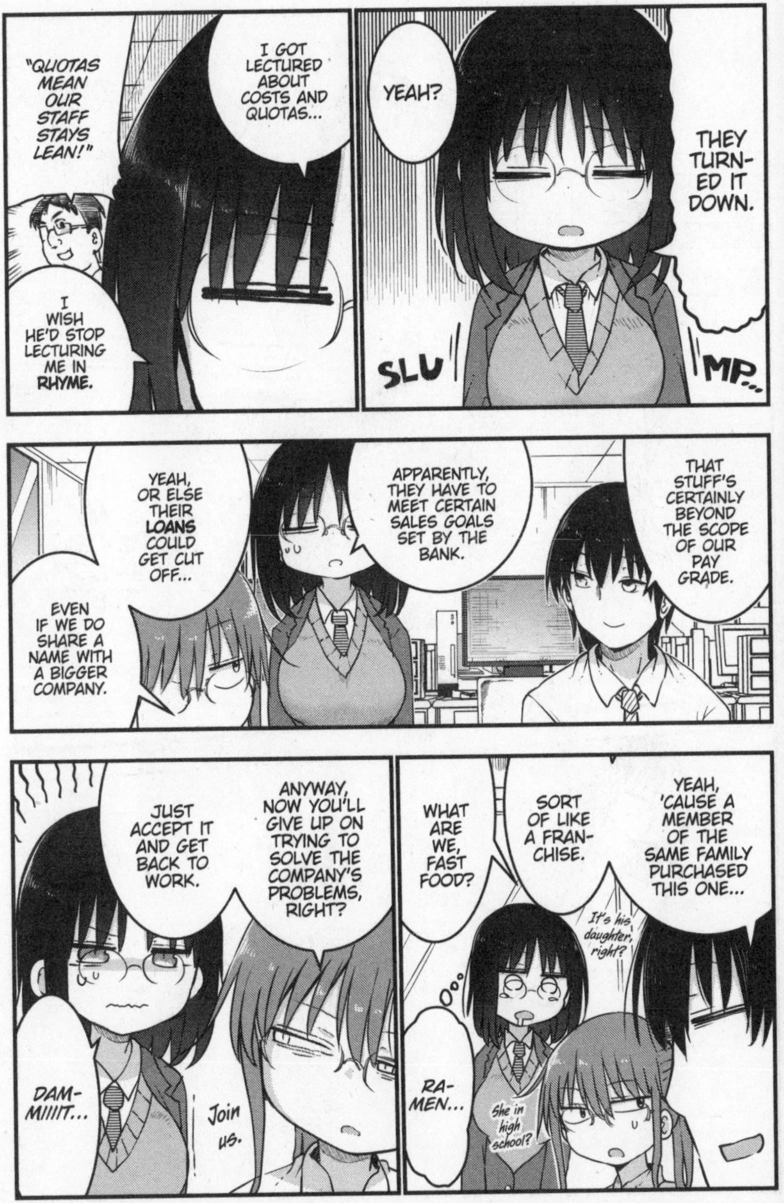
YEAH?
THEY TURNED IT DOWN.
SLUMP...
I GOT LECTURED ABOUT COSTS AND QUOTAS...
"QUOTAS MEAN OUR STAFF STAYS LEAN!"
I WISH HE'D STOP LECTURING ME IN RHYME.
THAT STUFF'S CERTAINLY BEYOND THE SCOPE OF OUR PAY GRADE.
APPARENTLY, THEY HAVE TO MEET CERTAIN SALES GOALS SET BY THE BANK.
YEAH, OR ELSE THEIR LOANS COULD GET CUT OFF...
EVEN IF WE DO SHARE A NAME WITH A BIGGER COMPANY.
YEAH, 'CAUSE A MEMBER OF THE SAME FAMILY PURCHASED THIS ONE...
SORT OF LIKE A FRANCHISE.
WHAT ARE WE, FAST FOOD?
It's his daughter, right?
RAMEN...
She in high school?
ANYWAY, NOW YOU'LL GIVE UP ON TRYING TO SOLVE THE COMPANY'S PROBLEMS, RIGHT?
JUST ACCEPT IT AND GET BACK TO WORK.
Join us.
DAMMIIIIT...

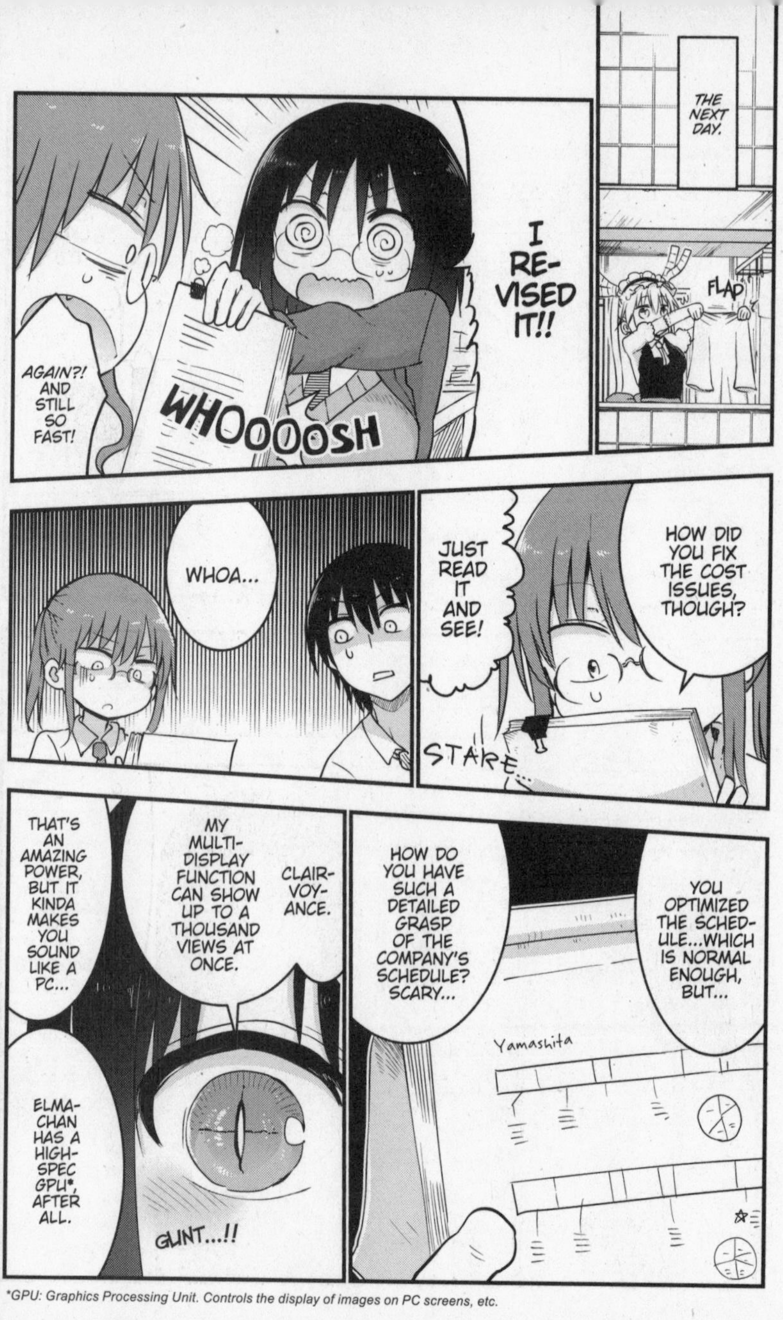
THE NEXT DAY.
FLAP
I RE-VISED IT!!
WHOOOOSH
AGAIN?! AND STILL SO FAST!
HOW DID YOU FIX THE COST ISSUES, THOUGH?
JUST READ IT AND SEE!
STARE...
WHOA...
YOU OPTIMIZED THE SCHEDULE...WHICH IS NORMAL ENOUGH, BUT...
HOW DO YOU HAVE SUCH A DETAILED GRASP OF THE COMPANY'S SCHEDULE? SCARY...
Yamashita
CLAIRVOYANCE.
MY MULTI-DISPLAY FUNCTION CAN SHOW UP TO A THOUSAND VIEWS AT ONCE.
THAT'S AN AMAZING POWER, BUT IT KINDA MAKES YOU SOUND LIKE A PC...
ELMA-CHAN HAS A HIGH-SPEC GPU*, AFTER ALL.
GLINT...!!

*GPU: Graphics Processing Unit. Controls the display of images on PC screens, etc.

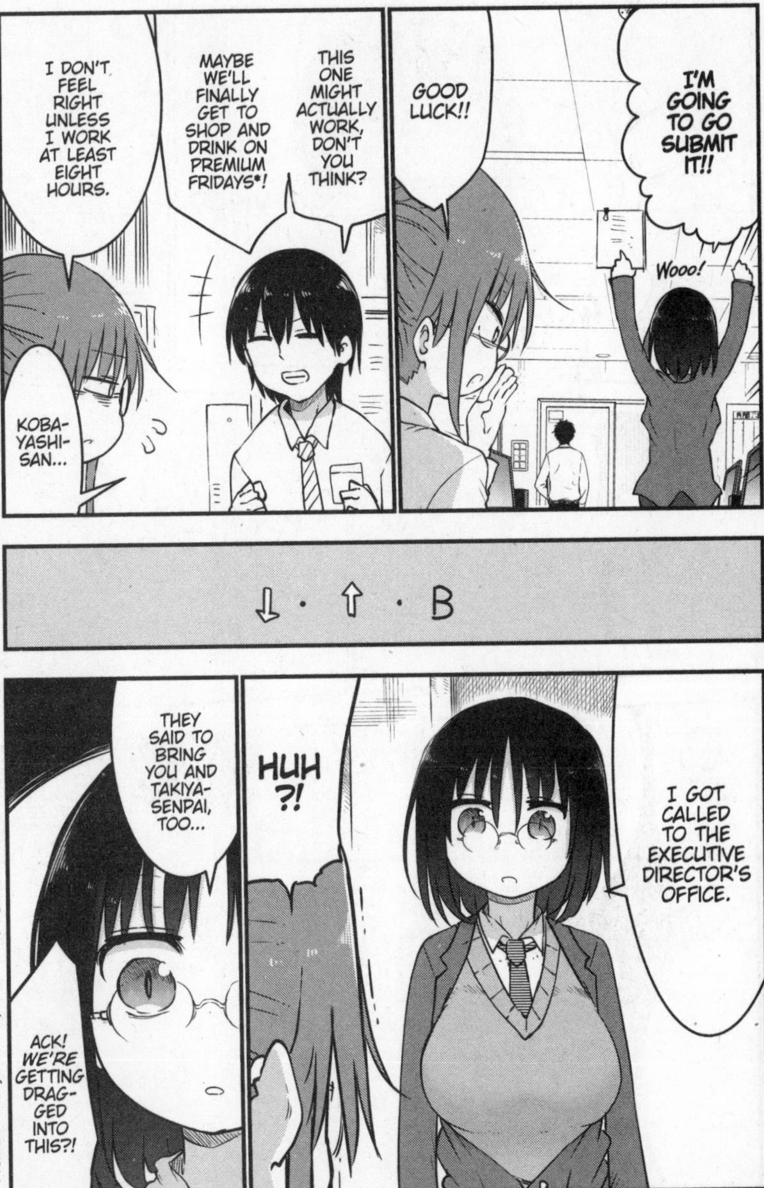
I'M GOING TO GO SUBMIT IT!!
Wooo!
GOOD LUCK!!
THIS ONE MIGHT ACTUALLY WORK, DON'T YOU THINK?
MAYBE WE'LL FINALLY GET TO SHOP AND DRINK ON PREMIUM FRIDAYS*!
I DON'T FEEL RIGHT UNLESS I WORK AT LEAST EIGHT HOURS.
KOBA-YASHI-SAN...
↓ · ↑ · B
I GOT CALLED TO THE EXECUTIVE DIRECTOR'S OFFICE.
HUH?!
THEY SAID TO BRING YOU AND TAKIYA-SENPAI, TOO...
ACK! WE'RE GETTING DRAG-GED INTO THIS?!

*"Premium Fridays" is a Japanese campaign to stimulate the economy by getting workers to leave early on the last Friday of every month so they can go spend money.

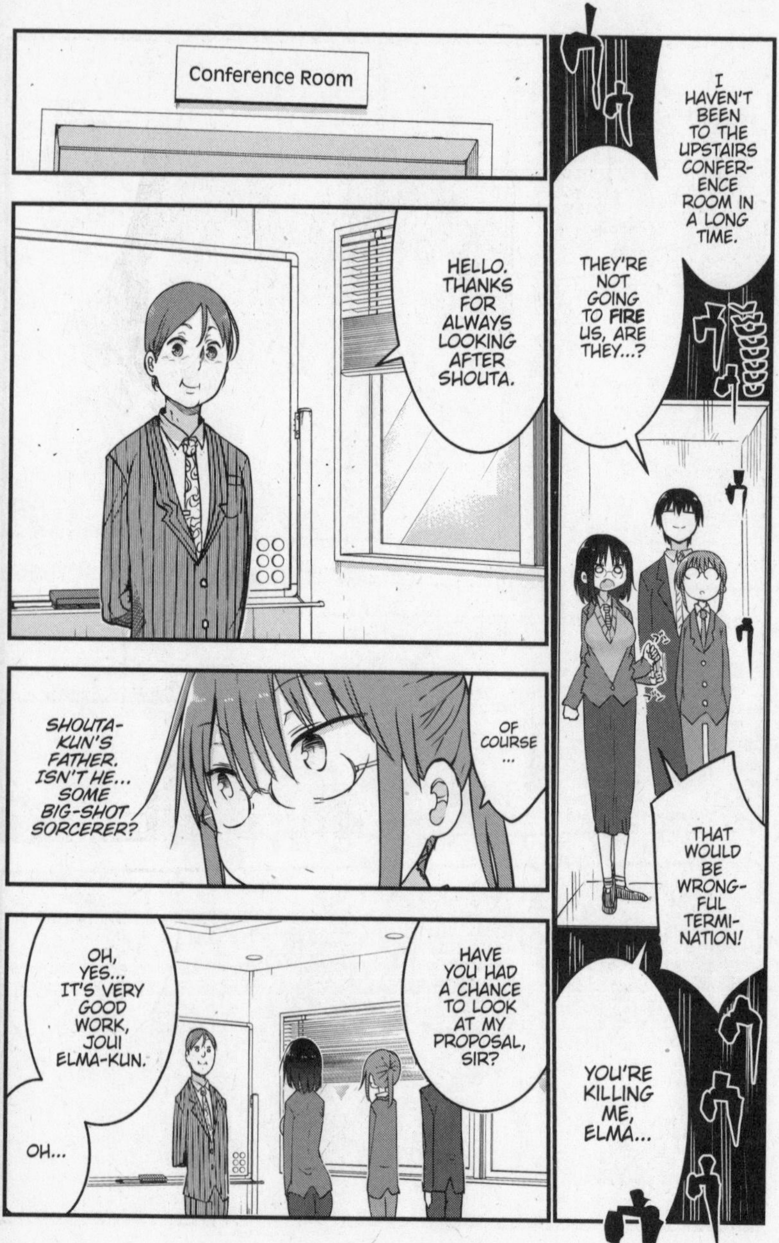
I HAVEN'T BEEN TO THE UPSTAIRS CONFERENCE ROOM IN A LONG TIME.
THEY'RE NOT GOING TO FIRE US, ARE THEY...?
THAT WOULD BE WRONGFUL TERMINATION!
YOU'RE KILLING ME, ELMA...
Conference Room
HELLO. THANKS FOR ALWAYS LOOKING AFTER SHOUTA.
OF COURSE ...
SHOUTA-KUN'S FATHER. ISN'T HE... SOME BIG-SHOT SORCERER?
HAVE YOU HAD A CHANCE TO LOOK AT MY PROPOSAL, SIR?
OH, YES... IT'S VERY GOOD WORK, JOUI ELMA-KUN.
OH...

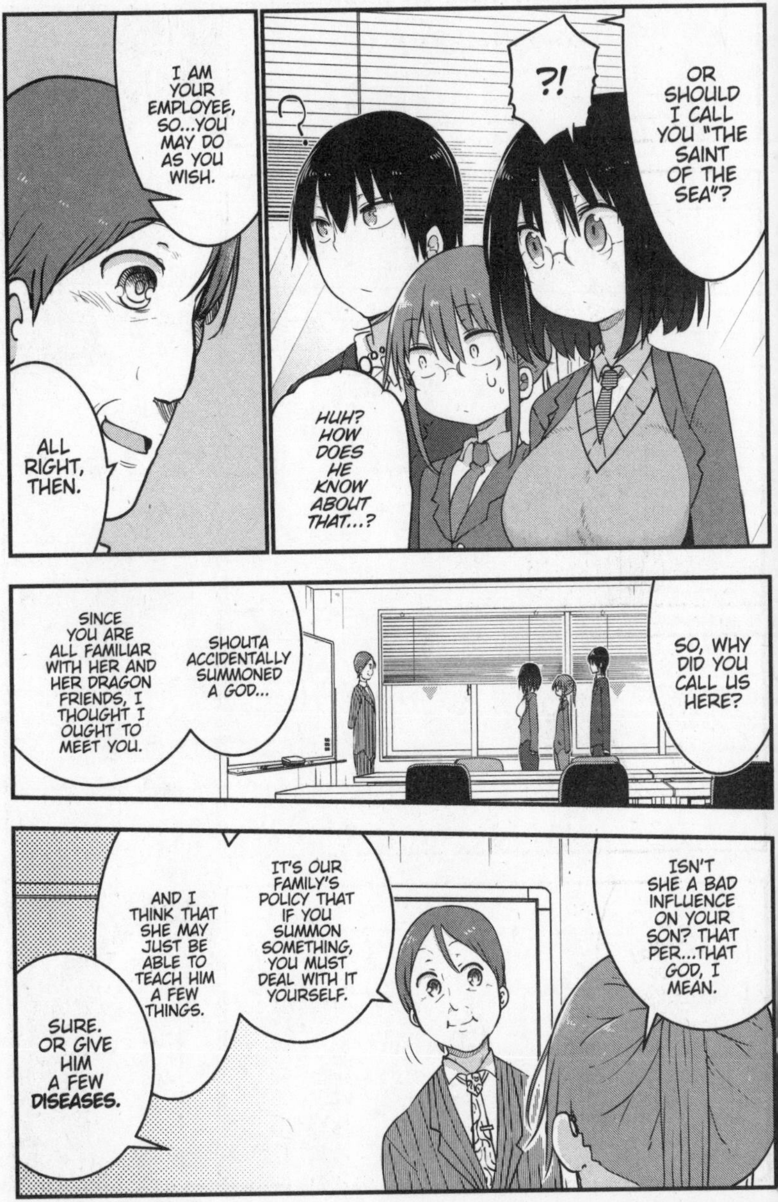
OR SHOULD I CALL YOU "THE SAINT OF THE SEA"?
?!
HUH? HOW DOES HE KNOW ABOUT THAT...?
I AM YOUR EMPLOYEE, SO...YOU MAY DO AS YOU WISH.
ALL RIGHT, THEN.
SO, WHY DID YOU CALL US HERE?
SHOUTA ACCIDENTALLY SUMMONED A GOD...
SINCE YOU ARE ALL FAMILIAR WITH HER AND HER DRAGON FRIENDS, I THOUGHT I OUGHT TO MEET YOU.
ISN'T SHE A BAD INFLUENCE ON YOUR SON? THAT PER...THAT GOD, I MEAN.
IT'S OUR FAMILY'S POLICY THAT IF YOU SUMMON SOMETHING, YOU MUST DEAL WITH IT YOURSELF.
AND I THINK THAT SHE MAY JUST BE ABLE TO TEACH HIM A FEW THINGS.
SURE. OR GIVE HIM A FEW DISEASES.

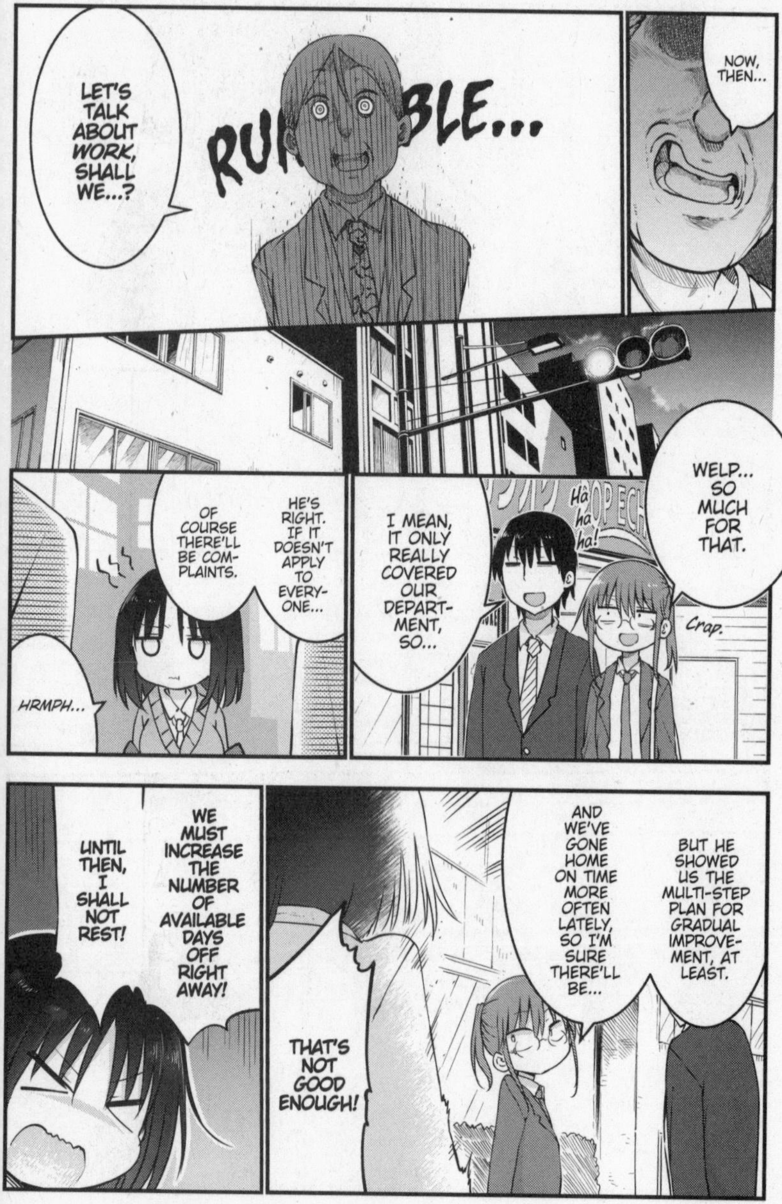
NOW, THEN...
LET'S TALK ABOUT WORK, SHALL WE...?
RU BLE...
WELP... SO MUCH FOR THAT.
Crap.
Ha ha ha!
I MEAN, IT ONLY REALLY COVERED OUR DEPARTMENT, SO...
HE'S RIGHT. IF IT DOESN'T APPLY TO EVERYONE...
OF COURSE THERE'LL BE COMPLAINTS.
HRMPH...
BUT HE SHOWED US THE MULTI-STEP PLAN FOR GRADUAL IMPROVEMENT, AT LEAST.
AND WE'VE GONE HOME ON TIME MORE OFTEN LATELY, SO I'M SURE THERE'LL BE...
THAT'S NOT GOOD ENOUGH!
WE MUST INCREASE THE NUMBER OF AVAILABLE DAYS OFF RIGHT AWAY!
UNTIL THEN, I SHALL NOT REST!

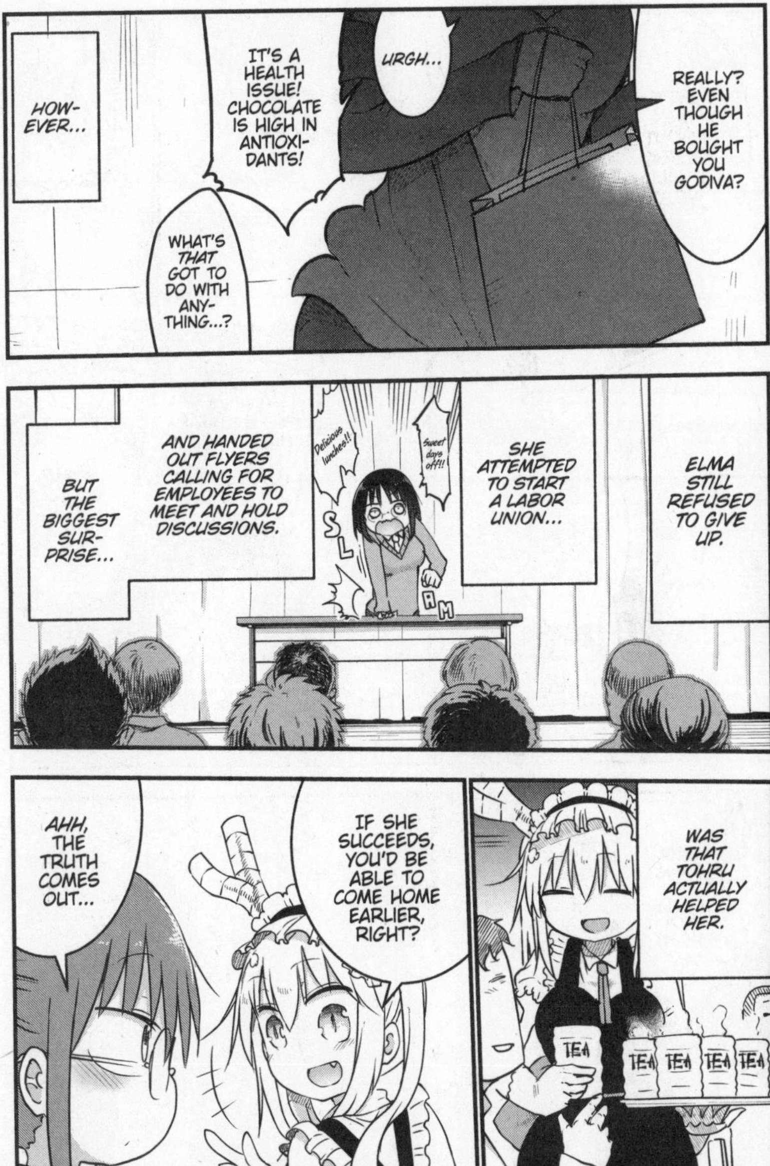
REALLY? EVEN THOUGH HE BOUGHT YOU GODIVA?
URGH...
IT'S A HEALTH ISSUE! CHOCOLATE IS HIGH IN ANTIOXIDANTS!
WHAT'S THAT GOT TO DO WITH ANYTHING...?
HOWEVER...
ELMA STILL REFUSED TO GIVE UP.
SHE ATTEMPTED TO START A LABOR UNION...
Sweet days off!!
Delicious lunches!!
SLAM
AND HANDED OUT FLYERS CALLING FOR EMPLOYEES TO MEET AND HOLD DISCUSSIONS.
BUT THE BIGGEST SURPRISE...
WAS THAT TOHRU ACTUALLY HELPED HER.
TEA
TEA
TEA
TEA
TEA
IF SHE SUCCEEDS, YOU'D BE ABLE TO COME HOME EARLIER, RIGHT?
AHH, THE TRUTH COMES OUT...

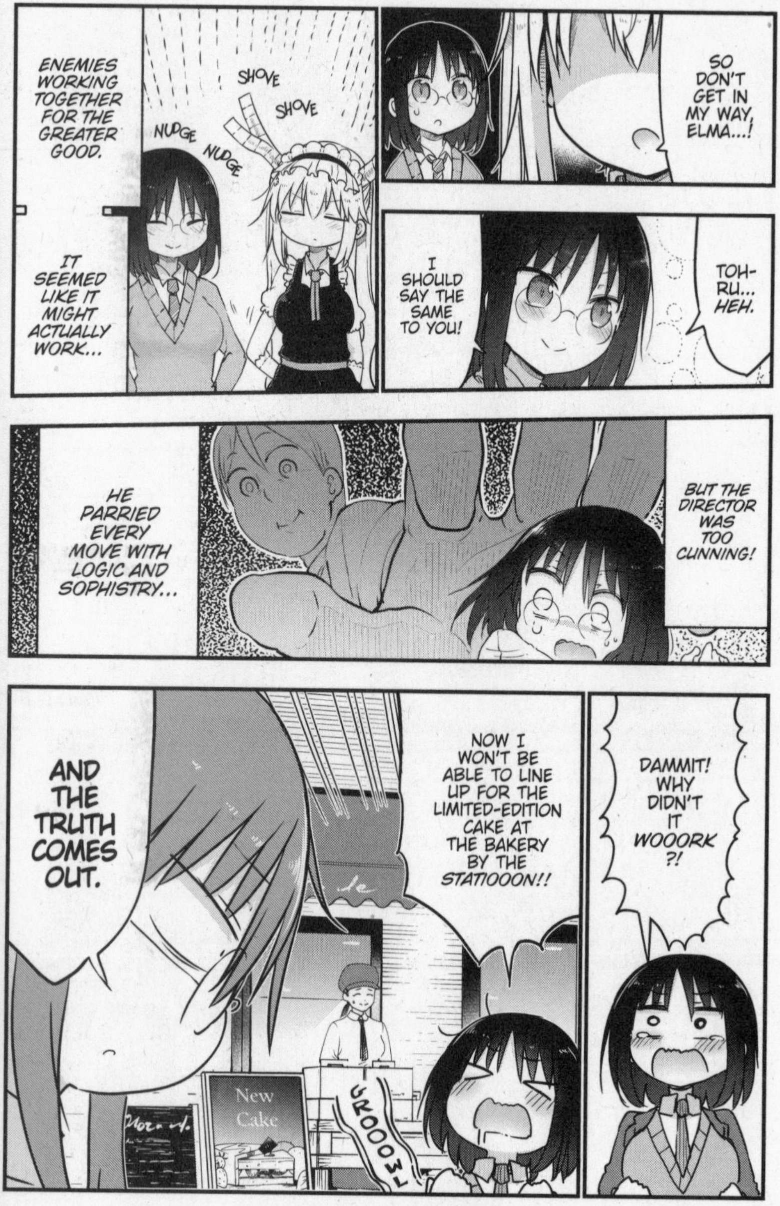
SO DON'T GET IN MY WAY, ELMA...!
TOH-RU... HEH.
I SHOULD SAY THE SAME TO YOU!
SHOVE
SHOVE
ENEMIES WORKING TOGETHER FOR THE GREATER GOOD.
NUDGE
NUDGE
IT SEEMED LIKE IT MIGHT ACTUALLY WORK...
BUT THE DIRECTOR WAS TOO CUNNING!
HE PARRIED EVERY MOVE WITH LOGIC AND SOPHISTRY...
DAMMIT! WHY DIDN'T IT WOOORK?!
NOW I WON'T BE ABLE TO LINE UP FOR THE LIMITED-EDITION CAKE AT THE BAKERY BY THE STATIOOON!!
AND THE TRUTH COMES OUT.
GROOOWL
New Cake

CHAPTER 55/END

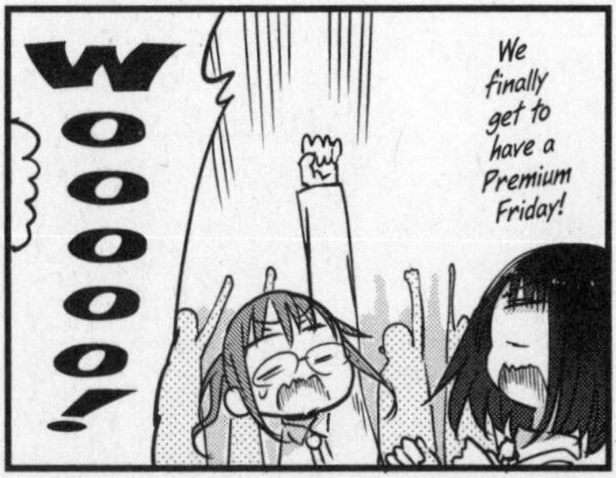
We finally get to have a Premium Friday!
WOOOOO!
It was a one-time thing.

Miss Kobayashi's Dragon Maid

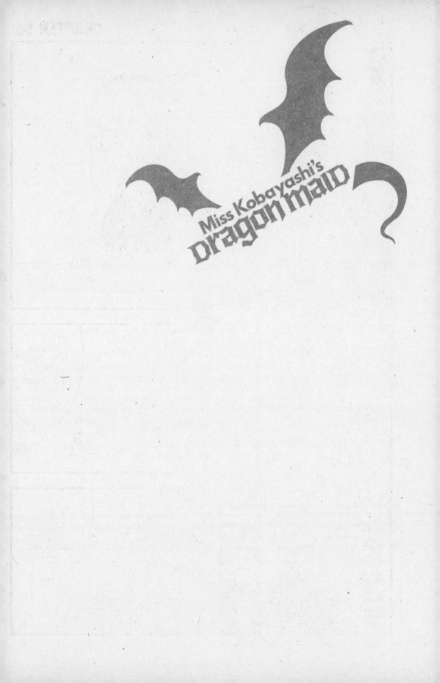

CHAPTER 56

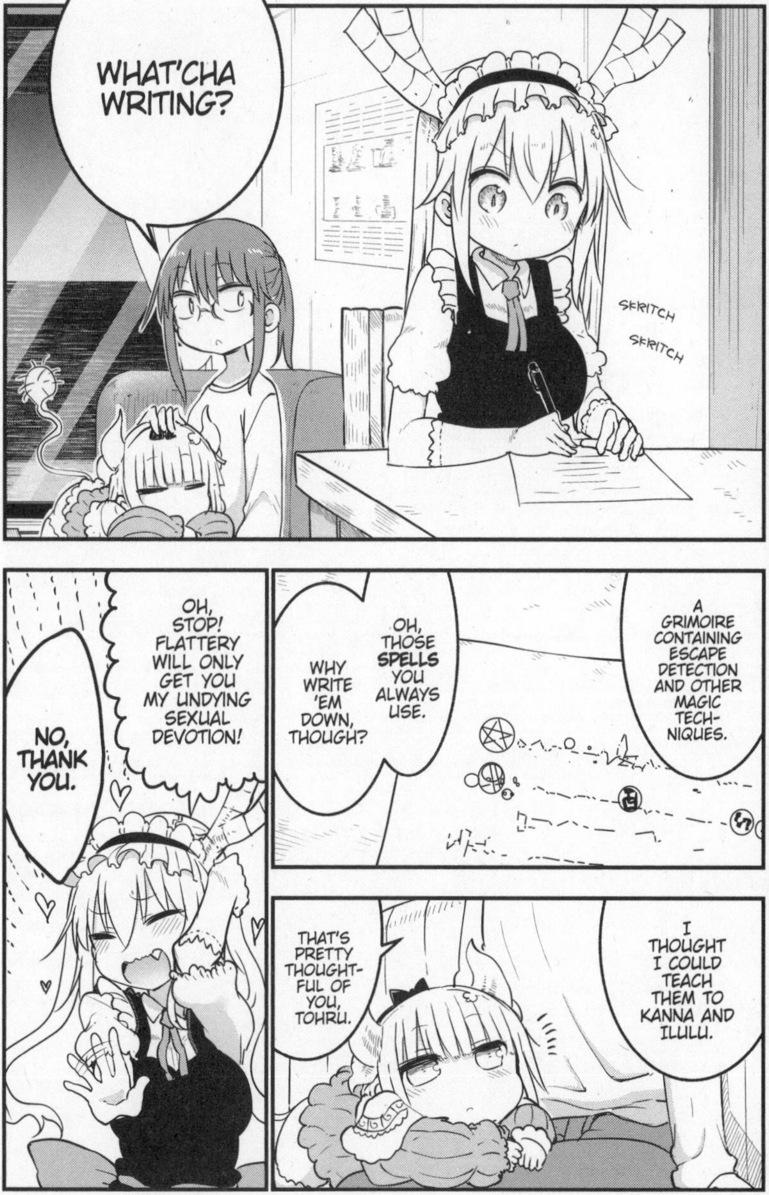
WHAT'CHA WRITING?
SKRITCH SKRITCH
A GRIMOIRE CONTAINING ESCAPE DETECTION AND OTHER MAGIC TECHNIQUES.
OH, THOSE **SPELLS** YOU ALWAYS USE.
WHY WRITE 'EM DOWN, THOUGH?
I THOUGHT I COULD TEACH THEM TO KANNA AND ILULU.
THAT'S PRETTY THOUGHTFUL OF YOU, TOHRU.
OH, STOP! FLATTERY WILL ONLY GET YOU MY UNDYING SEXUAL DEVOTION!
NO, THANK YOU.

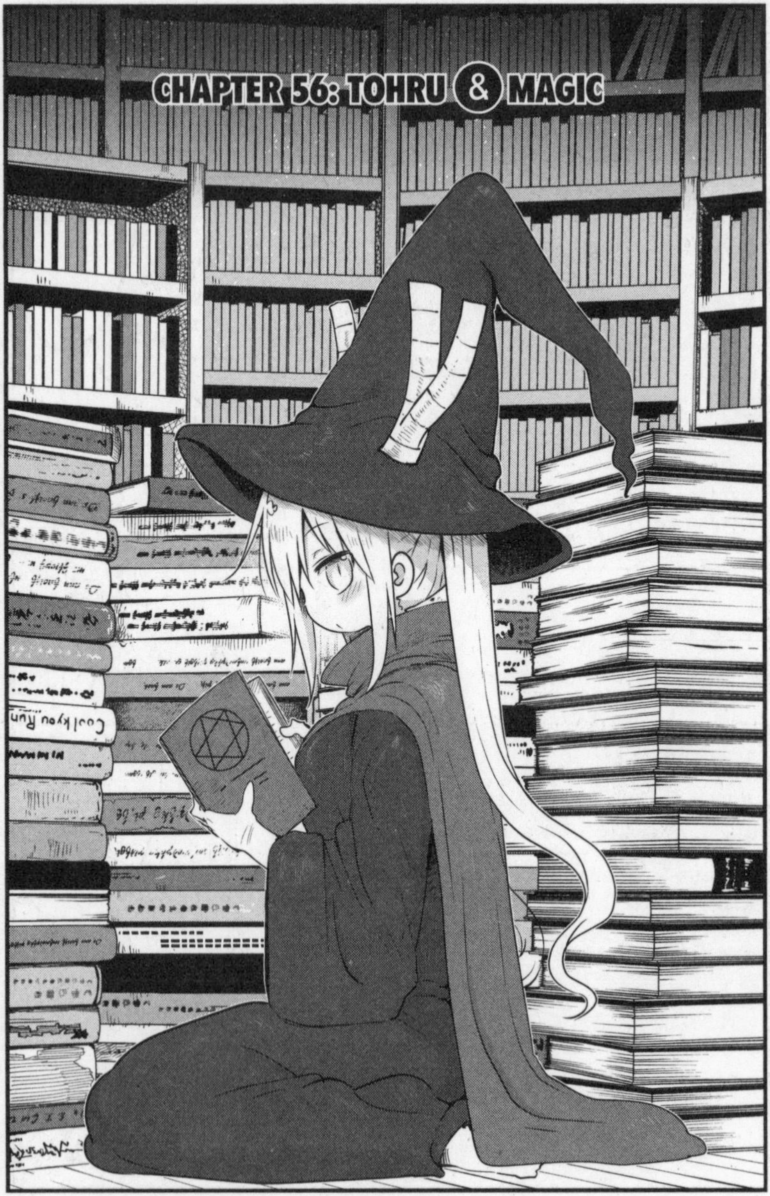
CHAPTER 56: TOHRU & MAGIC

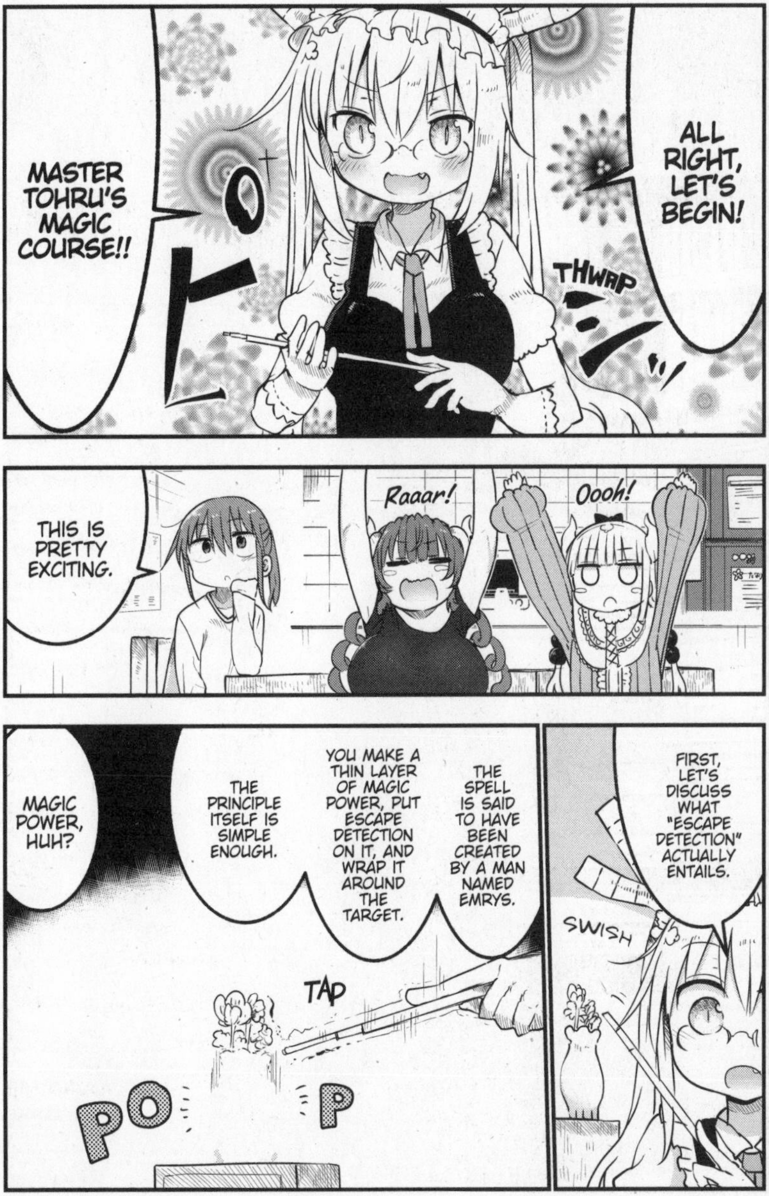
ALL RIGHT, LET'S BEGIN!
THWAP
MASTER TOHRU'S MAGIC COURSE!!
Oooh!
Raaar!
THIS IS PRETTY EXCITING.
FIRST, LET'S DISCUSS WHAT "ESCAPE DETECTION" ACTUALLY ENTAILS.
SWISH
THE SPELL IS SAID TO HAVE BEEN CREATED BY A MAN NAMED EMRYS.
YOU MAKE A THIN LAYER OF MAGIC POWER, PUT ESCAPE DETECTION ON IT, AND WRAP IT AROUND THE TARGET.
THE PRINCIPLE ITSELF IS SIMPLE ENOUGH.
TAP
POP
MAGIC POWER, HUH?

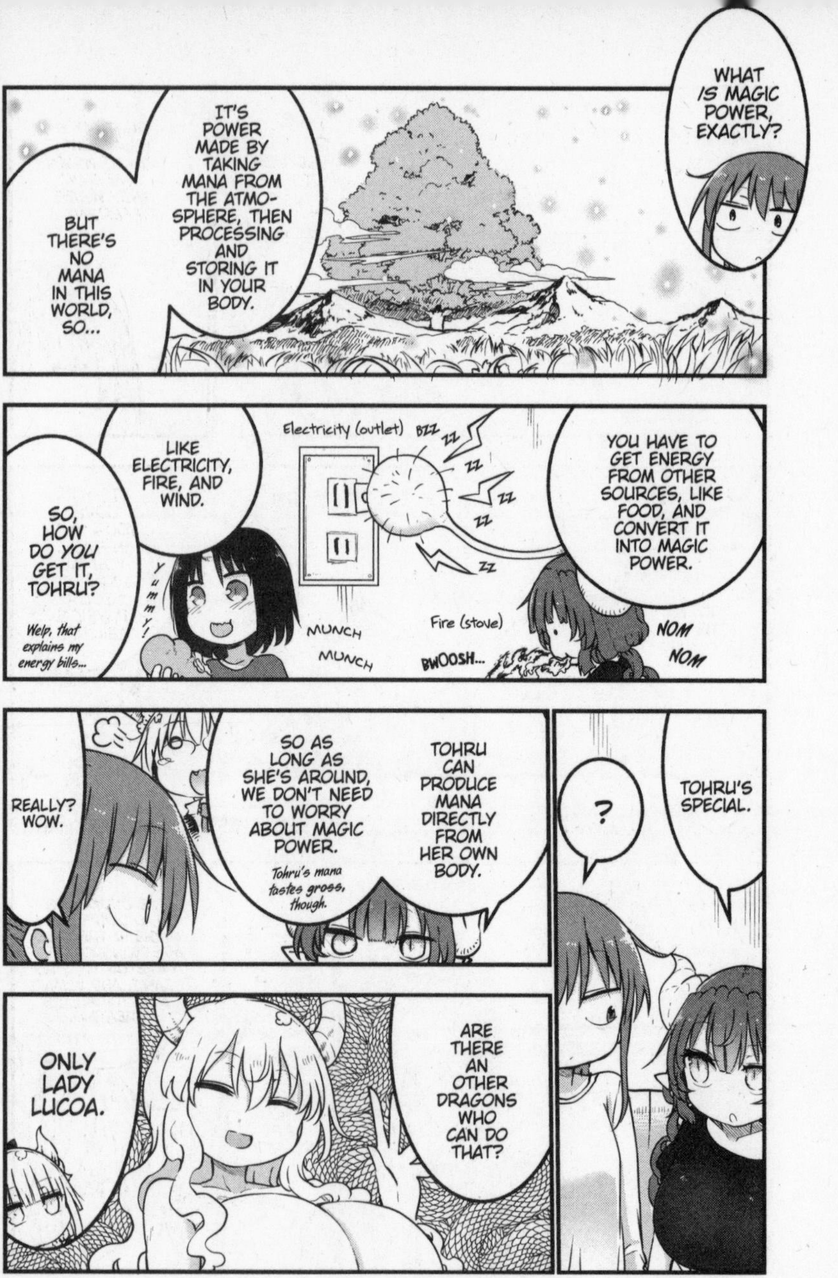
WHAT IS MAGIC POWER, EXACTLY?
IT'S POWER MADE BY TAKING MANA FROM THE ATMOSPHERE, THEN PROCESSING AND STORING IT IN YOUR BODY.
BUT THERE'S NO MANA IN THIS WORLD, SO...
YOU HAVE TO GET ENERGY FROM OTHER SOURCES, LIKE FOOD, AND CONVERT IT INTO MAGIC POWER.
Electricity (outlet)
BZZ
ZZ
ZZ
ZZ
ZZ
ZZ
NOM
NOM
Fire (stove)
BWOOSH...
MUNCH
MUNCH
LIKE ELECTRICITY, FIRE, AND WIND.
SO, HOW DO YOU GET IT, TOHRU?
Yummy!
Welp, that explains my energy bills...
TOHRU'S SPECIAL.
?
TOHRU CAN PRODUCE MANA DIRECTLY FROM HER OWN BODY.
SO AS LONG AS SHE'S AROUND, WE DON'T NEED TO WORRY ABOUT MAGIC POWER.
Tohru's mana tastes gross, though.
REALLY? WOW.
ARE THERE AN OTHER DRAGONS WHO CAN DO THAT?
ONLY LADY LUCOA.

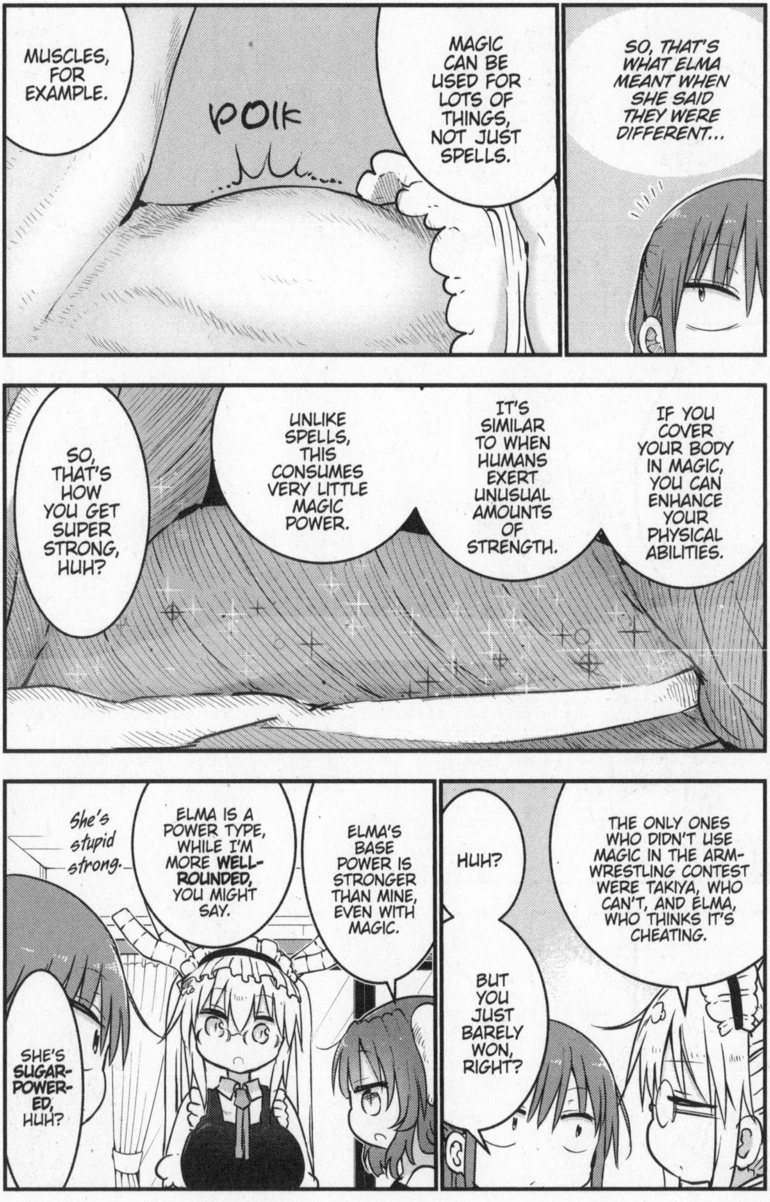
SO, THAT'S WHAT ELMA MEANT WHEN SHE SAID THEY WERE DIFFERENT...
MAGIC CAN BE USED FOR LOTS OF THINGS, NOT JUST SPELLS.
POIK
MUSCLES, FOR EXAMPLE.
IF YOU COVER YOUR BODY IN MAGIC, YOU CAN ENHANCE YOUR PHYSICAL ABILITIES.
IT'S SIMILAR TO WHEN HUMANS EXERT UNUSUAL AMOUNTS OF STRENGTH.
UNLIKE SPELLS, THIS CONSUMES VERY LITTLE MAGIC POWER.
SO, THAT'S HOW YOU GET SUPER STRONG, HUH?
THE ONLY ONES WHO DIDN'T USE MAGIC IN THE ARM-WRESTLING CONTEST WERE TAKIYA, WHO CAN'T, AND ELMA, WHO THINKS IT'S CHEATING.
HUH?
BUT YOU JUST BARELY WON, RIGHT?
ELMA'S BASE POWER IS STRONGER THAN MINE, EVEN WITH MAGIC.
ELMA IS A POWER TYPE, WHILE I'M MORE **WELL-ROUNDED,** YOU MIGHT SAY.
She's stupid strong.
SHE'S **SUGAR-POWERED,** HUH?

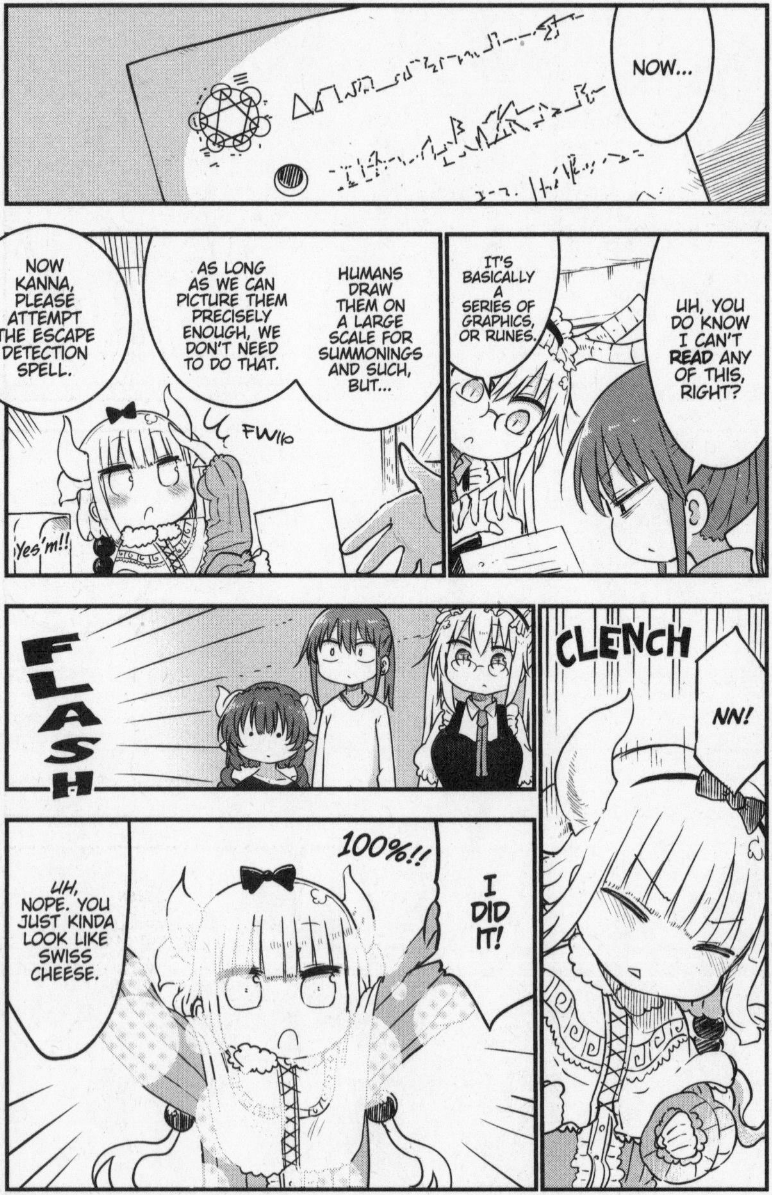
NOW...
UH, YOU DO KNOW I CAN'T READ ANY OF THIS, RIGHT?
IT'S BASICALLY A SERIES OF GRAPHICS, OR RUNES.
HUMANS DRAW THEM ON A LARGE SCALE FOR SUMMONINGS AND SUCH, BUT...
AS LONG AS WE CAN PICTURE THEM PRECISELY ENOUGH, WE DON'T NEED TO DO THAT.
FWIP
NOW KANNA, PLEASE ATTEMPT THE ESCAPE DETECTION SPELL.
Yes'm!!
CLENCH
NN!
FLASH
100%!!
I DID IT!
UH, NOPE. YOU JUST KINDA LOOK LIKE SWISS CHEESE.

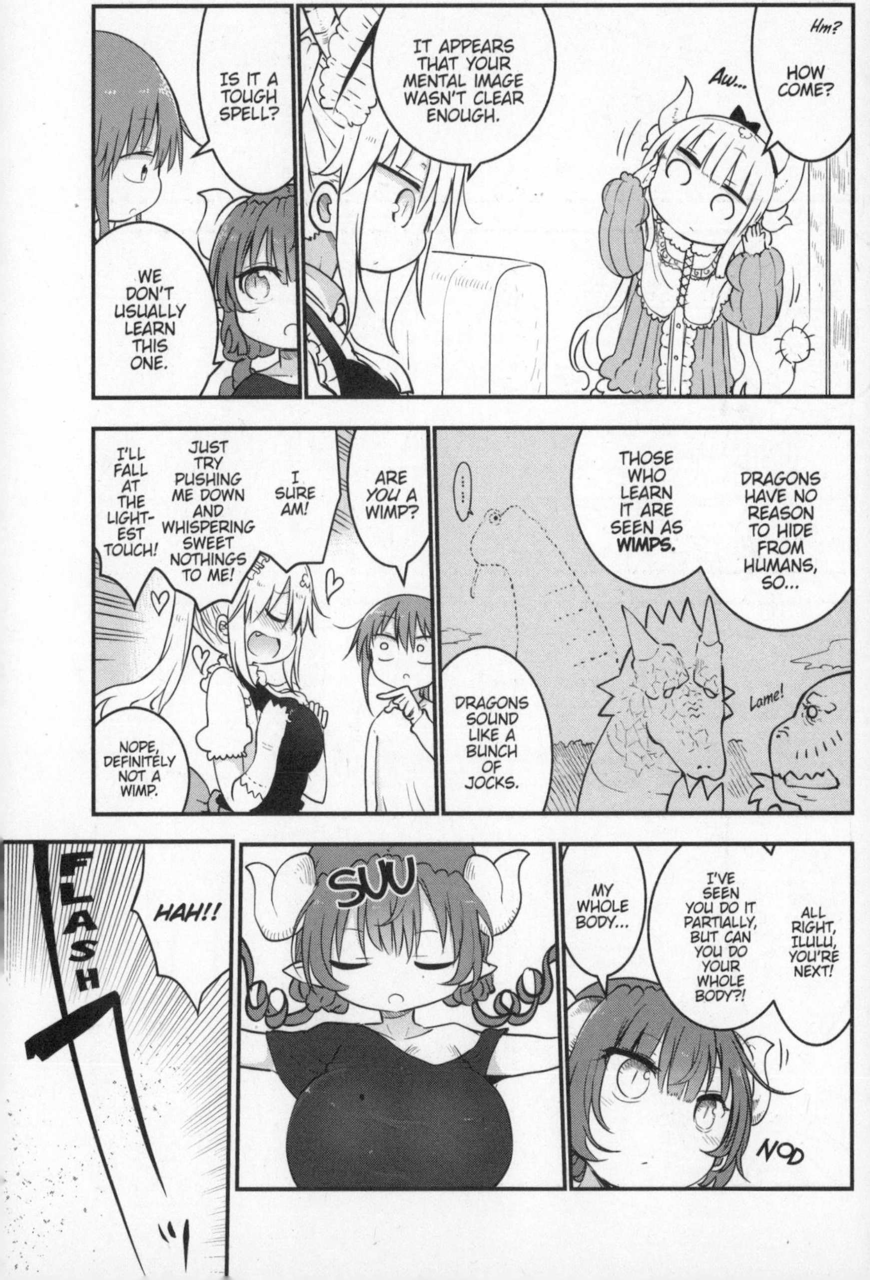
Hm?
HOW COME?
Aw...
IT APPEARS THAT YOUR MENTAL IMAGE WASN'T CLEAR ENOUGH.
IS IT A TOUGH SPELL?
WE DON'T USUALLY LEARN THIS ONE.
DRAGONS HAVE NO REASON TO HIDE FROM HUMANS, SO...
THOSE WHO LEARN IT ARE SEEN AS **WIMPS.**
...
Lame!
DRAGONS SOUND LIKE A BUNCH OF JOCKS.
ARE *YOU* A WIMP?
I SURE AM!
JUST TRY PUSHING ME DOWN AND WHISPERING SWEET NOTHINGS TO ME!
I'LL FALL AT THE LIGHT-EST TOUCH!
NOPE, DEFINITELY NOT A WIMP.
ALL RIGHT, ILULU, YOU'RE NEXT!
I'VE SEEN YOU DO IT PARTIALLY, BUT CAN YOU DO YOUR WHOLE BODY?!
MY WHOLE BODY...
NOD
SUU
HAH!!
FLASH

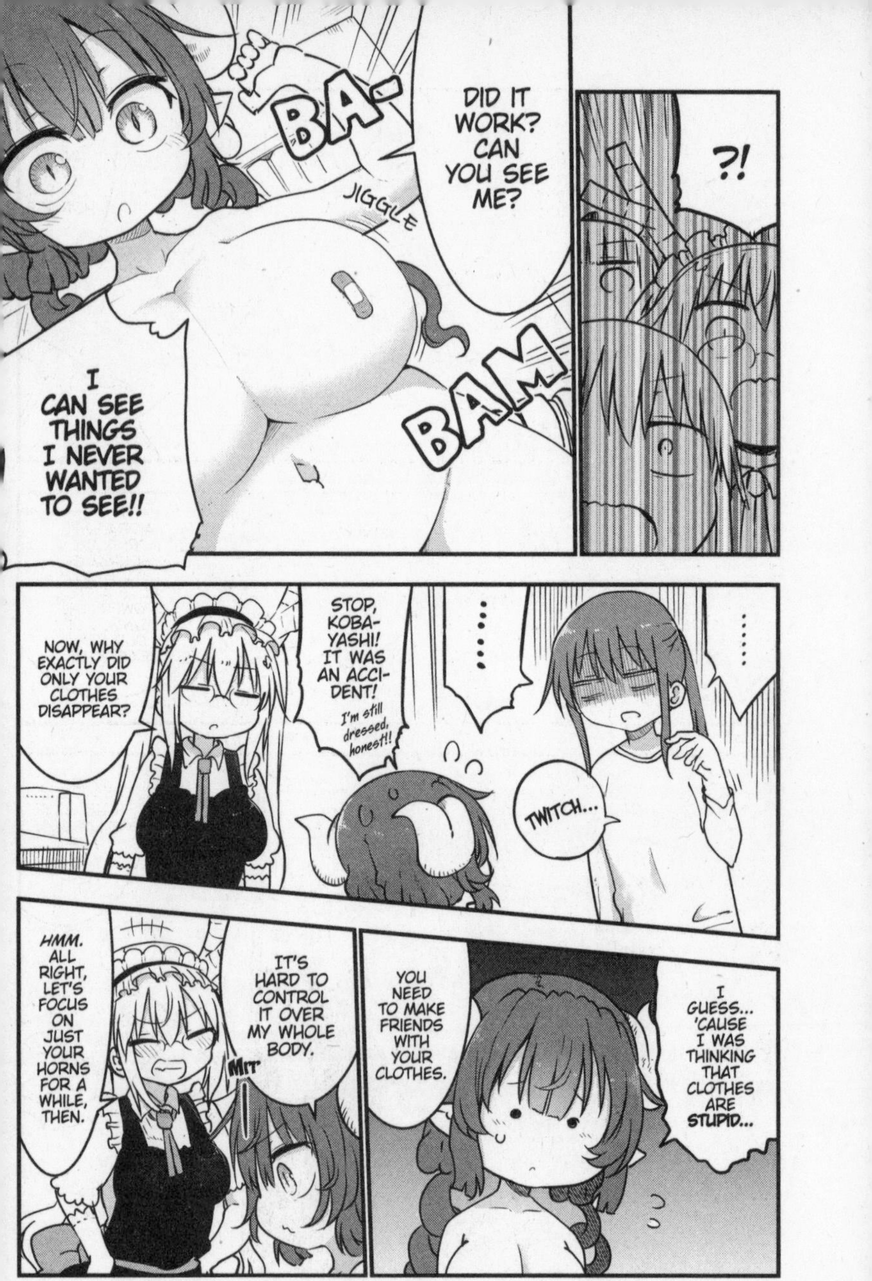
?!
DID IT WORK? CAN YOU SEE ME?
BA-
JIGGLE
BAM
I CAN SEE THINGS I NEVER WANTED TO SEE!!
......
TWITCH...
......
STOP, KOBA-YASHI! IT WAS AN ACCI-DENT!
I'm still dressed, honest!!
NOW, WHY EXACTLY DID ONLY YOUR CLOTHES DISAPPEAR?
I GUESS... 'CAUSE I WAS THINKING THAT CLOTHES ARE STUPID...
YOU NEED TO MAKE FRIENDS WITH YOUR CLOTHES.
IT'S HARD TO CONTROL IT OVER MY WHOLE BODY.
MIT
HMM. ALL RIGHT, LET'S FOCUS ON JUST YOUR HORNS FOR A WHILE, THEN.

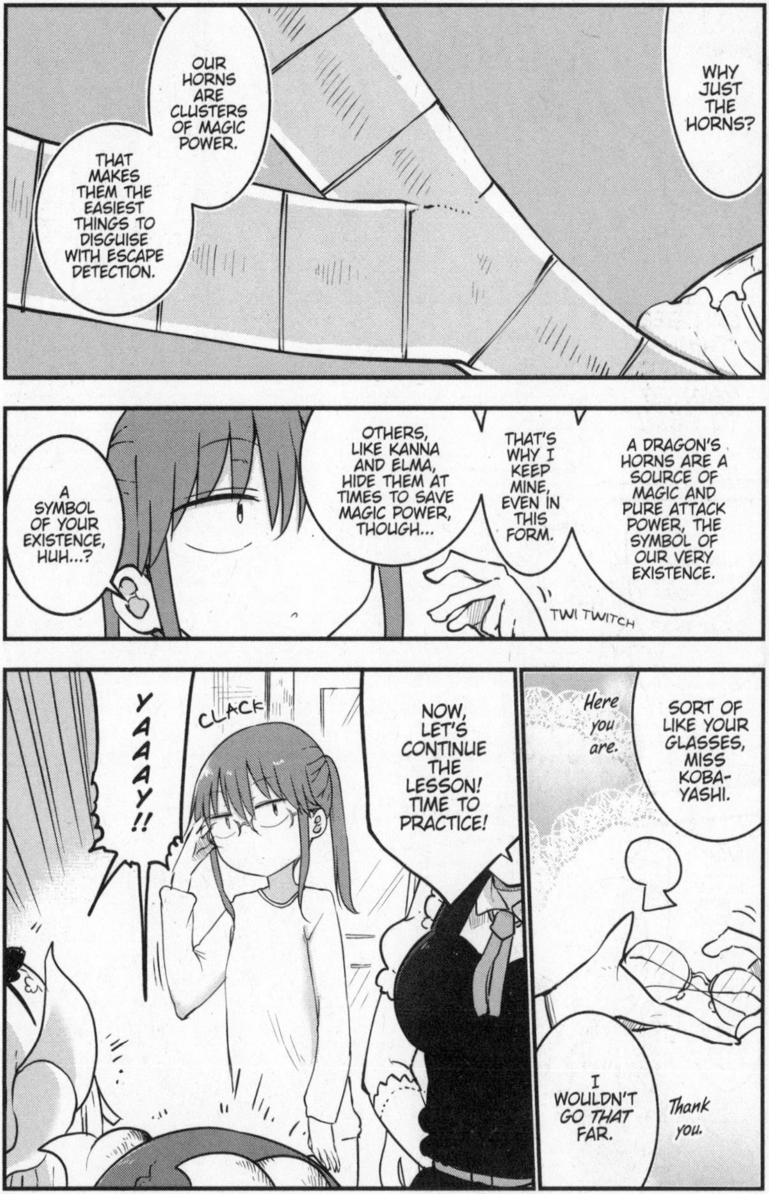
WHY JUST THE HORNS?
OUR HORNS ARE CLUSTERS OF MAGIC POWER.
THAT MAKES THEM THE EASIEST THINGS TO DISGUISE WITH ESCAPE DETECTION.
A DRAGON'S HORNS ARE A SOURCE OF MAGIC AND PURE ATTACK POWER, THE SYMBOL OF OUR VERY EXISTENCE.
THAT'S WHY I KEEP MINE, EVEN IN THIS FORM.
OTHERS, LIKE KANNA AND ELMA, HIDE THEM AT TIMES TO SAVE MAGIC POWER, THOUGH...
TWI TWITCH
A SYMBOL OF YOUR EXISTENCE, HUH...?
SORT OF LIKE YOUR GLASSES, MISS KOBA-YASHI.
Here you are.
Thank you.
I WOULDN'T GO *THAT* FAR.
NOW, LET'S CONTINUE THE LESSON! TIME TO PRACTICE!
CLACK
YAAAAY!!

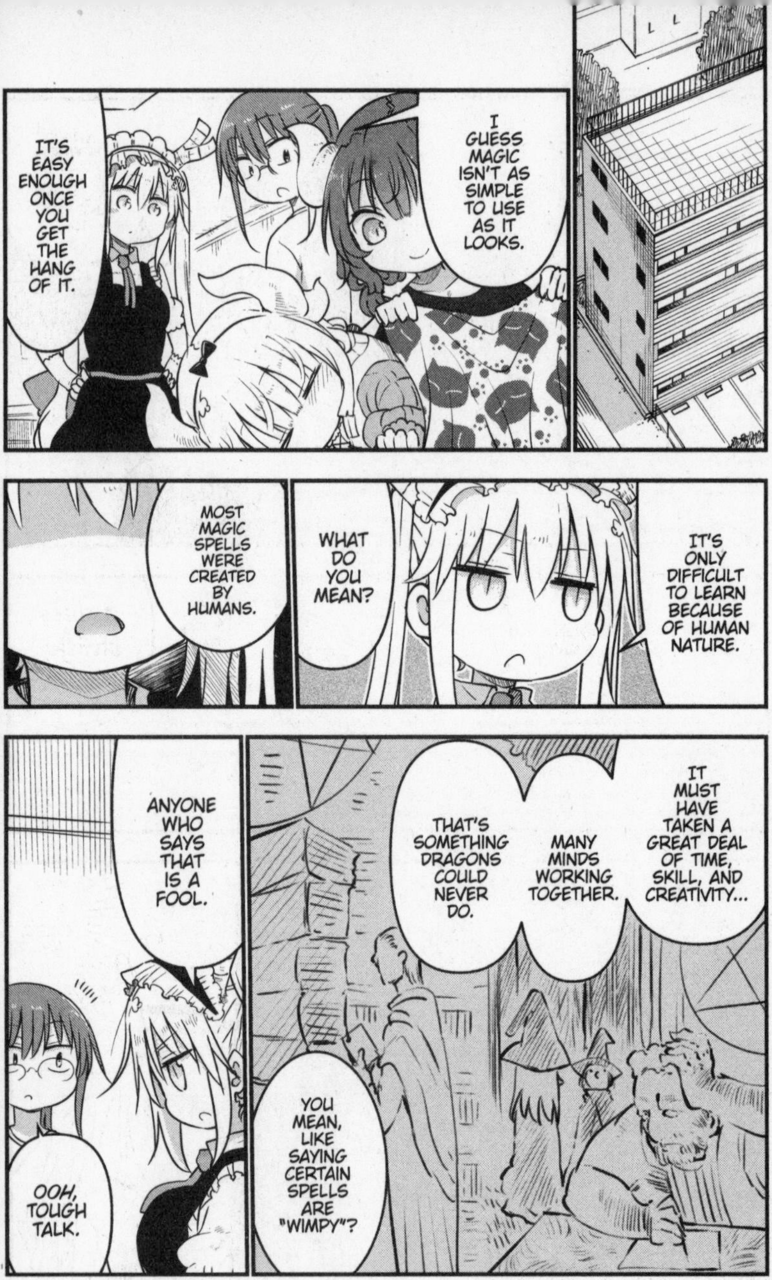
I GUESS MAGIC ISN'T AS SIMPLE TO USE AS IT LOOKS.
IT'S EASY ENOUGH ONCE YOU GET THE HANG OF IT.
IT'S ONLY DIFFICULT TO LEARN BECAUSE OF HUMAN NATURE.
WHAT DO YOU MEAN?
MOST MAGIC SPELLS WERE CREATED BY HUMANS.
IT MUST HAVE TAKEN A GREAT DEAL OF TIME, SKILL, AND CREATIVITY...
MANY MINDS WORKING TOGETHER.
THAT'S SOMETHING DRAGONS COULD NEVER DO.
YOU MEAN, LIKE SAYING CERTAIN SPELLS ARE "WIMPY"?
ANYONE WHO SAYS THAT IS A FOOL.
OOH, TOUGH TALK.

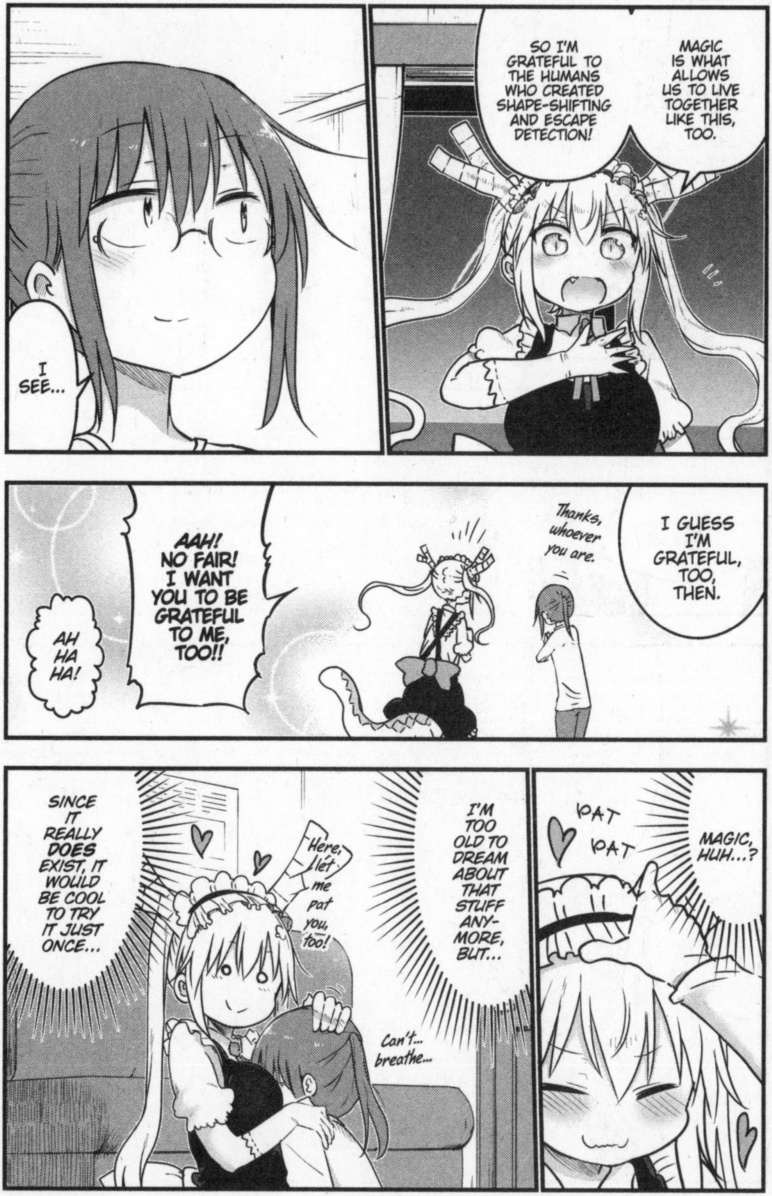
MAGIC IS WHAT ALLOWS US TO LIVE TOGETHER LIKE THIS, TOO.
SO I'M GRATEFUL TO THE HUMANS WHO CREATED SHAPE-SHIFTING AND ESCAPE DETECTION!
I SEE...
I GUESS I'M GRATEFUL, TOO, THEN.
Thanks, whoever you are.
AAH! NO FAIR! I WANT YOU TO BE GRATEFUL TO ME, TOO!!
AH HA HA!
MAGIC, HUH...?
PAT PAT
I'M TOO OLD TO DREAM ABOUT THAT STUFF ANY-MORE, BUT...
SINCE IT REALLY DOES EXIST, IT WOULD BE COOL TO TRY IT JUST ONCE...
Here, let me pat you, too!
Can't... breathe...

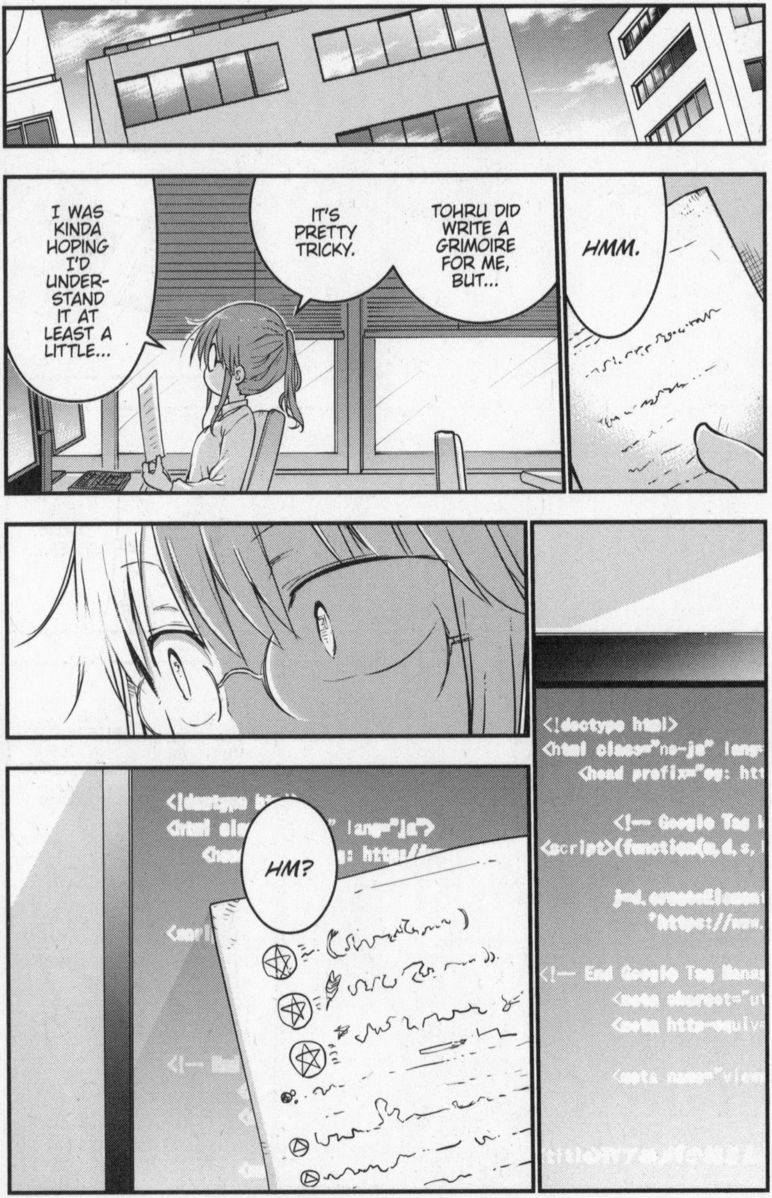
HMM.
TOHRU DID WRITE A GRIMOIRE FOR ME, BUT...
IT'S PRETTY TRICKY.
I WAS KINDA HOPING I'D UNDERSTAND IT AT LEAST A LITTLE...
<!doctype html>
HM?

CHAPTER 56/END

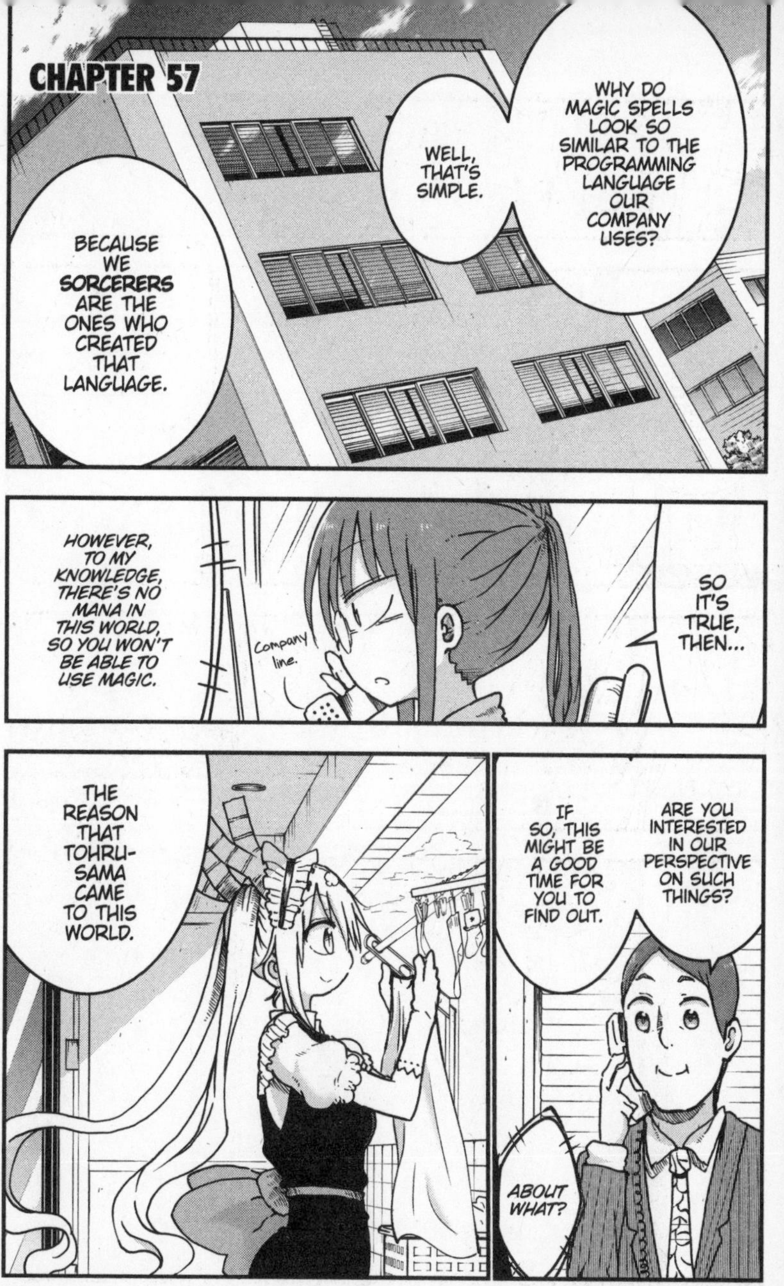
CHAPTER 57
WHY DO MAGIC SPELLS LOOK SO SIMILAR TO THE PROGRAMMING LANGUAGE OUR COMPANY USES?
WELL, THAT'S SIMPLE.
BECAUSE WE SORCERERS ARE THE ONES WHO CREATED THAT LANGUAGE.
SO IT'S TRUE, THEN...
HOWEVER, TO MY KNOWLEDGE, THERE'S NO MANA IN THIS WORLD, SO YOU WON'T BE ABLE TO USE MAGIC.
Company line.
ARE YOU INTERESTED IN OUR PERSPECTIVE ON SUCH THINGS?
IF SO, THIS MIGHT BE A GOOD TIME FOR YOU TO FIND OUT.
ABOUT WHAT?
THE REASON THAT TOHRU-SAMA CAME TO THIS WORLD.

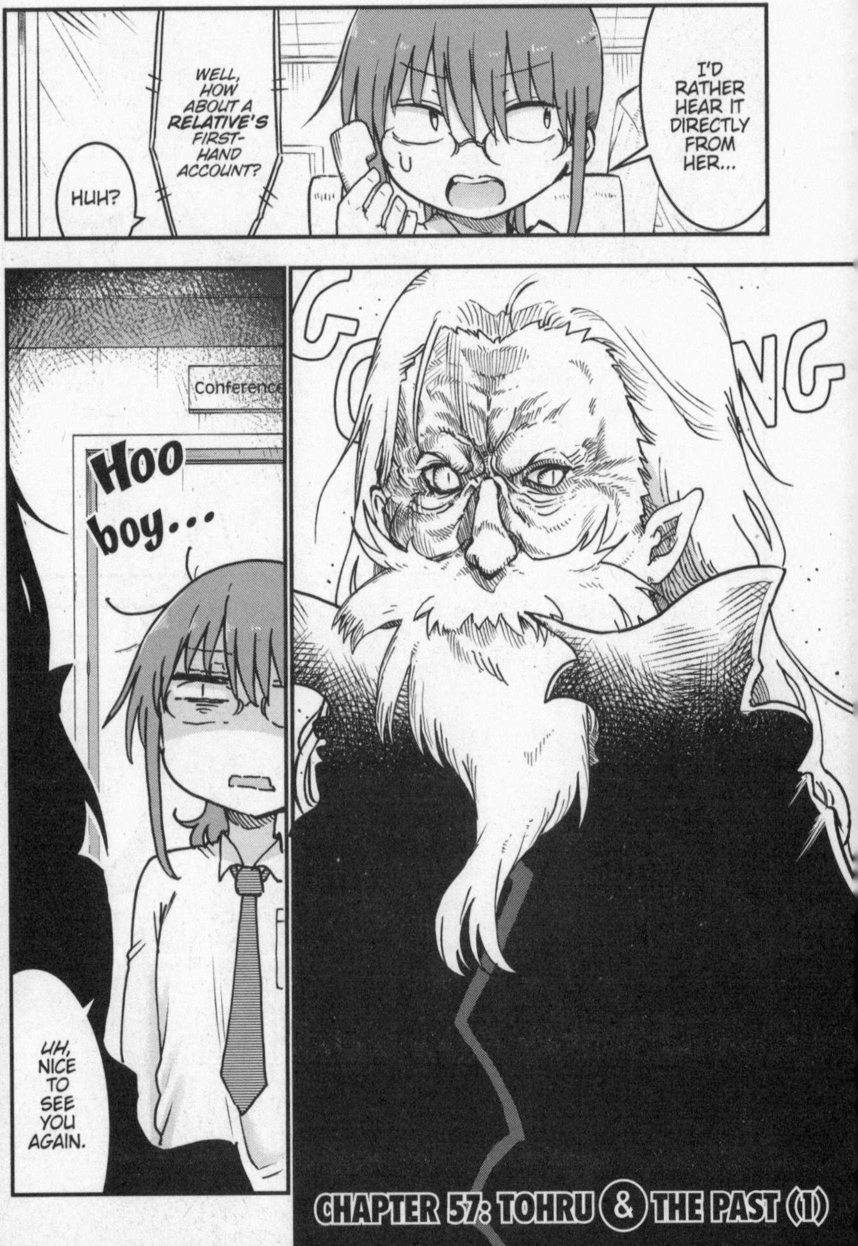
I'D RATHER HEAR IT DIRECTLY FROM HER...
WELL, HOW ABOUT A RELATIVE'S FIRST-HAND ACCOUNT?
HUH?
CHAPTER 57: TOHRU & THE PAST (1)
Conference
Hoo boy...
UH, NICE TO SEE YOU AGAIN.

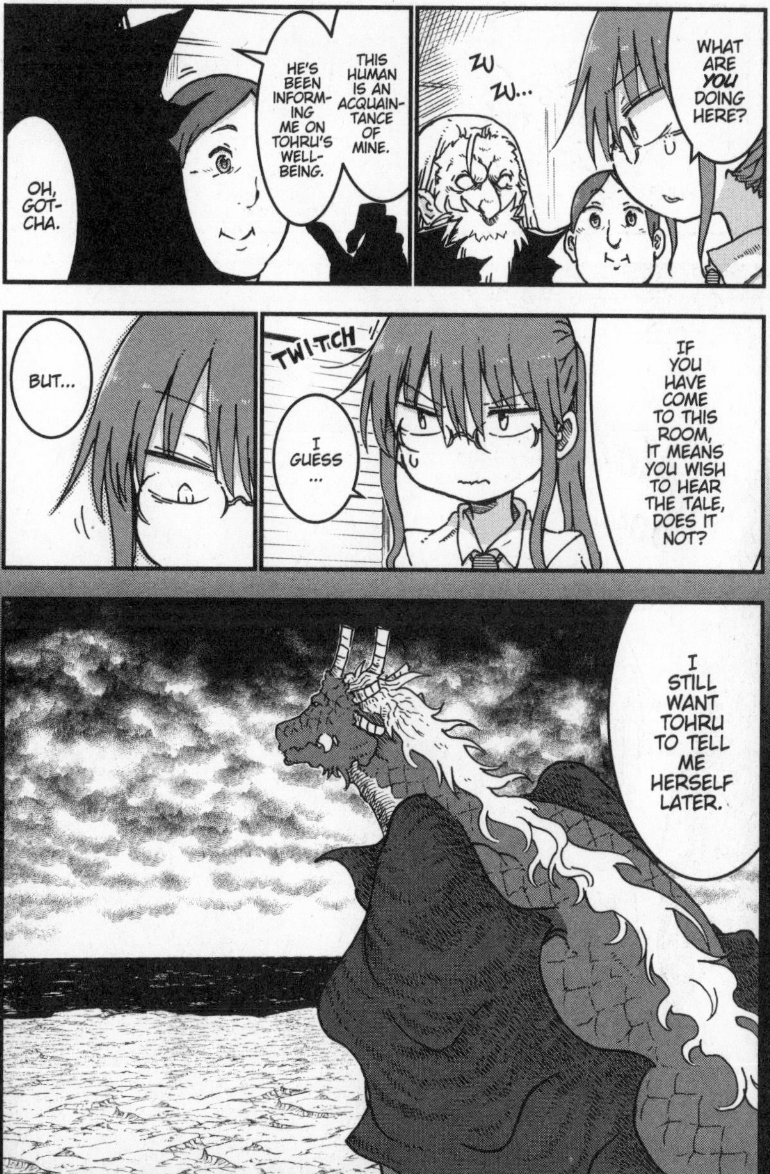
WHAT ARE *YOU* DOING HERE?
ZU ZU...
THIS HUMAN IS AN ACQUAINTANCE OF MINE.
HE'S BEEN INFORMING ME ON TOHRU'S WELL-BEING.
OH, GOTCHA.
IF YOU HAVE COME TO THIS ROOM, IT MEANS YOU WISH TO HEAR THE TALE, DOES IT NOT?
TWITCH
I GUESS...
BUT...
I STILL WANT TOHRU TO TELL ME HERSELF LATER.

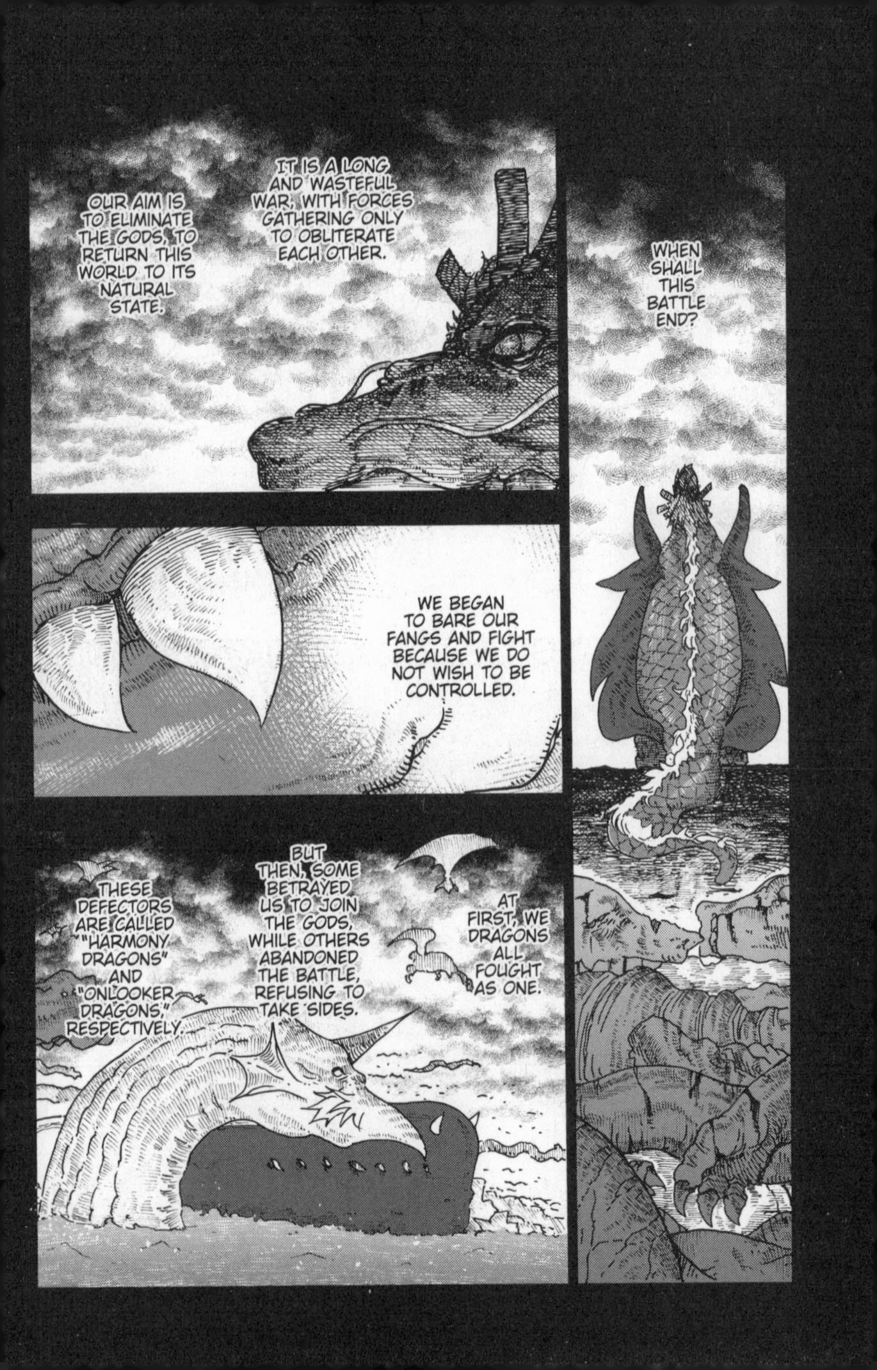
WHEN SHALL THIS BATTLE END?
IT IS A LONG AND WASTEFUL WAR, WITH FORCES GATHERING ONLY TO OBLITERATE EACH OTHER.
OUR AIM IS TO ELIMINATE THE GODS, TO RETURN THIS WORLD TO ITS NATURAL STATE.
WE BEGAN TO BARE OUR FANGS AND FIGHT BECAUSE WE DO NOT WISH TO BE CONTROLLED.
AT FIRST, WE DRAGONS ALL FOUGHT AS ONE.
BUT THEN, SOME BETRAYED US TO JOIN THE GODS, WHILE OTHERS ABANDONED THE BATTLE, REFUSING TO TAKE SIDES.
THESE DEFECTORS ARE CALLED "HARMONY DRAGONS" AND "ONLOOKER DRAGONS," RESPECTIVELY.

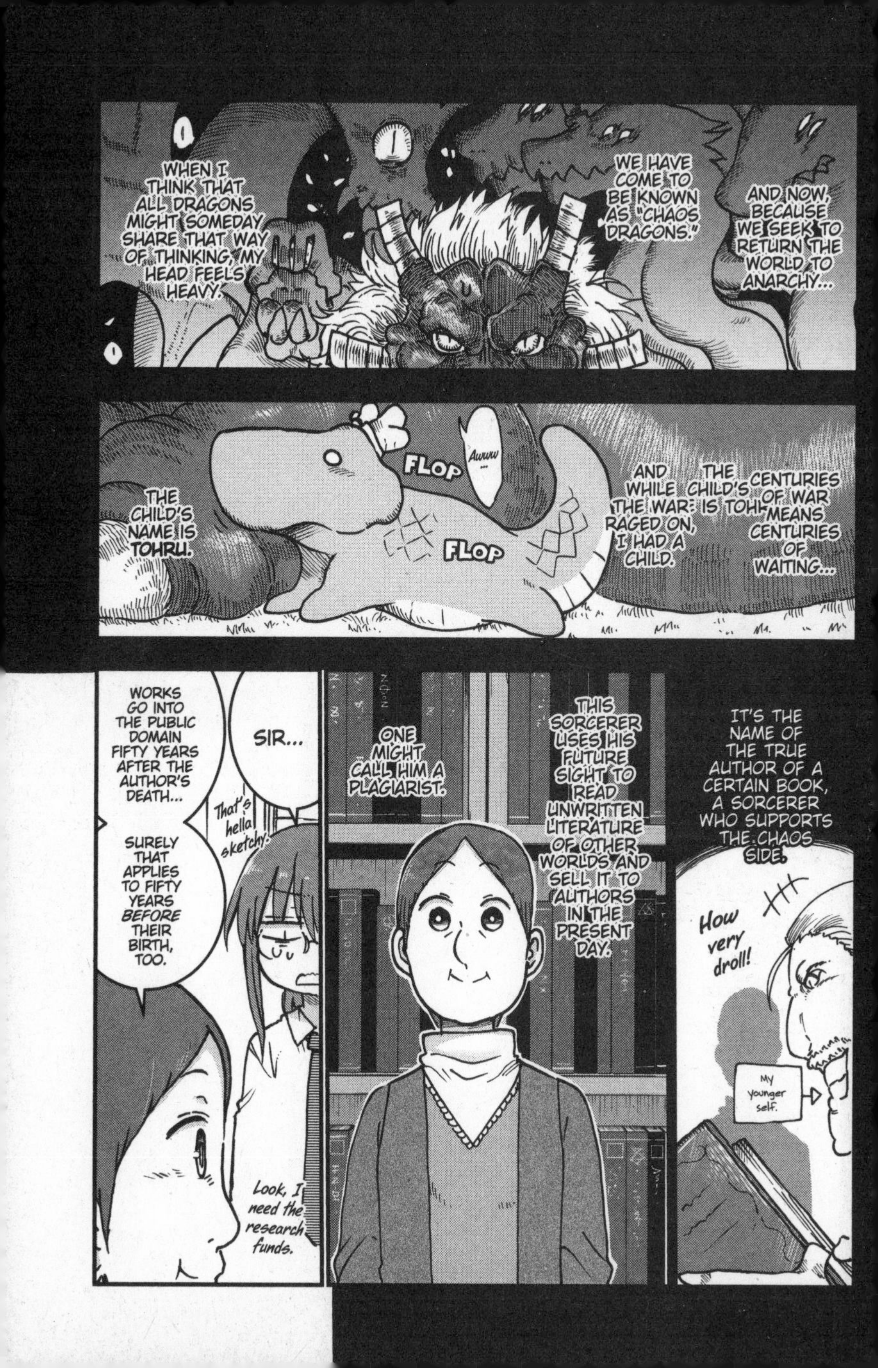
AND NOW, BECAUSE WE SEEK TO RETURN THE WORLD TO ANARCHY...
WE HAVE COME TO BE KNOWN AS "CHAOS DRAGONS."
WHEN I THINK THAT ALL DRAGONS MIGHT SOMEDAY SHARE THAT WAY OF THINKING, MY HEAD FEELS HEAVY.
CENTURIES OF WAR MEANS CENTURIES OF WAITING...
THE CHILD'S IS TOH
AND WHILE THE WAR RAGED ON, I HAD A CHILD.
Awuuu...
FLOP
FLOP
THE CHILD'S NAME IS TOHRU.
IT'S THE NAME OF THE TRUE AUTHOR OF A CERTAIN BOOK, A SORCERER WHO SUPPORTS THE CHAOS SIDE.
How very droll!
My younger self.
THIS SORCERER USES HIS FUTURE SIGHT TO READ UNWRITTEN LITERATURE OF OTHER WORLDS AND SELL IT TO AUTHORS IN THE PRESENT DAY.
ONE MIGHT CALL HIM A PLAGIARIST.
SIR...
WORKS GO INTO THE PUBLIC DOMAIN FIFTY YEARS AFTER THE AUTHOR'S DEATH...
SURELY THAT APPLIES TO FIFTY YEARS BEFORE THEIR BIRTH, TOO.
That's hella sketchy.
Look, I need the research funds.

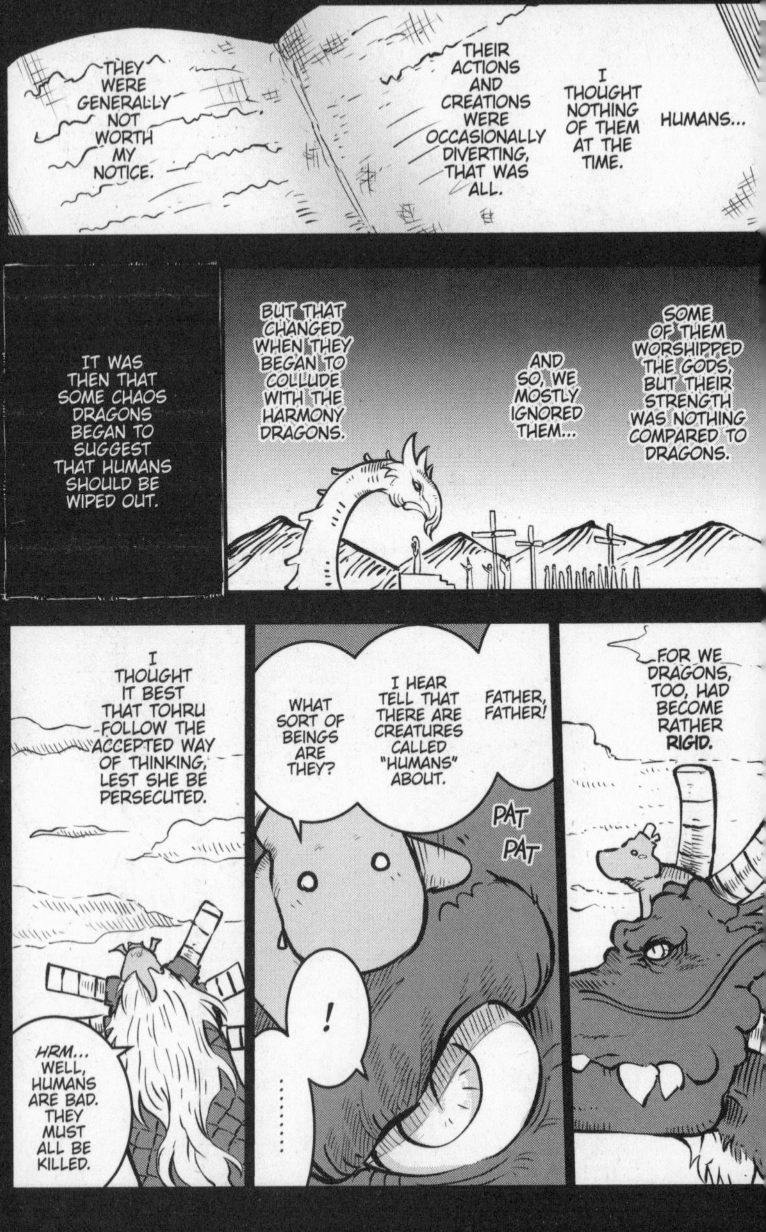
HUMANS...
I THOUGHT NOTHING OF THEM AT THE TIME.
THEIR ACTIONS AND CREATIONS WERE OCCASIONALLY DIVERTING, THAT WAS ALL.
THEY WERE GENERALLY NOT WORTH MY NOTICE.
SOME OF THEM WORSHIPPED THE GODS, BUT THEIR STRENGTH WAS NOTHING COMPARED TO DRAGONS.
AND SO, WE MOSTLY IGNORED THEM...
BUT THAT CHANGED WHEN THEY BEGAN TO COLLUDE WITH THE HARMONY DRAGONS.
IT WAS THEN THAT SOME CHAOS DRAGONS BEGAN TO SUGGEST THAT HUMANS SHOULD BE WIPED OUT.
FOR WE DRAGONS, TOO, HAD BECOME RATHER **RIGID.**
FATHER, FATHER!
I HEAR TELL THAT THERE ARE CREATURES CALLED "HUMANS" ABOUT.
WHAT SORT OF BEINGS ARE THEY?
PAT PAT
!
......
I THOUGHT IT BEST THAT TOHRU FOLLOW THE ACCEPTED WAY OF THINKING, LEST SHE BE PERSECUTED.
HRM... WELL, HUMANS ARE BAD. THEY MUST ALL BE KILLED.

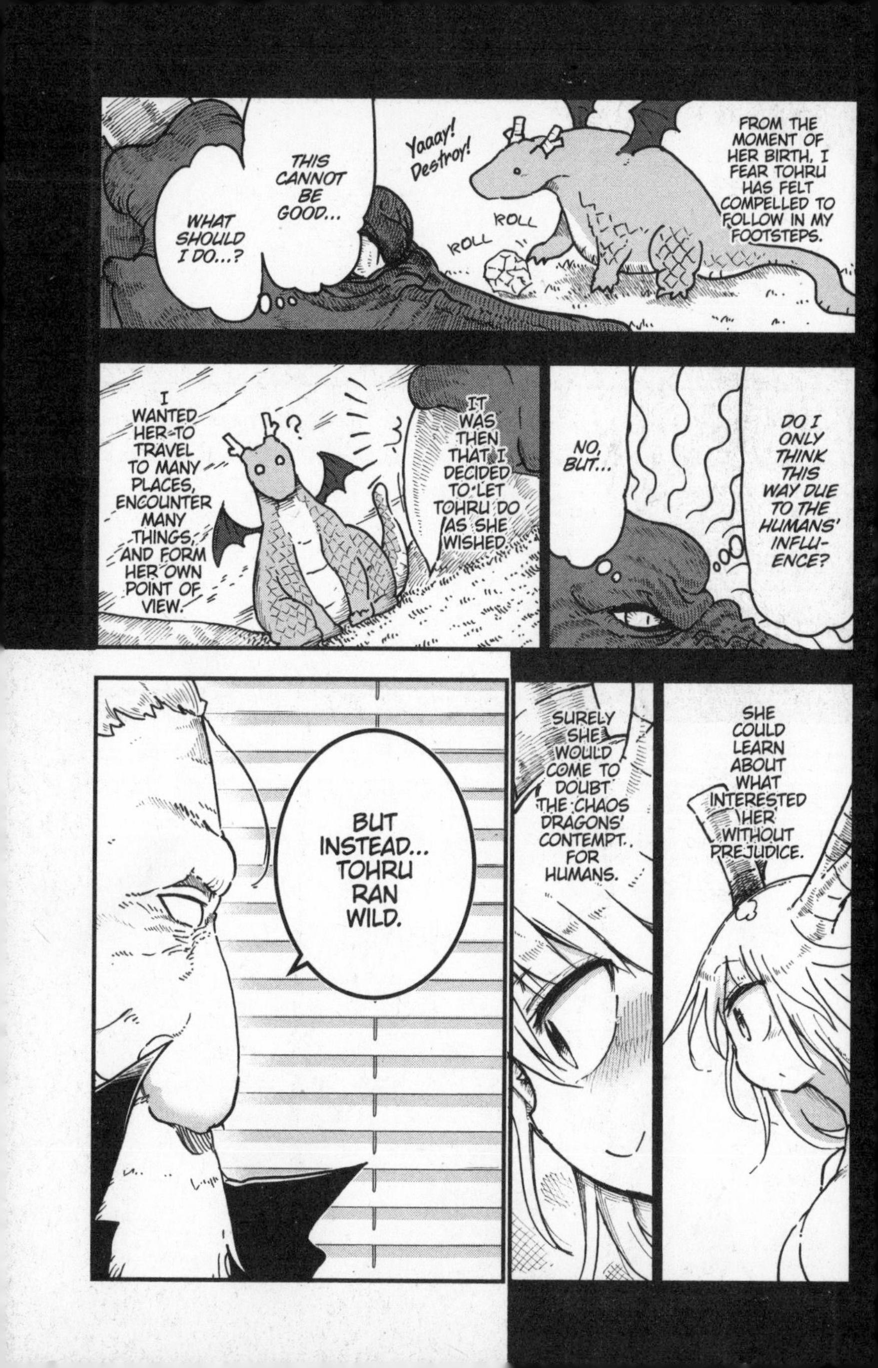
FROM THE MOMENT OF HER BIRTH, I FEAR TOHRU HAS FELT COMPELLED TO FOLLOW IN MY FOOTSTEPS.
Yaaay! Destroy!
ROLL
ROLL
THIS CANNOT BE GOOD...
WHAT SHOULD I DO...?
DO I ONLY THINK THIS WAY DUE TO THE HUMANS' INFLU-ENCE?
NO, BUT...
IT WAS THEN THAT I DECIDED TO LET TOHRU DO AS SHE WISHED.
?
I WANTED HER TO TRAVEL TO MANY PLACES, ENCOUNTER MANY THINGS, AND FORM HER OWN POINT OF VIEW.
SHE COULD LEARN ABOUT WHAT INTERESTED HER WITHOUT PREJUDICE.
SURELY SHE WOULD COME TO DOUBT THE CHAOS DRAGONS' CONTEMPT FOR HUMANS.
BUT INSTEAD... TOHRU RAN WILD.

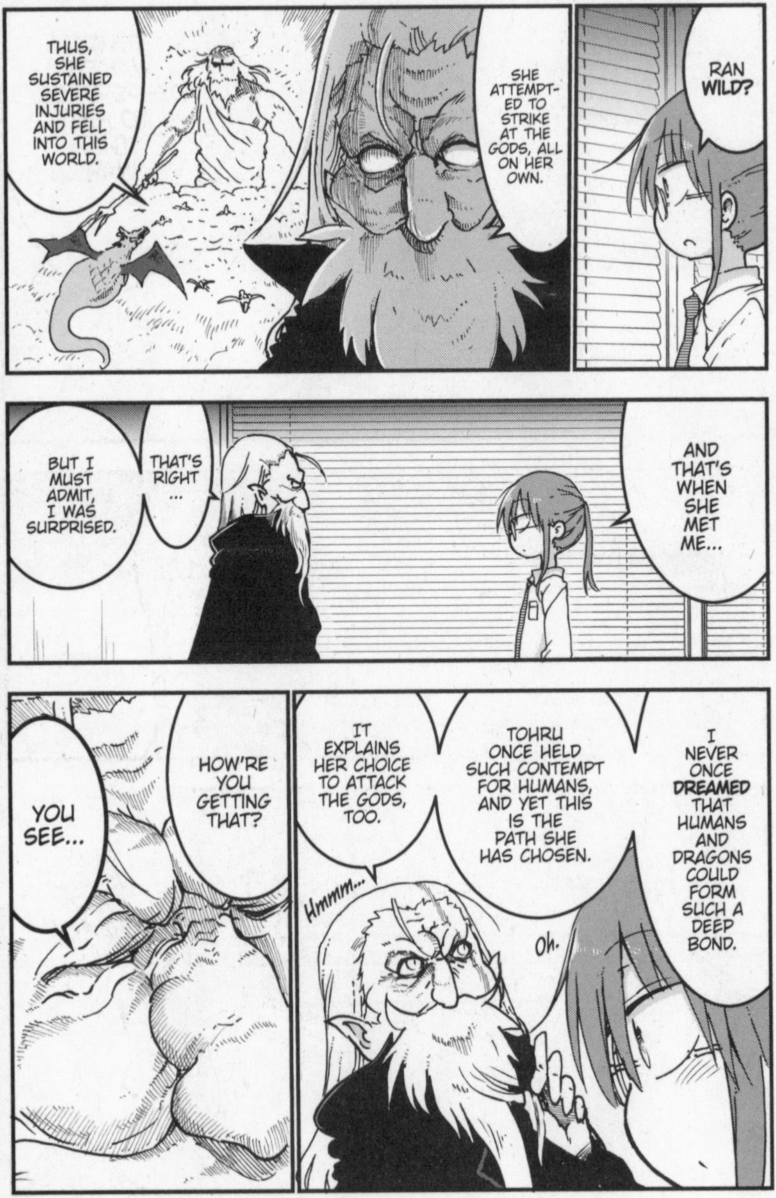
RAN WILD?
SHE ATTEMPTED TO STRIKE AT THE GODS, ALL ON HER OWN.
THUS, SHE SUSTAINED SEVERE INJURIES AND FELL INTO THIS WORLD.
AND THAT'S WHEN SHE MET ME...
THAT'S RIGHT ...
BUT I MUST ADMIT, I WAS SURPRISED.
I NEVER ONCE **DREAMED** THAT HUMANS AND DRAGONS COULD FORM SUCH A DEEP BOND.
TOHRU ONCE HELD SUCH CONTEMPT FOR HUMANS, AND YET THIS IS THE PATH SHE HAS CHOSEN.
IT EXPLAINS HER CHOICE TO ATTACK THE GODS, TOO.
Hmmm...
Oh.
HOW'RE YOU GETTING THAT?
YOU SEE...

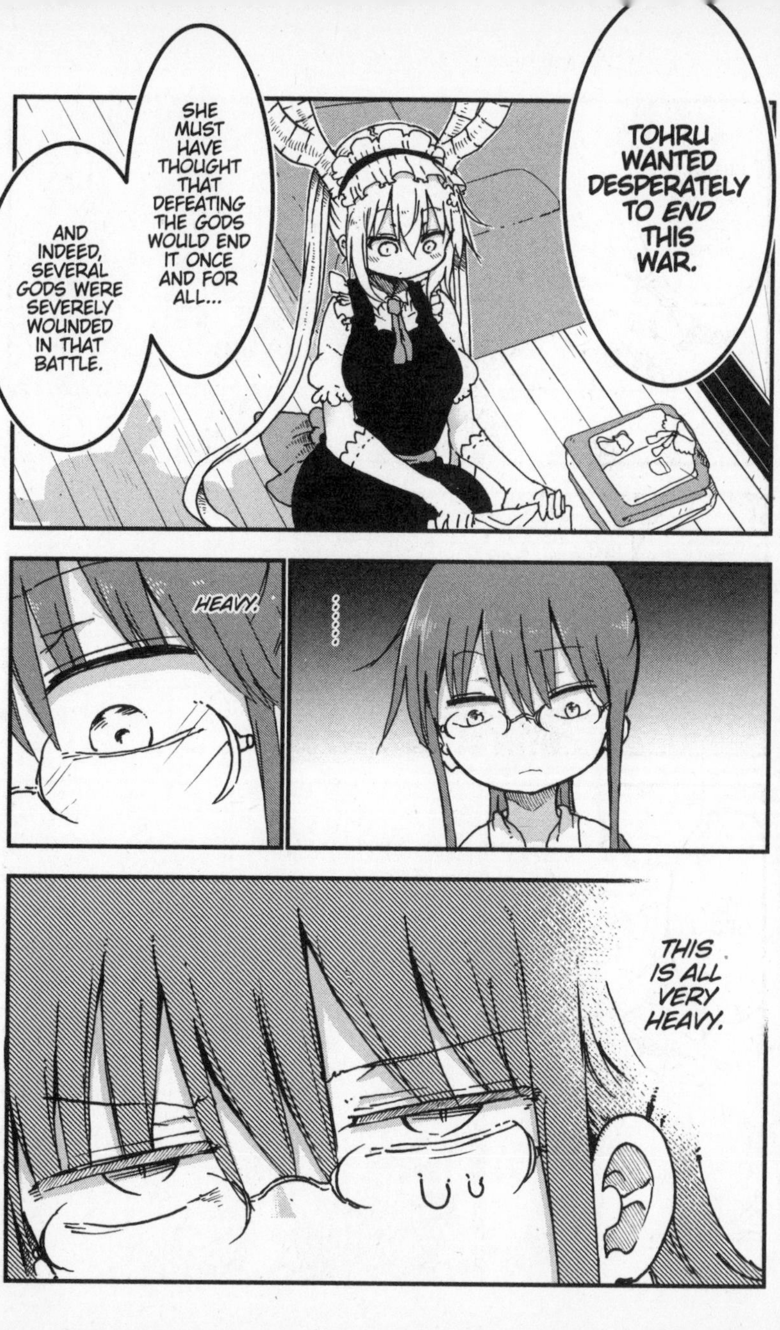
TOHRU WANTED DESPERATELY TO *END* THIS WAR.
SHE MUST HAVE THOUGHT THAT DEFEATING THE GODS WOULD END IT ONCE AND FOR ALL...
AND INDEED, SEVERAL GODS WERE SEVERELY WOUNDED IN THAT BATTLE.
......
HEAVY.
THIS IS ALL VERY HEAVY.

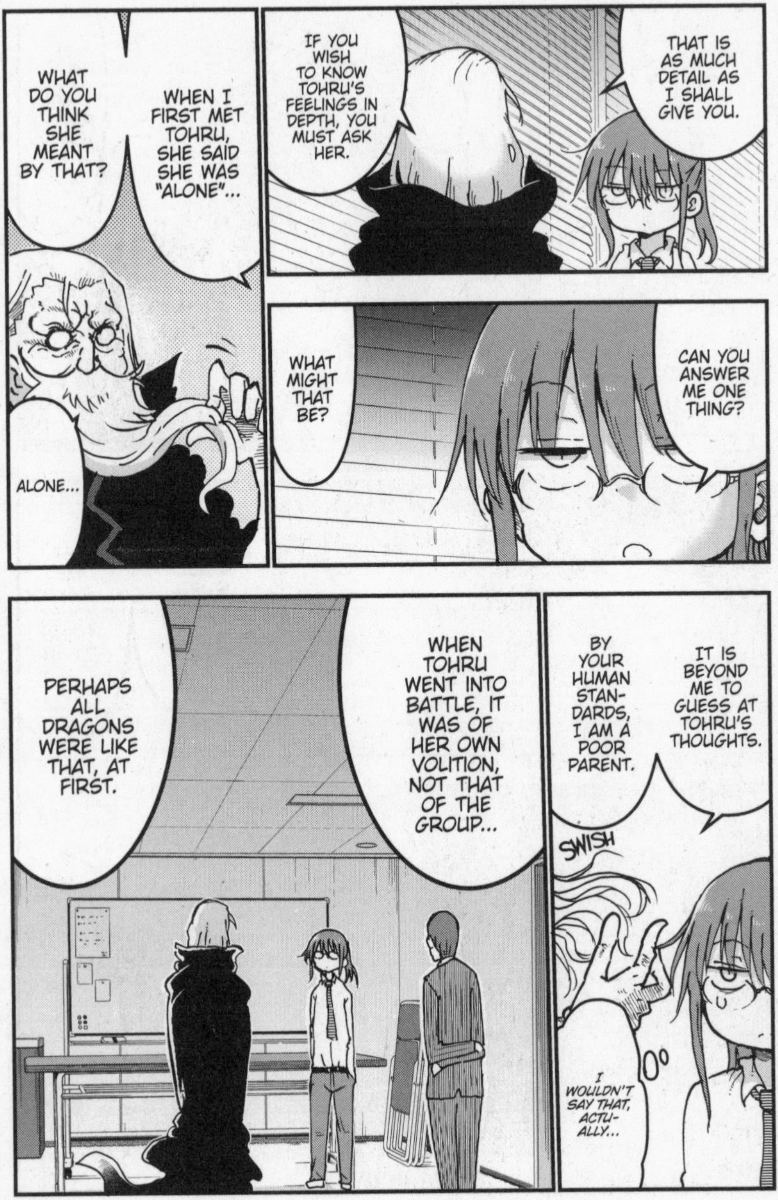
THAT IS AS MUCH DETAIL AS I SHALL GIVE YOU.
IF YOU WISH TO KNOW TOHRU'S FEELINGS IN DEPTH, YOU MUST ASK HER.
CAN YOU ANSWER ME ONE THING?
WHAT MIGHT THAT BE?
WHEN I FIRST MET TOHRU, SHE SAID SHE WAS "ALONE"...
WHAT DO YOU THINK SHE MEANT BY THAT?
ALONE...
IT IS BEYOND ME TO GUESS AT TOHRU'S THOUGHTS.
BY YOUR HUMAN STANDARDS, I AM A POOR PARENT.
SWISH
I WOULDN'T SAY THAT, ACTU-ALLY...
WHEN TOHRU WENT INTO BATTLE, IT WAS OF HER OWN VOLITION, NOT THAT OF THE GROUP...
PERHAPS ALL DRAGONS WERE LIKE THAT, AT FIRST.

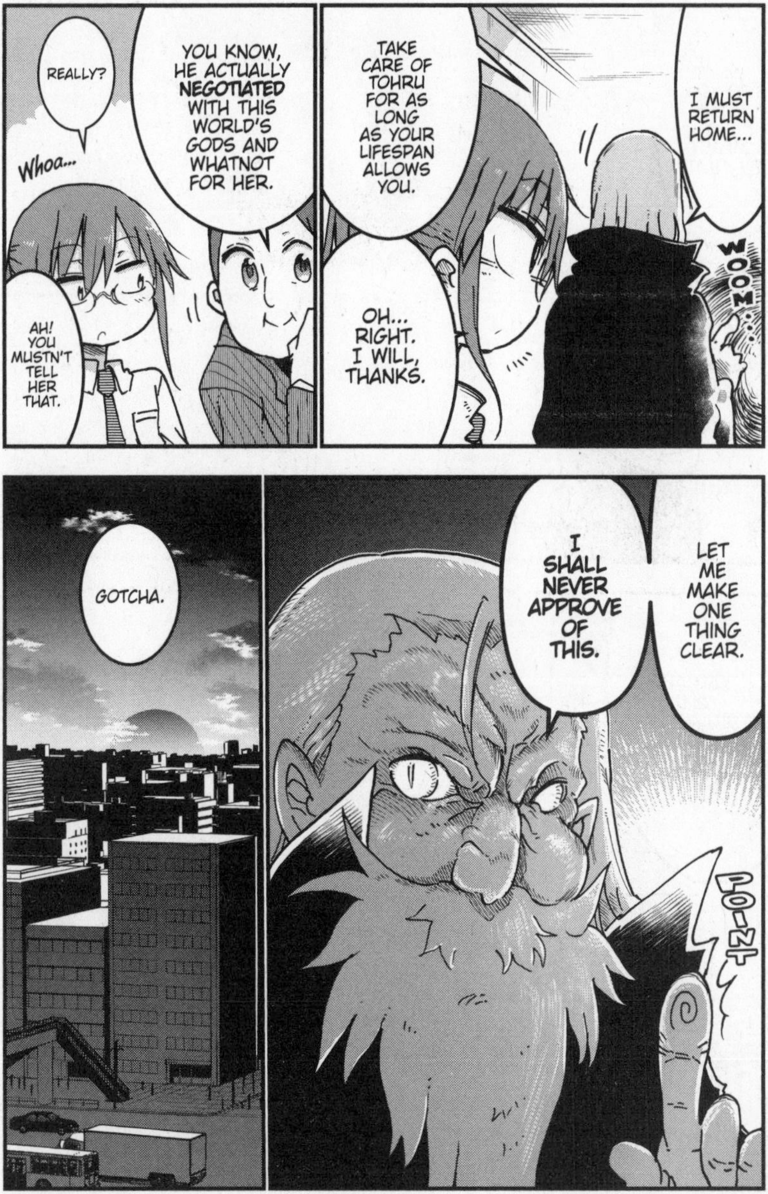
I MUST RETURN HOME...
WOOM...
TAKE CARE OF TOHRU FOR AS LONG AS YOUR LIFESPAN ALLOWS YOU.
OH... RIGHT. I WILL, THANKS.
YOU KNOW, HE ACTUALLY **NEGOTIATED** WITH THIS WORLD'S GODS AND WHATNOT FOR HER.
REALLY?
Whoa...
AH! YOU MUSTN'T TELL HER THAT.
LET ME MAKE ONE THING CLEAR.
I SHALL NEVER APPROVE OF THIS.
POINT
GOTCHA.

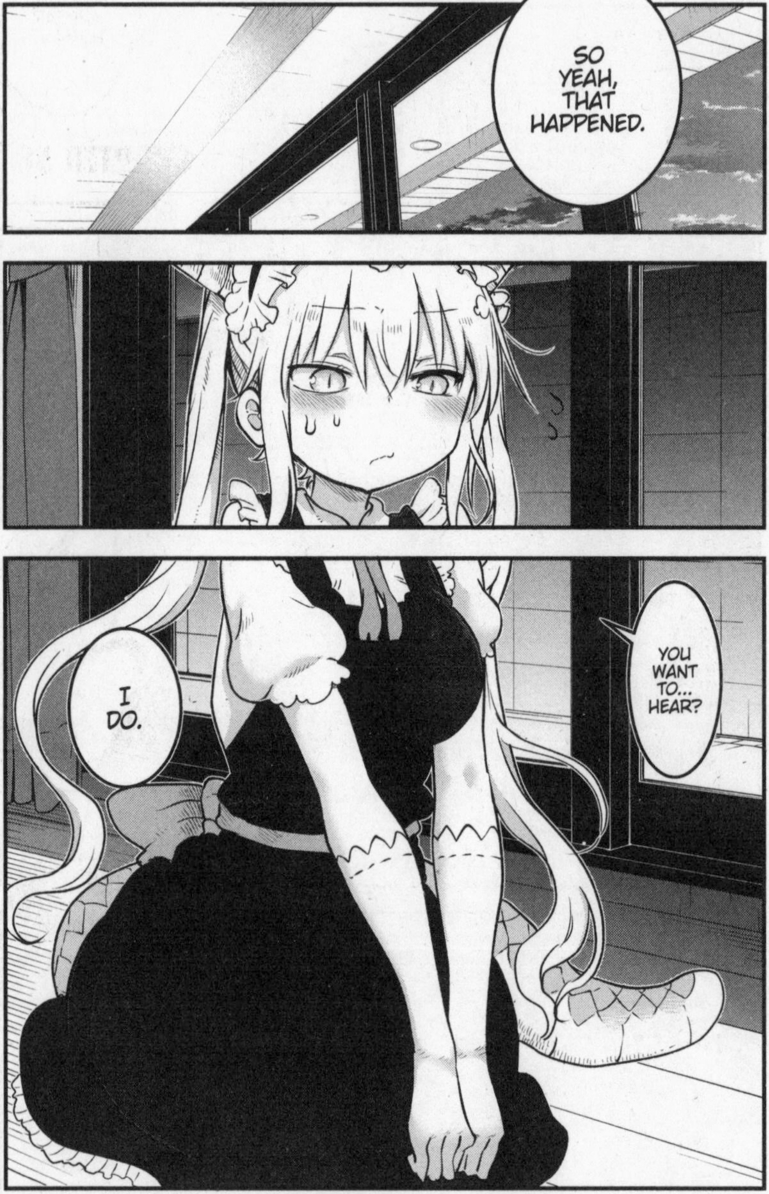
SO YEAH, THAT HAPPENED.
YOU WANT TO... HEAR?
I DO.

CHAPTER 57/END

CHAPTER 58

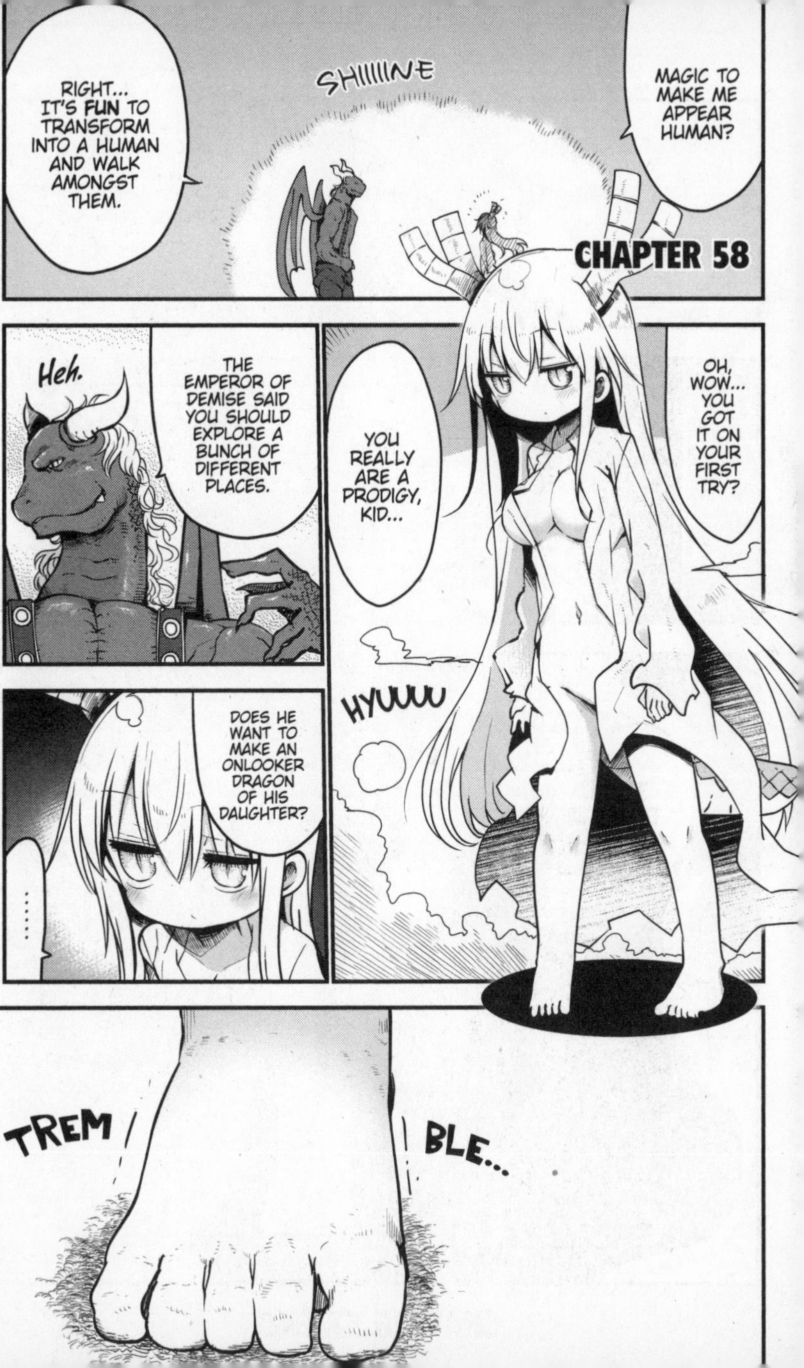
MAGIC TO MAKE ME APPEAR HUMAN?
SHIIIIINE
RIGHT... IT'S **FUN** TO TRANSFORM INTO A HUMAN AND WALK AMONGST THEM.
OH, WOW... YOU GOT IT ON YOUR FIRST TRY?
YOU REALLY ARE A PRODIGY, KID...
HYUUUU
THE EMPEROR OF DEMISE SAID YOU SHOULD EXPLORE A BUNCH OF DIFFERENT PLACES.
Heh.
DOES HE WANT TO MAKE AN ONLOOKER DRAGON OF HIS DAUGHTER?
......
TREM
BLE...

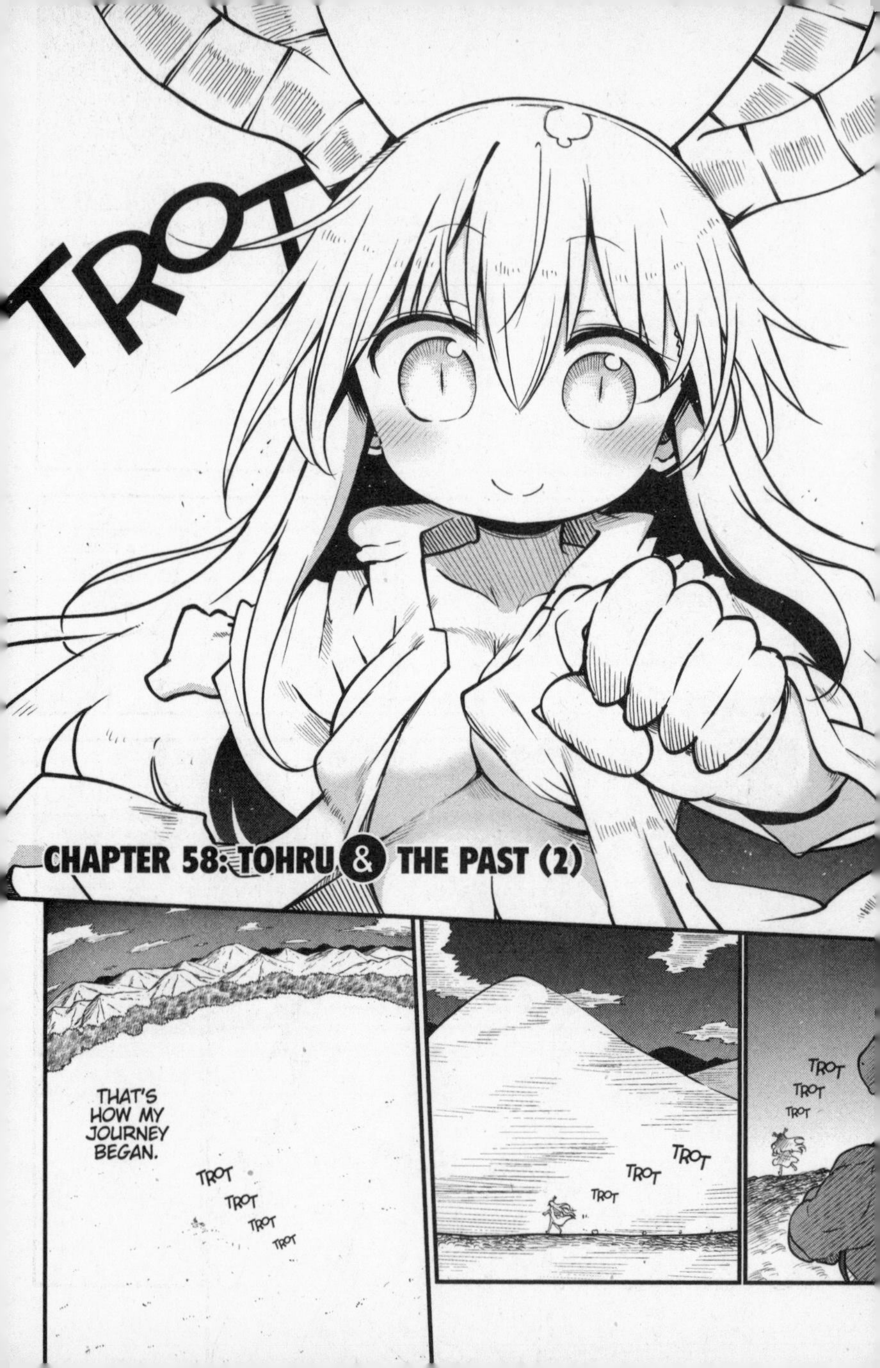
TROT
CHAPTER 58: TOHRU & THE PAST (2)
TROT
TROT
TROT
TROT
TROT
TROT
THAT'S HOW MY JOURNEY BEGAN.
TROT
TROT
TROT
TROT

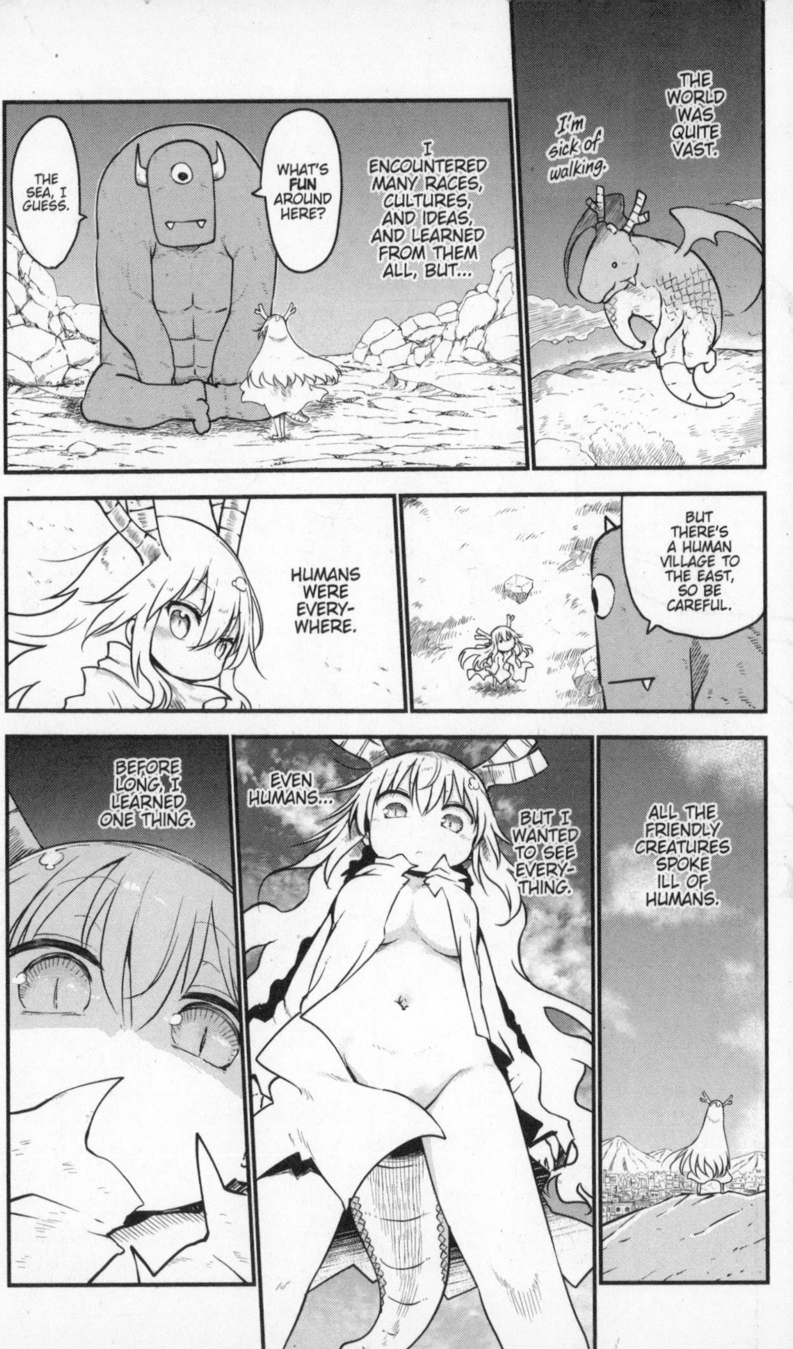
THE WORLD WAS QUITE VAST.
I'm sick of walking.
I ENCOUNTERED MANY RACES, CULTURES, AND IDEAS, AND LEARNED FROM THEM ALL, BUT...
WHAT'S **FUN** AROUND HERE?
THE SEA, I GUESS.
BUT THERE'S A HUMAN VILLAGE TO THE EAST, SO BE CAREFUL.
HUMANS WERE EVERY-WHERE.
ALL THE FRIENDLY CREATURES SPOKE ILL OF HUMANS.
BUT I WANTED TO SEE EVERY-THING.
EVEN HUMANS...
BEFORE LONG, I LEARNED ONE THING.

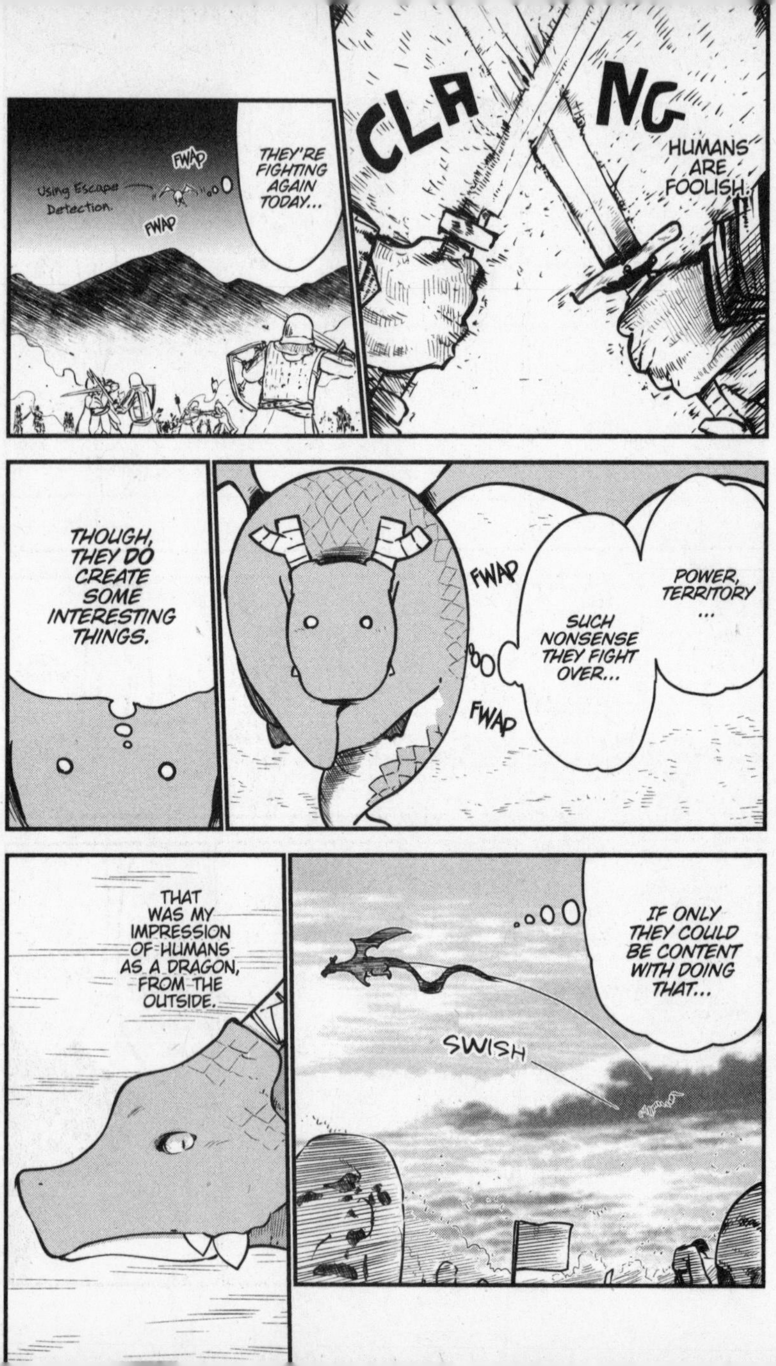
CLA NG
HUMANS ARE FOOLISH.
THEY'RE FIGHTING AGAIN TODAY...
FWAP
Using Escape Detection.
FWAP
POWER, TERRITORY ...
SUCH NONSENSE THEY FIGHT OVER...
FWAP
FWAP
THOUGH, THEY DO CREATE SOME INTERESTING THINGS.
IF ONLY THEY COULD BE CONTENT WITH DOING THAT...
SWISH
THAT WAS MY IMPRESSION OF HUMANS AS A DRAGON, FROM THE OUTSIDE.

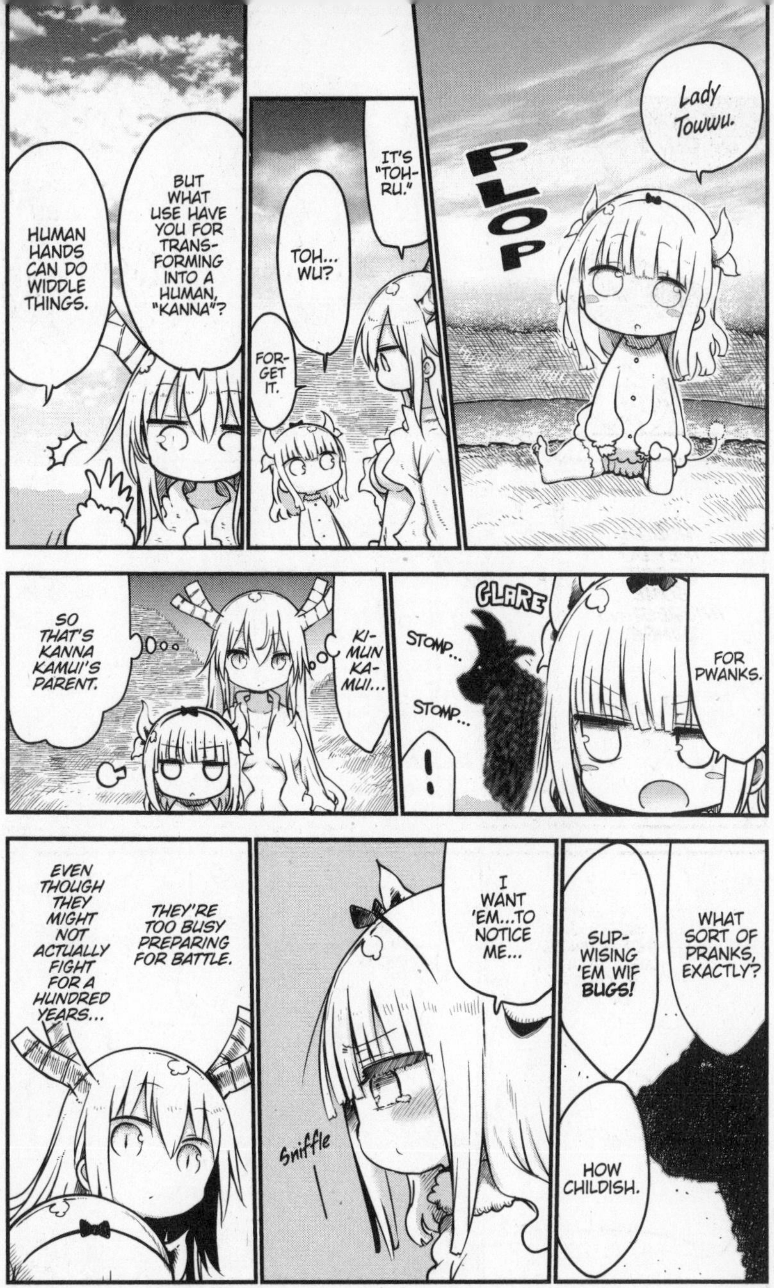
Lady Towwu.
PLOP
IT'S "TOH-RU."
TOH... WU?
FOR-GET IT.
BUT WHAT USE HAVE YOU FOR TRANS-FORMING INTO A HUMAN, "KANNA"?
HUMAN HANDS CAN DO WIDDLE THINGS.
FOR PWANKS.
GLARE
STOMP...
STOMP...
!
KI-MUN KA-MUI...
SO THAT'S KANNA KAMUI'S PARENT.
WHAT SORT OF PRANKS, EXACTLY?
SUP-WISING 'EM WIF BUGS!
HOW CHILDISH.
I WANT 'EM...TO NOTICE ME...
Sniffle
THEY'RE TOO BUSY PREPARING FOR BATTLE.
EVEN THOUGH THEY MIGHT NOT ACTUALLY FIGHT FOR A HUNDRED YEARS...

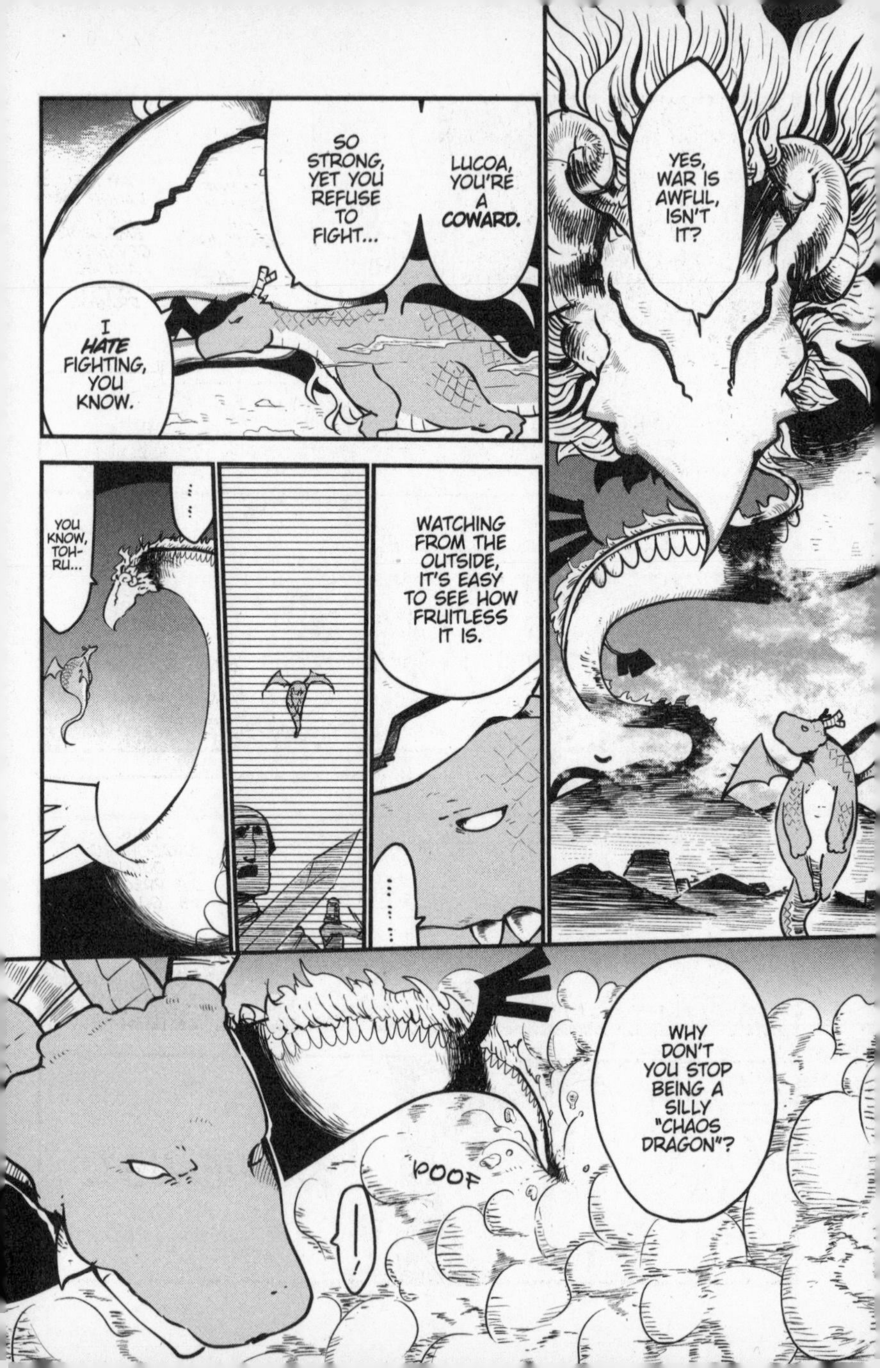
YES, WAR IS AWFUL, ISN'T IT?
LUCOA, YOU'RE A COWARD.
SO STRONG, YET YOU REFUSE TO FIGHT...
I *HATE* FIGHTING, YOU KNOW.
WATCHING FROM THE OUTSIDE, IT'S EASY TO SEE HOW FRUITLESS IT IS.
... ...
...
YOU KNOW, TOHRU...
WHY DON'T YOU STOP BEING A SILLY "CHAOS DRAGON"?
POOF
!

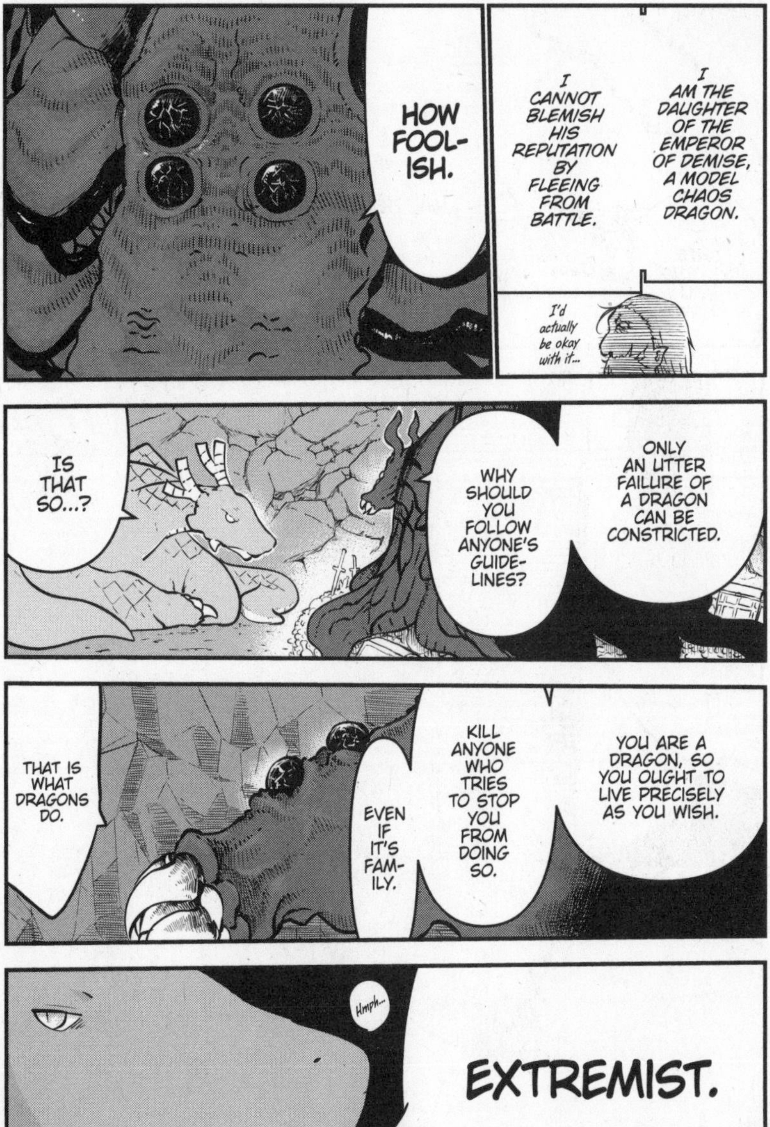
I AM THE DAUGHTER OF THE EMPEROR OF DEMISE, A MODEL CHAOS DRAGON.
I CANNOT BLEMISH HIS REPUTATION BY FLEEING FROM BATTLE.
I'd actually be okay with it...
HOW FOOL-ISH.
ONLY AN UTTER FAILURE OF A DRAGON CAN BE CONSTRICTED.
WHY SHOULD YOU FOLLOW ANYONE'S GUIDE-LINES?
IS THAT SO...?
YOU ARE A DRAGON, SO YOU OUGHT TO LIVE PRECISELY AS YOU WISH.
KILL ANYONE WHO TRIES TO STOP YOU FROM DOING SO.
EVEN IF IT'S FAM-ILY.
THAT IS WHAT DRAGONS DO.
EXTREMIST.
Hmph...

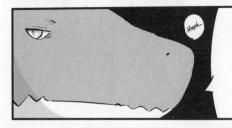

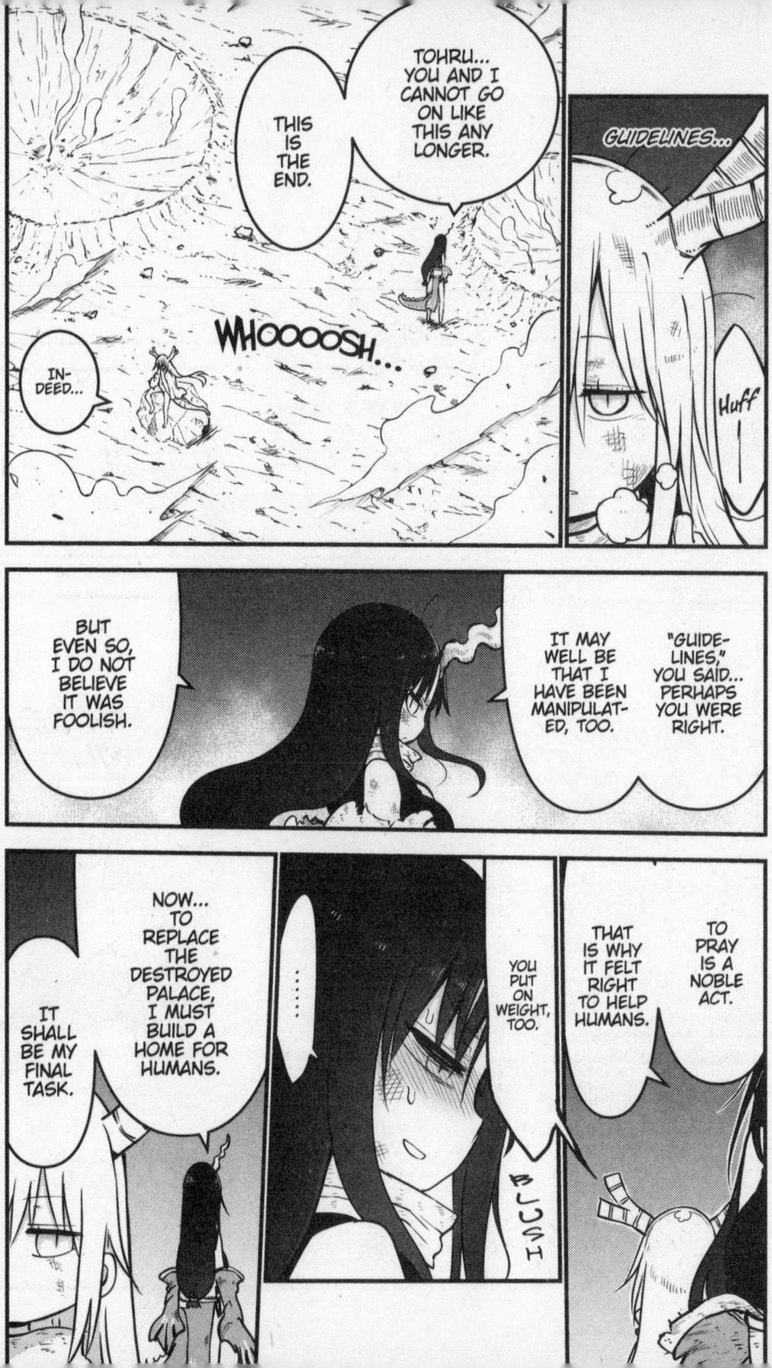
GUIDELINES...
Huff
TOHRU... YOU AND I CANNOT GO ON LIKE THIS ANY LONGER.
THIS IS THE END.
WHOOOOSH...
IN-DEED...
"GUIDE-LINES," YOU SAID... PERHAPS YOU WERE RIGHT.
IT MAY WELL BE THAT I HAVE BEEN MANIPULAT-ED, TOO.
BUT EVEN SO, I DO NOT BELIEVE IT WAS FOOLISH.
TO PRAY IS A NOBLE ACT.
THAT IS WHY IT FELT RIGHT TO HELP HUMANS.
YOU PUT ON WEIGHT, TOO.
......
BLUSH
NOW... TO REPLACE THE DESTROYED PALACE, I MUST BUILD A HOME FOR HUMANS.
IT SHALL BE MY FINAL TASK.

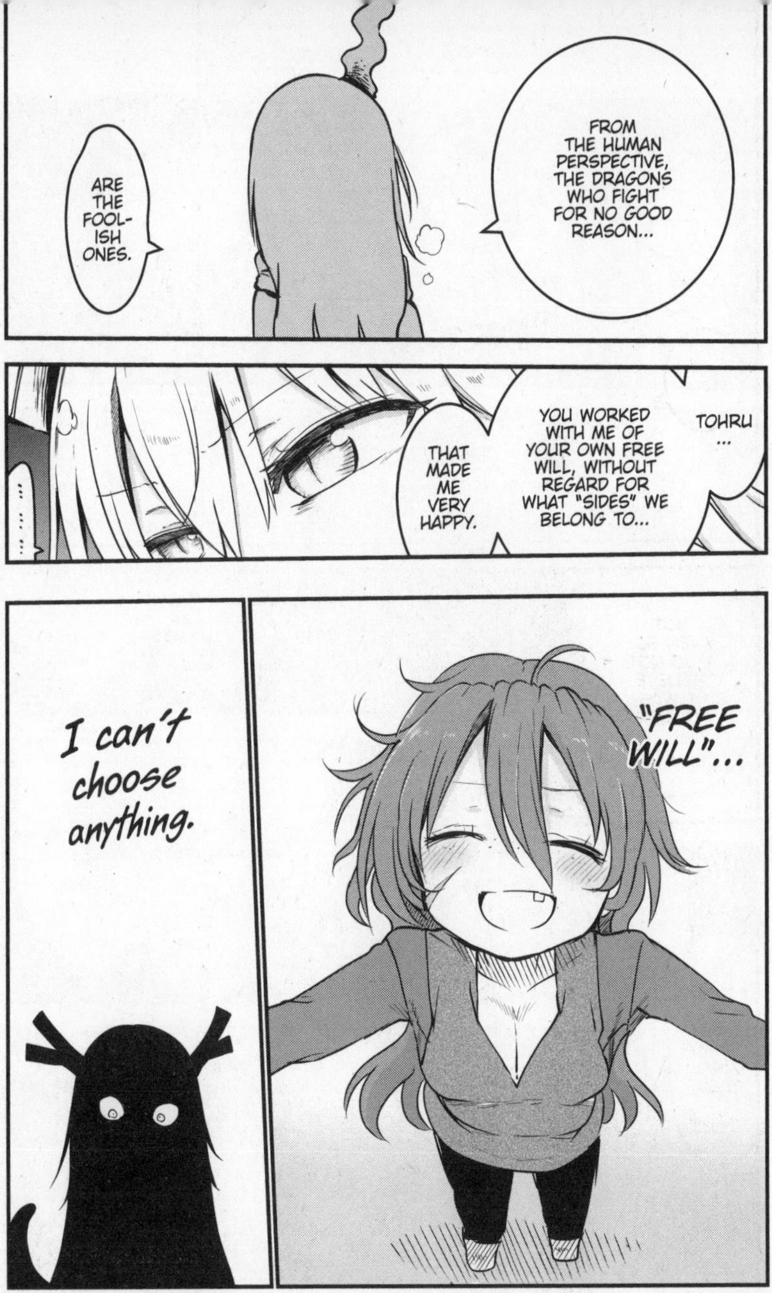
FROM THE HUMAN PERSPECTIVE, THE DRAGONS WHO FIGHT FOR NO GOOD REASON...
ARE THE FOOL-ISH ONES.
TOHRU ...
YOU WORKED WITH ME OF YOUR OWN FREE WILL, WITHOUT REGARD FOR WHAT "SIDES" WE BELONG TO...
THAT MADE ME VERY HAPPY.
......
"FREE WILL"...
I can't choose anything.

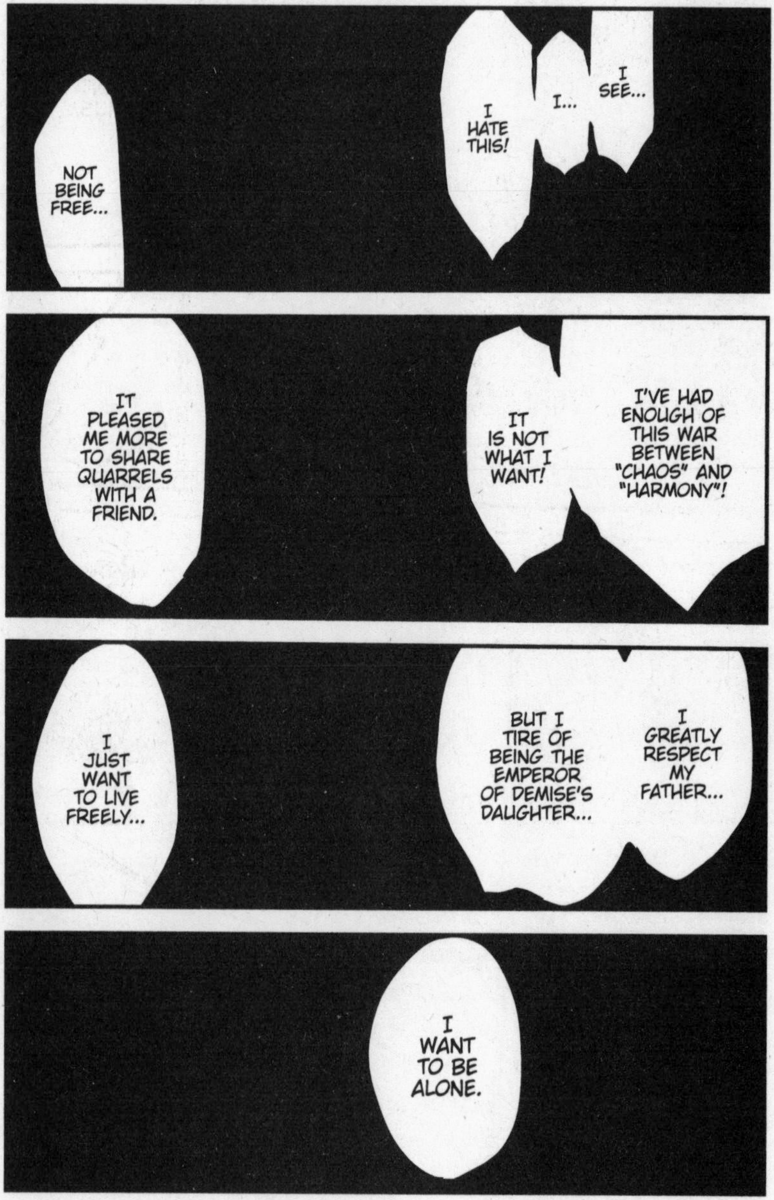
I SEE...
I...
I HATE THIS!
NOT BEING FREE...
I'VE HAD ENOUGH OF THIS WAR BETWEEN "CHAOS" AND "HARMONY"!
IT IS NOT WHAT I WANT!
IT PLEASED ME MORE TO SHARE QUARRELS WITH A FRIEND.
I GREATLY RESPECT MY FATHER...
BUT I TIRE OF BEING THE EMPEROR OF DEMISE'S DAUGHTER...
I JUST WANT TO LIVE FREELY...
I WANT TO BE ALONE.

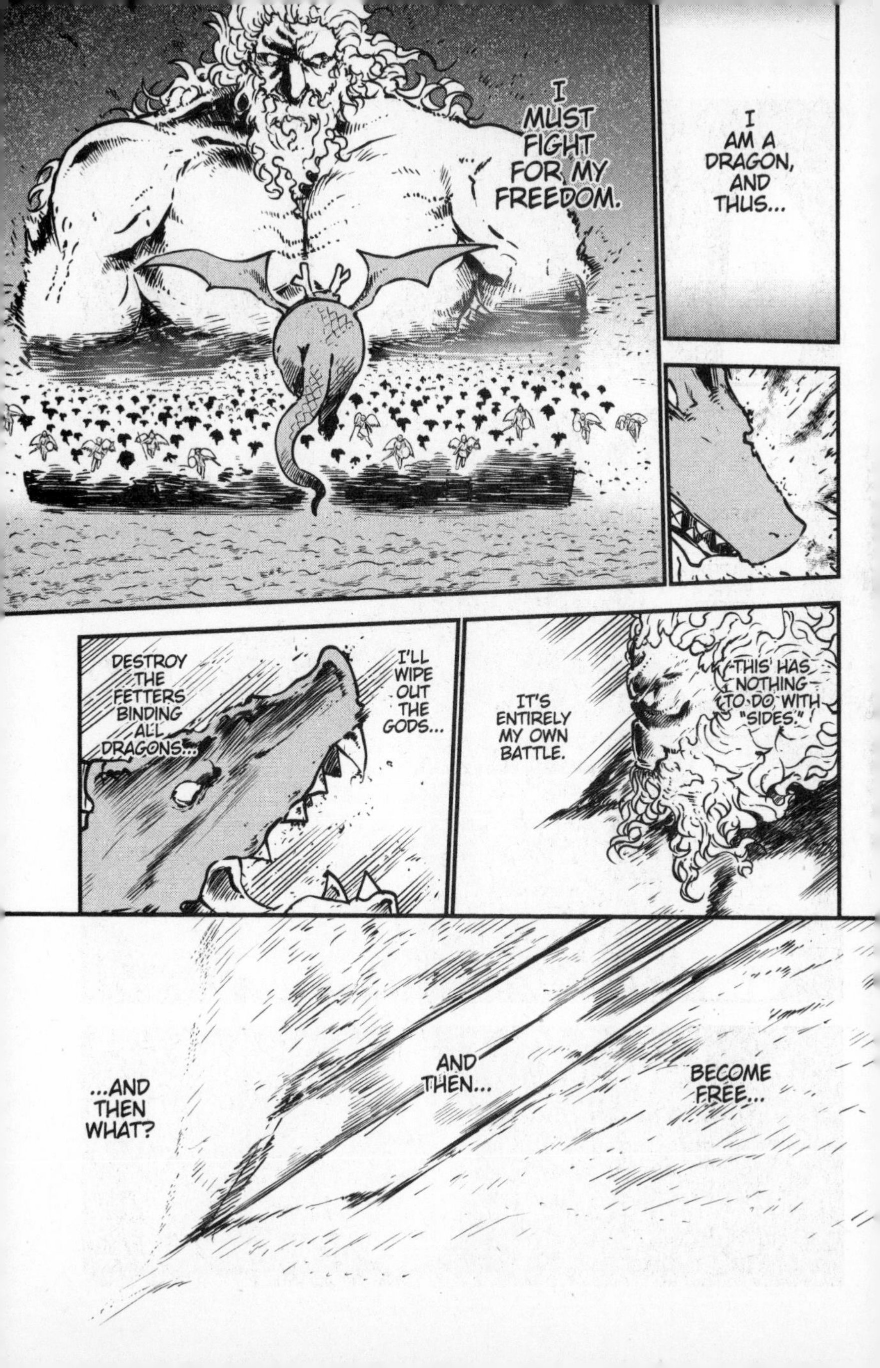
I AM A DRAGON, AND THUS...
I MUST FIGHT FOR MY FREEDOM.
THIS HAS NOTHING TO DO WITH "SIDES."
IT'S ENTIRELY MY OWN BATTLE.
I'LL WIPE OUT THE GODS...
DESTROY THE FETTERS BINDING ALL DRAGONS...
BECOME FREE...
AND THEN...
...AND THEN WHAT?

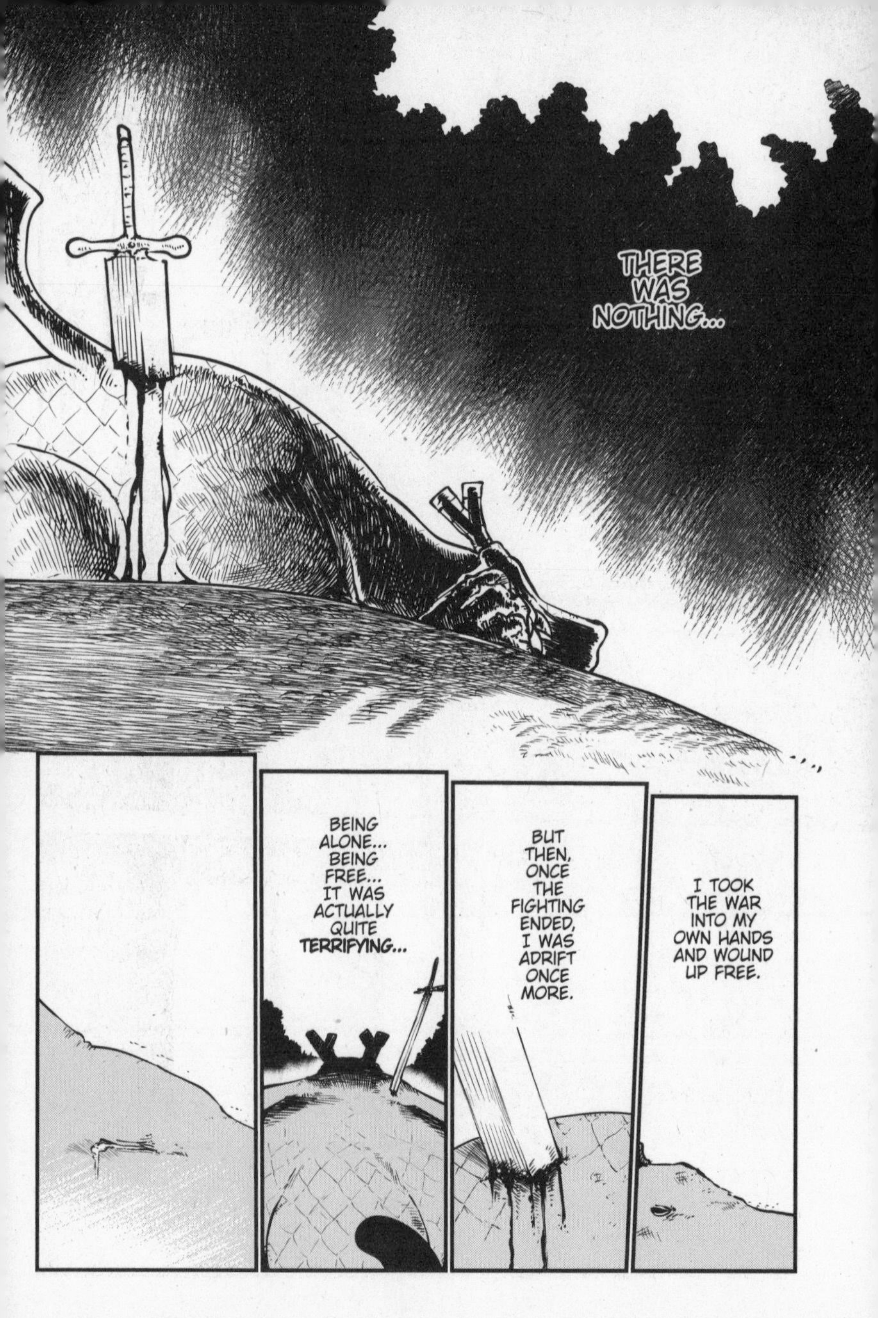
THERE WAS NOTHING...
I TOOK THE WAR INTO MY OWN HANDS AND WOUND UP FREE.
BUT THEN, ONCE THE FIGHTING ENDED, I WAS ADRIFT ONCE MORE.
BEING ALONE... BEING FREE... IT WAS ACTUALLY QUITE **TERRIFYING...**

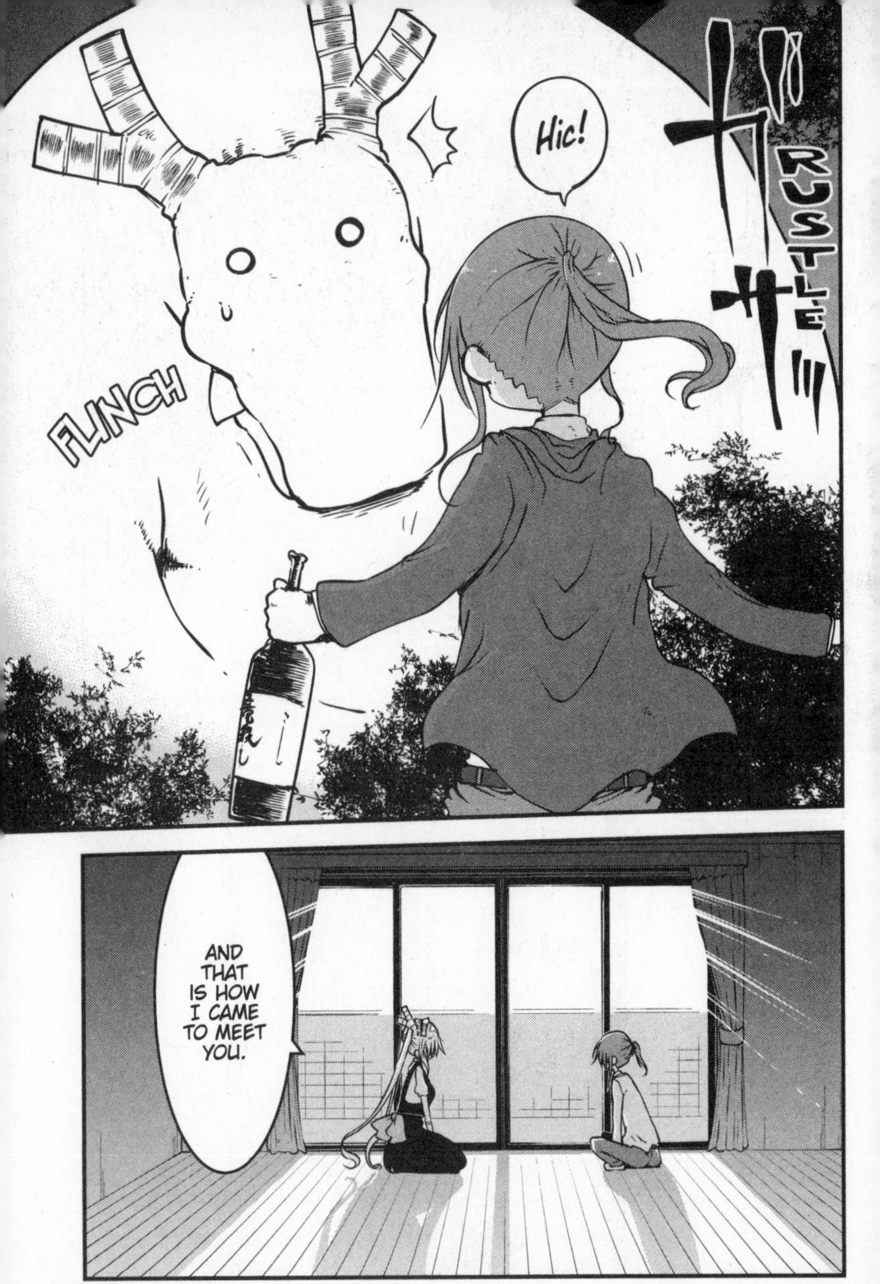
RUSTLE
Hic!
FLINCH
AND THAT IS HOW I CAME TO MEET YOU.

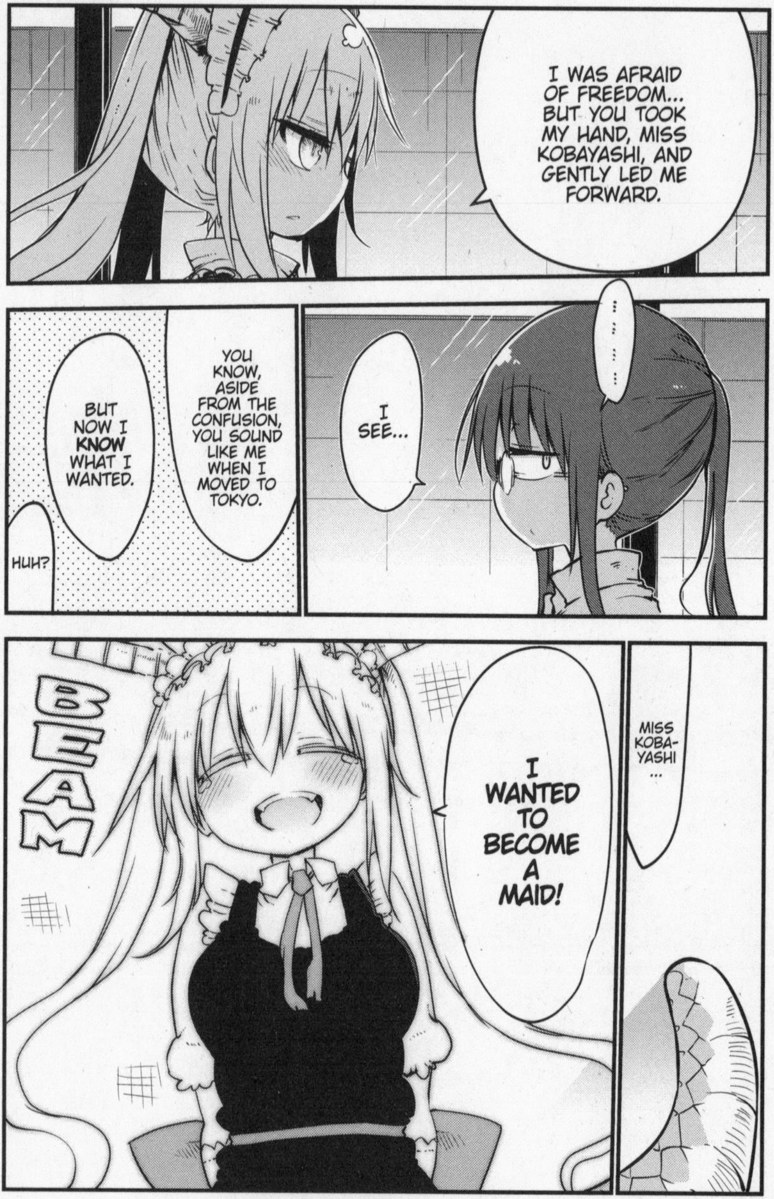
I WAS AFRAID OF FREEDOM... BUT YOU TOOK MY HAND, MISS KOBAYASHI, AND GENTLY LED ME FORWARD.
......
I SEE...
YOU KNOW, ASIDE FROM THE CONFUSION, YOU SOUND LIKE ME WHEN I MOVED TO TOKYO.
BUT NOW I **KNOW** WHAT I WANTED.
HUH?
MISS KOBAYASHI...
I WANTED TO BECOME A MAID!
BEAM

CHAPTER 58/END

Miss Kobayashi's
DRAGON MAID

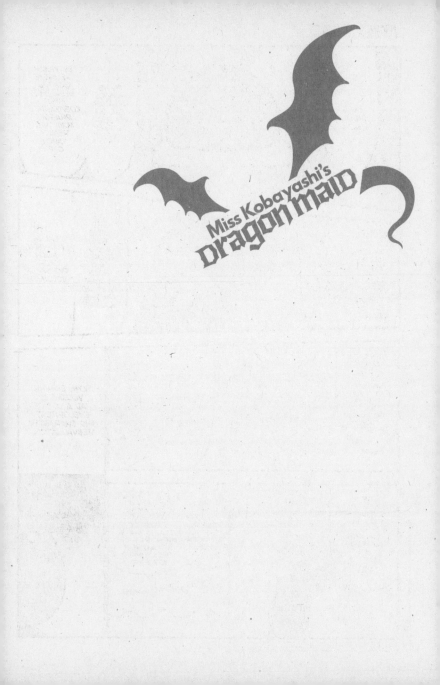

AFTERWORD

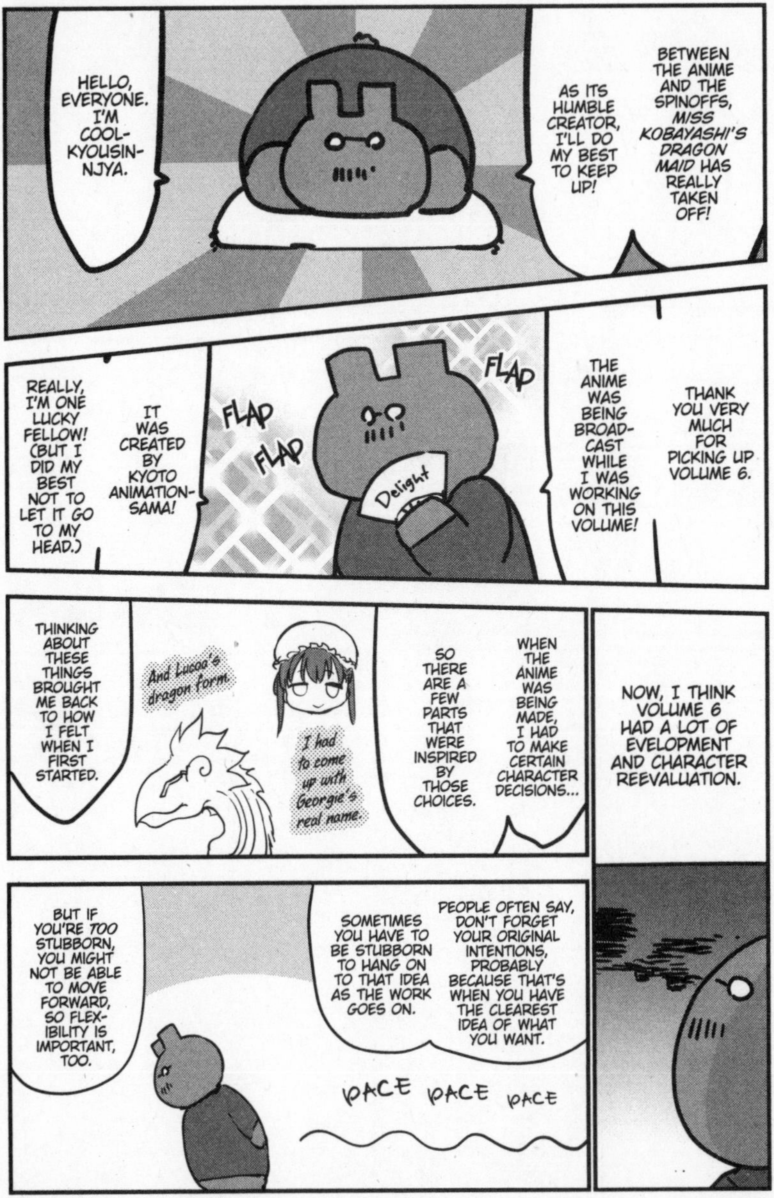
BETWEEN THE ANIME AND THE SPINOFFS, *MISS KOBAYASHI'S DRAGON MAID* HAS REALLY TAKEN OFF!
AS ITS HUMBLE CREATOR, I'LL DO MY BEST TO KEEP UP!
HELLO, EVERYONE. I'M COOL-KYOUSIN-NJYA.
THANK YOU VERY MUCH FOR PICKING UP VOLUME 6.
THE ANIME WAS BEING BROAD-CAST WHILE I WAS WORKING ON THIS VOLUME!
FLAP
FLAP
FLAP
Delight
IT WAS CREATED BY KYOTO ANIMATION-SAMA!
REALLY, I'M ONE LUCKY FELLOW! (BUT I DID MY BEST NOT TO LET IT GO TO MY HEAD.)
NOW, I THINK VOLUME 6 HAD A LOT OF EVELOPMENT AND CHARACTER REEVALUATION.
WHEN THE ANIME WAS BEING MADE, I HAD TO MAKE CERTAIN CHARACTER DECISIONS...
SO THERE ARE A FEW PARTS THAT WERE INSPIRED BY THOSE CHOICES.
I had to come up with Georgie's real name.
And Lucoa's dragon form
THINKING ABOUT THESE THINGS BROUGHT ME BACK TO HOW I FELT WHEN I FIRST STARTED.
PEOPLE OFTEN SAY, DON'T FORGET YOUR ORIGINAL INTENTIONS, PROBABLY BECAUSE THAT'S WHEN YOU HAVE THE CLEAREST IDEA OF WHAT YOU WANT.
SOMETIMES YOU HAVE TO BE STUBBORN TO HANG ON TO THAT IDEA AS THE WORK GOES ON.
PACE PACE PACE
BUT IF YOU'RE *TOO* STUBBORN, YOU MIGHT NOT BE ABLE TO MOVE FORWARD, SO FLEX-IBILITY IS IMPORTANT, TOO.

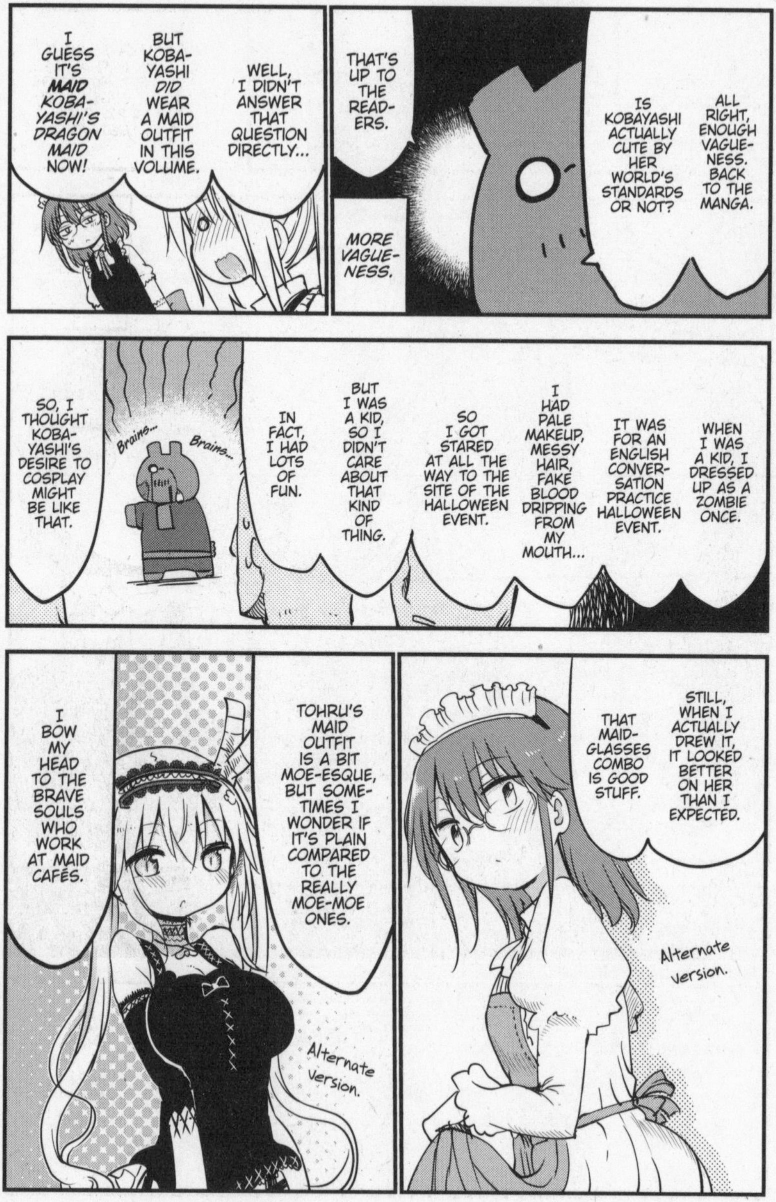
ALL RIGHT, ENOUGH VAGUENESS. BACK TO THE MANGA.
IS KOBAYASHI ACTUALLY CUTE BY HER WORLD'S STANDARDS OR NOT?
THAT'S UP TO THE READERS.
MORE VAGUENESS.
WELL, I DIDN'T ANSWER THAT QUESTION DIRECTLY...
BUT KOBAYASHI *DID* WEAR A MAID OUTFIT IN THIS VOLUME.
I GUESS IT'S ***MAID*** KOBAYASHI'S DRAGON MAID NOW!
WHEN I WAS A KID, I DRESSED UP AS A ZOMBIE ONCE.
IT WAS FOR AN ENGLISH CONVERSATION PRACTICE HALLOWEEN EVENT.
I HAD PALE MAKEUP, MESSY HAIR, FAKE BLOOD DRIPPING FROM MY MOUTH...
SO I GOT STARED AT ALL THE WAY TO THE SITE OF THE HALLOWEEN EVENT.
BUT I WAS A KID, SO I DIDN'T CARE ABOUT THAT KIND OF THING.
IN FACT, I HAD LOTS OF FUN.
Brains...
Brains...
SO, I THOUGHT KOBAYASHI'S DESIRE TO COSPLAY MIGHT BE LIKE THAT.
STILL, WHEN I ACTUALLY DREW IT, IT LOOKED BETTER ON HER THAN I EXPECTED.
THAT MAID-GLASSES COMBO IS GOOD STUFF.
Alternate Version.
TOHRU'S MAID OUTFIT IS A BIT MOE-ESQUE, BUT SOMETIMES I WONDER IF IT'S PLAIN COMPARED TO THE REALLY MOE-MOE ONES.
I BOW MY HEAD TO THE BRAVE SOULS WHO WORK AT MAID CAFÉS.
Alternate Version.

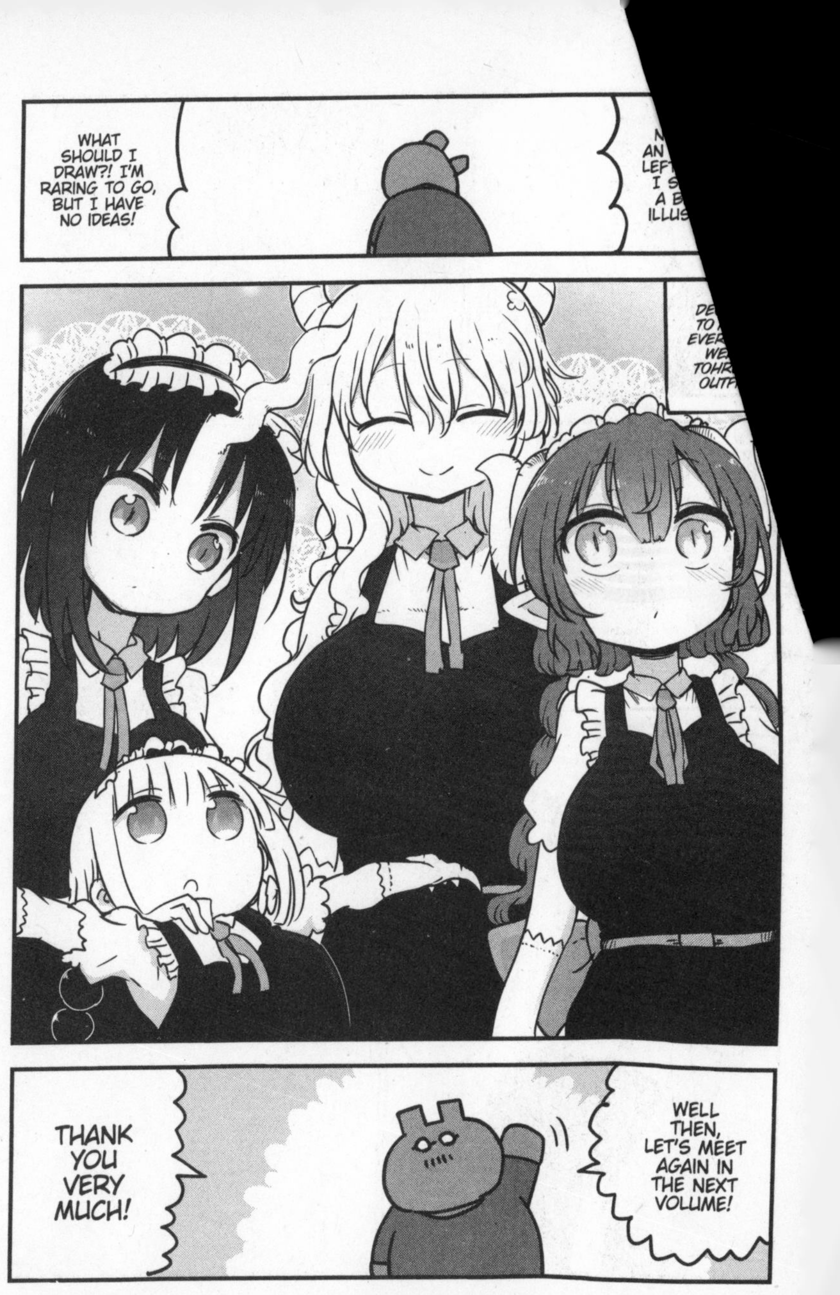
WHAT SHOULD I DRAW?! I'M RARING TO GO, BUT I HAVE NO IDEAS!
WELL THEN, LET'S MEET AGAIN IN THE NEXT VOLUME!
THANK YOU VERY MUCH!

Miss Kobayashi's Dragon Maid

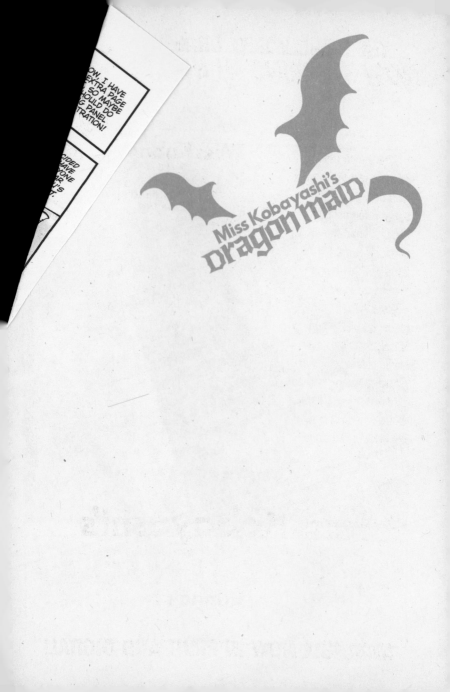